...AND THE

Lotus Opened

To book Marie for a consultation, session, speech, or workshop, please contact her at (800) 337-7682 or padmalifecoaching.com.

...AND THE
Lotus Opened

A MEMOIR

Marie O'Neill

Personal History
PRODUCTIONS LLC

This book is a memoir and reflects the author's present recollections of experiences over time. Some names and characteristics have been changed, some events compressed, and some dialogue recreated.

ISBN 978-1-952932-06-9 (hardcover)
ISBN 978-1-952932-07-6 (paperback)

Produced by Personal History Productions LLC

ersonal History
P R O D U C T I O N S LLC

www.personalhistoryproductions.com
707.888.3446

*To all who are seeking to discover their authentic self
and in so doing experience what Freedom really is*

Contents

CONTENTS

CONTENTS

Foreword

I have many happy memories of time spent with Marie O'Neill, but here's my favorite. Let me set the stage because the stage itself is a character in the story . . .

Picture a tumbledown resort hidden in the tangled, tinder-laden forests near Calistoga, California. It was called Mountain Home Ranch—and I say "was" because it finally burned to the ground in the devastating Tubbs fire of 2017. For years, every March and every September, I would teach a four-day astrology class there with maybe fifty people in attendance. Marie was always there, and always one of my sharpest students.

These meetings were serious classes, with me lecturing for seven hours a day. But the nights were all about fun. There was a serve-yourself bar in the basement, and serve ourselves we did. The Saturday night entertainment was always the "talent show," an event for which actual talent was always an optional *accoutrement*. When applause wasn't merited, at least forgiveness was. We also had a piano player, the inimitable "Professor Griffanzohead," Robert Griffin—a true pro, skilled enough on the keyboard even to follow my own wandering sense of rhythm.

We pressed Marie to sing a tune. She responded with the requisite apologies and protests, claiming that she couldn't sing a note. Well, that wasn't good enough for any of us—a lack of talent obviously had not stopped anyone else, so why should we let it stop her? We pressed her. Finally, with obvious reluctance, Marie stepped up to the microphone—and gave us such a spine-chilling, spell-binding, transcendent rendition of George Gershwin's classic, "Summertime," that I am confident that none of us will ever forget it.

I am fond of saying that "there are people with cameras, and there are photographers." In the same vein, there are people who know the lyrics and can hit all the notes of "Summertime." Meanwhile, there are true *singers* who can make the song itself *sing*—singers who can claim the melody as their own, despite us all having heard it a million times. Marie rules that second box. She was goosebump-amazing that night.

Only in reading . . . *and the Lotus Opened* did I come to a full appreciation of the saga of soul-growth in the face of appalling adversity that led Marie to mount that stage and to belt out that tune that night. It turns out that there was a time that she didn't even believe she could sing at all.

I will not steal her fire by recounting the details of the bad hand she was dealt as a child. I won't belabor the damaging horrors of racism in America, both in its southern variety and its northern one, and how that old poison impacted her sensitive spirit. I will say, as a male, that I am embarrassed by my gender for the cruelty and abuse that men, almost without exception, heaped upon her.

All of that you will read for yourself in her own words in the pages that follow.

What I will say is that, from a spiritual perspective, there is almost nothing so inspiring as a truly, honestly examined life. Each person's challenges are different, and we all must thread our own path through the labyrinths of our wounds, whether they are self-inflicted or visited upon us by the nightmares this world can dish up.

Marie cannot do that brave work for any of us, but she has done the next best thing—she has offered us a success story. She is unpretentious in her telling of it, so let me blow the trumpet for her. The story she tells is a hero's tale. We may not be able to walk in her footsteps—they are her footsteps, not our own—but we can be encouraged, guided, and inspired by them.

That is what . . . *and the Lotus Opened* ultimately is—a map of how to get to heaven . . . via hell if necessary. Marie's faith will uplift you and her honesty will scare you. I keep thinking of her in that basement bar deep in the soon-to-be-toast forest near Calistoga, singing . . .

One of these mornings
you're gonna rise up singing.
You're gonna spread your wings
and take to the sky

If Marie had sung that lyric when she was twelve, it would have qualified as prophecy. Singing those words in her fifties, they are nothing but pure autobiography.

Steven Forrest
author of *The Inner Sky*

Introduction

A Lotus Unfolding

Over the years when I get to know someone, we talk about our lives. The same questions invariably arise as they seek to tease out the details of my story. They want to know how I managed to survive living in Salt Lake City, Utah, as a Black woman from Chicago, with a Jack Mormon man 28 years older than I was. They ask every conceivable follow-up question: How did you do this for so long? Why did you do it? How did you survive? What was it like? What was your life like there? Were you insane or something? How did you become a Buddhist? An astrologer? How did you get an MBA? Initially, these questions perplexed me. "This is just my life," I thought. "Why would there be anything unique about it? Why might I need to account for my experience so others can understand me?"

After a while, it began to dawn on me that my life was really unusual for so many reasons. I'm not insane, but I understand why people might think so. In many facets of my experience, I have challenged the expected scripts for a Black woman. I moved out of my hometown, following my own compass. My life has been complex and filled with adversity.

As I contemplated how to begin my memoir, I saw the story of my life like the growth of a lotus flower, with various cycles that proceed in order until the petals release their perfume and a new cycle begins again. The idea of using the lotus flower to symbolize my life came easily to me. The lotus is my plant teacher, aka totem. Everyone has a plant, an animal, and a tree teacher that symbolizes their identity in the respective kingdom. I learned about totems while studying with a Native American medicine woman. She was the person who introduced me to The Great Mother. Until my training with her, I had no idea there was a feminine aspect to The Divine. She also taught me about nature and the interconnectedness of all things. I had been a city girl, so it took me a long time to develop—or should I say, see—myself as a part of nature. She taught me quite a lot in the four years I trained with her.

By the time I began studying Buddhism, I already had a solid foundation in The Mother. I had learned what my animal and tree teachers were, along with how to talk to trees, minerals, and water. I knew how to read Sign and Symbol in nature. Having this foundation made my Buddhist studies much easier. It took many years for me to realize that the lotus was my plant teacher, even though I had been drawn to it for years. At that point, I had also become certified as a Journey Practitioner, learned astrology, and traveled to Malta and Delphi—places that honored the feminine. It wasn't until I was ready to open my business as a Life Coach that the realization dawned. I had been searching internally but didn't know it. The feminine part of me had been severely damaged, and it wasn't until I had healed to a certain point that my plant teacher was revealed.

Our connection to The Divine in the physical world is through nature. We can't get the connection unless we understand the symbolism of nature. This is how we understand the symbolism as it relates to us as individuals. So in 2005 I choose the white lotus as the symbol for my business. The white lotus represents purity. I had been searching for truth—not New Age truth, but Truth with a capital *T*. I wanted it to be pure and not tainted in any way. This is the truth I planned to bring to every session with a client. I now use the color pink, which symbolizes devotion to the Path. The Path represents the road we travel consciously to know ourselves. Afterall, knowing who we really are is the ultimate goal of all human beings.

Our Soul comes into life with an agenda—that is the seed. In order for this agenda to be fulfilled, the Soul has to be placed in the mud of life. The Soul has chosen to grow on the physical plane. There is no guarantee that the Soul will reach the blossom stage. There are many hazards, obstacles, and ways to derail its growth. Earth for the Soul can feel heavy, dense, and immovable.

Once the lotus seed germinates, the underwater tuber begins to grow. This is the same for humans. Our seeds, aka roots, are our bank of memories. The mind of the child with all of its memories is the foundation that anchors the Soul. The influence of these roots determines how many resources the Soul has to reach the top.

Just as the tuber of the lotus grows, so does the human Soul. This is done by the Soul gaining more experience from life and all the other lifetimes it has passed through. It has to grow and expand with each experience.

I like to relate the stem of the lotus to the ruler that a parent puts against the wall to measure the child's growth. The stem marks our way through life. The Soul makes it through different periods of life, and at each stage it is still being fed by its roots—stored memories. The stems are trying to get through the day-to-day murkiness of water and the human Soul is trying to get through the day-to-day murkiness of life, always trying to figure things out.

As the stem of the lotus grows, it begins to reach for the light. The lotus feels the light as the murky water clears closer to the surface. Water surrounding the rising lotus stem is represented in humans as emotions. Throughout life we are always learning to evolve and work with them. The water is much clearer on the surface of the pond the lotus is growing in, and for humans the correlation is that our emotions are becoming more balanced.

Now, the light of the sun helps the leaf nodes and leaves to grow. The sun feeds the lotus plant from above through photosynthesis, which is pulled down into the plant, giving it strength to form the bud and blossom. Likewise, the Soul knows it has to push toward the light. It is the only way to produce another seed. At this stage, the Soul gathers more experiences and continues maturing. We do this by reaching outside of ourselves for knowledge. This is the food and energy we use to sustain our lives and to keep developing.

The lotus bud is the protective casing for each developing petal. It is a rough, thick coating that gives the petals protection as they develop. The encapsulated flower looks like praying hands. I liken the petals of the lotus to the many facets of a person. These facets, or parts of us, are being purified within the protective casing we put around ourselves. Even with this protective casing, there is no guarantee the lotus will blossom—and this is the same for people. The harshness of life can disrupt our blossoming at any point during the process. As a person accomplishes the great work of knowing oneself, blooming occurs. Each opening petal represents one facet of a person's past being purified or healed. As the petals open, the full beauty of the blossom is evident to all around, and the perfume of the plant is naturally released, sweetening the air that can be smelled by anyone nearby. For us, when we bloom, we radiate our true selves out into the world, and this in turn helps others on their journey to know themselves.

My life has been like the petals of the lotus unfolding. In Eastern spiritual traditions, namely Buddhism and Hinduism, the many-layered lotus symbolizes spiritual awakening and rising from the mud of existence to a divine consciousness. Throughout my life, the lotus of my understanding has unfolded across time and space. I have awakened to many truths. My Soul has become aware of the interconnectedness of my life and its purpose as a part of nature. One of my gifts is being able to ask questions. I always want to know why. Gaining the answer to one question usually leads to another query and another. However, my thirst to know truth has carried me to the surface of the water and caused the leaf nodes and blossoms to open many times. I love having the lotus as my plant teacher.

As I have encountered and overcome adversity, I have gained a deeper awareness of who I am, along with realizing basic truths about how to flow with life. It has been a long journey to knowing I am loved unconditionally and that, like the lotus, I am unique and divinely beautiful. I have learned many spiritual truths through my experiences and through observation, and I share a few of them here to show you what lies ahead on life's journey of spiritual transformation:

First, just because a person has internal sight, can heal, is intuitive, or is spot on with predictions, doesn't mean they are enlightened. They are learning lessons just like the rest of us. They have developed a skill and are using it. There is nothing to be in awe of.

Second, the guru is yourself, that internal part of you that is called the Soul or Higher Mind.

Third, what is given can be taken away. If a person has a spiritual gift and they are sharing that gift with others, their intention has to be honorable, above board. If the person has put themselves out in the world as a spiritual teacher and they intentionally misuse their gifts, The Divine takes the gift away—that is, it can't be used by the person until they learn whatever lesson it is that caused them to misuse the skill.

Fourth, there are karmic interactions, which means sometimes we are predestined to meet certain people. Sometimes you or the other person has a karmic imbalance that has to be corrected. There is good and not-so-good Karma.

Fifth, The Divine speaks to us through nature. This is one of the reasons it's important to learn the traits of animals, plants, elements, and the rest of nature.

Sixth, we create our own lives. We really are creating our reality with our thoughts and deeds.

Seventh, when a door opens and you decide not to walk through it, it could be a long time before that door opens again, if ever. At the same time, if you walk through a door that is not optimal, it could be a long time before the door opens for you to exit.

Eighth, there is a rhythm to the Universe. Our job is to learn that rhythm and keep step with it, not fight against it. The Universe is constantly sending us signals to get in the flow of this rhythm, and we cause ourselves much more suffering than necessary by holding on to what is ready to be released, which keeps us from being in this rhythm.

Ninth, wisdom comes from what we might think of as failure. Failure is important for our growth.

Tenth, we are to do our best in any situation, have good intentions, and let go of the need to control outcomes.

Eleventh, each of us is loved unconditionally regardless of our actions.

I've learned other lessons as well, but these are the most important ones. One thing is for sure: I'm not someone who believes in airing her dirty laundry, or anyone else's, in public. I've never played the blame game—although I certainly could have—or felt like a victim. No matter what situations arise in our lives, we have the option to respond by taking the high road or the low road. When I was a teenager, my mother shared one of the few pieces of wisdom I ever learned from her. She said, "Girl, fat meat is greasy." I thought, "Doesn't everyone know fat meat is greasy?" I translated this advice to mean, "Don't believe what you're told." I knew I would have to experience something to glean my own truth, and many of these experiences are contained in the pages of this book.

I share my story and my search for truth with you in the hope that it inspires and helps you on your path to heal yourself. By telling you how I healed from the traumas I experienced for so many years, I hope you will learn to work with and heal the traumas of your life. My intention is to show you a blueprint that you can follow to learn about nature and how The Divine speaks to us through it. I want to inspire you to learn all that you can about who you really are. Doing so will open you to a joy you never knew was possible. I believe this spiritual journey is available to all who seek, and I hope to share the lessons of my spiritual transformation with you through the story of my life. I hope my telling will inspire you to live life on your own terms and to let your petals unfold.

You may notice that when I talk about the Soul, I usually capitalize it. This may seem unconventional; however, in Buddhism, there is no *soul* as there is in Western theology. The Western definition of *soul* conveys a narrower understanding of the Soul, or internal part of us, that is connected to the larger all-encompassing soul of the Universe. I sometimes use a variety of terms to describe the overarching universal soul: The Great All, Great Spirit, The Divine, Higher Mind. The words I use depend on my audience. Since I am a Westerner and was raised Christian, I also still use *Soul* and *soul*. I don't use *Soul* or *soul* if I am talking to anyone from the East because they don't use that language. In the Eastern traditions, *Higher Mind* or *Buddha Nature* are two terms that mean *Soul*. I capitalize *Soul* throughout this manuscript to make my meaning clear to everyday readers.

Nutrient-Rich Soil

It is the physical plane (earth) where the Soul has
chosen to develop. In order to have the Soul's
purpose fulfilled, each of us must be
dumped in the mud of life. The
quality of the soil is a key
component in determining
how the Soul will
progress.

1

First Six Years

Let me take you back to the beginning, to the soil I grew out of. My mom's name was Orastine. I have never heard of anyone else having that name. She saw me as fundamentally different from her and reflected that back to me with hurtful words. "If you didn't look like me," she said, "I wouldn't know you were my kid." She only said it once, but those words have stayed with me. When your mother sees you as different—not in a good way—you can be sure your life is going to be interesting, to say the least. As far as I know, my mother was the first woman in the family to have a child out of wedlock. Today, it's not a big deal, but back then it was a huge deal. On top of that, I was conceived while she was having an affair with a married man.

My mom lived in the North, in Chicago, alone. Her family was all in Louisiana. She moved north in the 1940s as a very young adult for several reasons. One, she wanted to have a better life. Two, she was escaping from her alcoholic mother. I met my maternal grandmother once as a little kid when my mother and I traveled to visit her family in Bogalusa, Louisiana. I was maybe three years old, so I don't remember what she was like. My memory of childhood is very good, so I find it odd that I don't remember the trip. Over the years, however, my cousins have filled me in on the missing pieces of my family history. She was a take-no-prisoners kind of woman with a big, ferocious temper, who loved and doted on her grandchildren. I could have used some doting on back then. What I got was far different from that.

I was born in 1961. The fact that I was born is nothing short of amazing. My father wanted my mom to have an abortion. I can understand why. I was an inconvenience. However, my mother didn't do it. To this day, I don't know for sure why she chose to go through with having me. Of course, I'm glad she did, but being born in these circumstances also meant that I was born with two strikes against me. First, there was the bastard label, and then there was being the child of a married man label. I'm sure tongues were wagging. I was also born with an extra finger on the upper outer edge of my left pinky. This, thank God, was taken care of. I assume it was removed before I left the hospital, leaving a small, nearly unnoticeable indentation on my finger. Growing up with an extra finger would have added extra difficulty to an already tough situation.

Whether you believe it or not, America has its own caste system. A person can move from one caste to another, which is a positive thing, but people put labels on others based on their caste. The expectations from family, community, and society as a whole are based on this system. I was born into an impoverished caste, and there was additional stigma because of how I was conceived. Another significant strike against me in this caste system was the fact that I was born Black. No one in the community or larger society would expect me to achieve anything in life. How could I? My pedigree was substandard.

My mother, I'm sure, had to be scared to death being responsible for a baby. When I came along, she was 34 years old—old to be having a baby back then. Her first job was to find me a babysitter, since she worked every day. She traveled two hours each way to Skokie, Illinois, to work in a dry cleaner's. That's four hours of commute time every day, six days a week. In her mind, I'm sure this was a step up from being a maid, and she wasn't qualified for the other careers available to Black women back then—that of a teacher or a nurse. She only had a ninth-grade education. You do what you have to do to survive, a trait I obviously inherited from her.

The first babysitter she found for me was a doozy. The babysitter didn't want to be bothered with my crying, so she fed me beer to make me sleep all day. No wonder I don't like beer today. I had my fill as an infant. When my mother discovered this, which took approximately 10 months, she had to find another babysitter. I was told many years later that a friend of a friend knew someone who might take on the job, which turned out to be true. Now my mom had the task of taking me to a new babysitter who lived on the South Side of Chicago. We were West Side people. I'm sure this was no fun because my mother had to make this trek twice a day before and after her two-hour commute to Skokie. Now, that's a feat in and of itself. I have a memory of being carried by my mother on one of these long treks, and I find it amazing that I remember it.

My new babysitter's name was Louisiana Monger. Now that's a name. She lived in a set of rooms in the basement of a six-flat on Prairie Avenue. I can remember every detail of the apartment layout, too. The entrance was down a flight of stairs on the side of the building. Once down the stairs, we could go straight through a breezeway to the backyard. Or we could enter the basement through a door on the right. Louisiana lived in the front of two apartments, although in my opinion there was only one real apartment in the back of the basement. She had a studio and a bedroom, which were separated from one another by the hallway that led to the back of the basement. In the studio, there was a sleeping area to the left as you walked through the door. The cooking area, akin to a studio kitchen, was to the right. A curtain served to separate the two areas, but most of the time the curtain was open and not used. I have no idea where the bathroom was, but there had to be one. I do remember a laundry room in the basement. I remember being given baths in one of those big stone wash tubs, of which there were two.

I like to imagine that when Louisiana met me, it was love at first sight, although I actually have no idea what it was like for her meeting me. What I do know is that she took on the job. She probably felt sorry for my mom and for me. I was 10 months old and so fragile and small that she had to hold me on a pillow to make sure I didn't get injured. My brain was injured by the diet of alcohol my first babysitter fed me, and it stunted my growth and affected my developing motor skills. Thank goodness there weren't any other effects, that I know of. This is what a diet of beer can do to an infant.

My life with Louisiana (or Granny, as I called her) had begun. I don't remember when I started calling her Granny because I don't remember calling her by any other name. She was born in 1910, which made her over 50 years old when she took me on. Granny was one of those light-skinned Black women. I say "those" because in the Black community being light skinned meant you were special. You were sought after. I have no idea if Granny was sought after. I do know she was married at 13 years old to a man who was 50 years old. I know the marriage didn't last because when I arrived, she was with Booker T. Monger, who was closer to her age.

I like that name, and I liked him. Booker was always nice to me. He used to pick me up in his arms and carry me to the local store to buy me a Hostess Fruit Pie when I was in trouble for something and Granny was determined to whip me. We would usually end up at the corner tavern, where I would sit on a stool eating my pie while he drank whatever it was he drank while smoking a cigar. Back then a tavern was not off limits for a kid. It was innocent, and he was doing his best to keep me away from the apartment until Granny cooled down. He couldn't stand seeing me being punished.

Booker T. was the first father figure I had. He was from the South—I think Mississippi. The story that Granny told me was that he was having an affair with a white woman, and when the Klan found out, he had to leave town fast—that day. He was told if he ever came back to town he would be killed. So he made his way to Chi Town. I have no idea how long Granny and Booker T. had been together. It was, however, long enough for Granny to take on his last name. Although I'm sure they were never legally married, it was a common-law marriage. Years later I looked him up when

I was searching for my birth father. His nickname was Boo, which was short for Booker. Boo lived in the same neighborhood as he did when I was a kid, probably in the same apartment. There were hundreds and hundreds of 45s in his living room. He obviously loved jazz. I love jazz, too. We listened to a few tunes together and chatted. That was the last time I saw him.

One of the ways Granny made money was by making lunches for people who worked in the neighborhood. Men would come by her apartment and pick up a paper bag filled with whatever it was she cooked for them that day. Granny also had a bookie. Yes, a bookie. She usually played the numbers, or whatever else bookies were selling, in the hope of hitting it big. No one thought anything of this back then. I sure didn't. I also have no idea if she ever won anything or if she did, how much. The bookie would come in with one of those small note pads, just like they did in the old movies. I never got to see what was written in it, but Granny would tell him how much she was putting down on whatever she was putting the money on and he would write in the little note pad. Her bets were no more than 50 cents.

The Barkleys lived down the hall in the other basement apartment. They had a little girl named Charlotte, who was my same age. Charlotte was my first friend. We would play together daily in the hallway or in her apartment. As a little kid, I was a daredevil, climbing on things that I could jump from. Once while playing, I had the brilliant idea to climb on top of the dresser in Charlotte's bedroom, jump off, and land on the bed. At three or four years old, I knew this was achievable. Charlotte stood by watching. Well, I made the jump and almost stuck the landing on the bed. The upper part of my body made it to the bed. However, my feet landed on the floor with one foot planted squarely on a paw of Charlotte's dog, who instinctively bit me on the leg. This was my first and only dog bite. The moral of the story for me was, if I'm going to do something like this, I need to make sure the dog isn't standing between the dresser and the bed. I graduated from scaling the dresser to climbing the tree in the front of the building. I fell out of it, too. My knee still bears the hyperpigmentation from that fall.

My mind was always at work. Of course, I thought I was as smart as any adult. I don't know when my mom started leaving me at Granny's overnight, but I know it wasn't long after she began taking care of me. The times Mom would take me home with her became infrequent. There were also times when Mom would stay over. We would sleep in the same bed in the room across the hall from the kitchen/studio. On one of these occasions, I lay awake in bed needing to use the bathroom. I couldn't have been younger than three because I had been potty trained. I had seen a mouse, or it could have been a rat, climbing on the screen door to the bedroom, and I didn't like them and wasn't about to get near them. On this particular morning as I lay in bed, I contemplated what to do about using the bathroom. My decision had nothing to do with the possibility of seeing a mouse—it was pure laziness. The bed was warm, and I didn't want to get up, so I decided to urinate in the bed. At the time, in my little mind, it was the optimal solution. That morning Granny asked me, "Who wet the bed?" "Mom did," I replied. I had come up with a brilliant response, I thought. Granny said she was going to ask my mother that evening if she wet the bed. I'm not sure if Granny ever asked because I didn't get a whipping for it, which was surely warranted.

I don't remember when the whippings started in earnest, but I do know they had begun by the time we moved to the first-floor apartment in the same building. By this time, I was about five years old, and I was living with Granny full time. My mom would come by from time to time, and sometimes she would stay the night. I remember lying next to her, holding onto the strap of her slip so that she wouldn't be able to leave in the morning without waking me up. My plan didn't work, of course. I'd wake up and she'd be gone. The parenting job was solely in Granny's hands. My mom never interfered. How could she? She was rarely ever around.

By the time we moved to the first-floor apartment, I had already begun the Head Start program and had my first pair of glasses. I loved school but hated the glasses. As a matter of fact, I deliberately broke the first pair by dropping them in the stone sink. It didn't do me any good to have broken them—my mother just bought another pair. I may have seemed like a willful kid, but I don't think I was. I was curious and used logic, even if that logic didn't bear itself out. All the same, I was using my mind to deduce how to achieve my goals. Parenting me would have been so much easier if the adults in my life had talked to me using logic rather than laying down the law. "Don't do this" or "Don't go there" was not an effective strategy to use with me. I needed to be told why I should or shouldn't do something and then be allowed to make up my own mind, within reason. If I wanted to eat glass or put my finger in the fire, I would need to be stopped. However, those aren't the sorts of things I was doing or attempting to do. A parent's job is to prepare a child for the world, and to do this, the kid has to learn how to take calculated risks. Most kids are fearless until their parents transfer their own fears to them, causing the kid to grow up with that same fear. As a little one, I didn't know this. What I knew was that telling me no without an explanation wasn't good enough to satisfy my understanding. Each kid is so different, and parenting styles really need to fit the kid.

Back then, children couldn't, or perhaps more accurately weren't supposed to, talk back to their elders. I didn't understand that unspoken principle, either. Why shouldn't I respectfully say what was on my mind? I did not observe honest communication from my elders. My mom taught me, through her actions, that she was a liar. She would promise me this or that and not follow through on her promises. One day Mom, Granny, and I were in Granny's studio apartment. Mom was sitting in a chair in the sitting and sleeping area, and I was standing next to her. Granny was in the kitchen area. My mother was making yet another promise to me. I flat-out said to her that she was lying. That comment went over like a ton of bricks. It was true. She was lying. Why should I get in trouble for telling the truth? Mom took her shoe off to beat me, but Granny stopped her, saying, "You know she's telling the truth."

I know that I was a kid and that adults were charged with the responsibility of raising me. I didn't have much say in the matter of *how* they raised me. What the adults in my life wanted me to do, without realizing the implications of their behavior, was for me to fit into their world. I know now that I was just trying to be me without being shackled with their beliefs, which would stunt my growth. I didn't realize it at the time, and I was just confused by their actions. I wanted to live honestly—true to myself. The process of unlearning their limiting beliefs has taken a lifetime.

This, of course, was the perfect nutrient-rich soil for me to grow in. There is no way I could be who I am today without it. My basic needs of food, shelter, and clothing were taken care of, which meant I felt secure enough not to worry about them. On the other hand, my emotional and spiritual needs were not being met. Because of this, I developed an internal muscle for being able to endure trauma and to question what I was being told as compared to what I felt internally. It was this soil that gave me the strength years later to go on the quest to find my true self. Without this soil, I wouldn't have had the courage or strength to seek my truth. I also wouldn't be able to stay on course as an adult.

In the first-floor apartment, I had a pet parrot and then a pet dog. The parrot entered my life first. I don't remember her name, but I do remember that she was yellow. Her cage was in the kitchen on a stand that was taller than I was, so I couldn't reach her easily. One day Granny and I were changing the water in her cage, and the parrot got out because her wings hadn't been clipped. I don't think Granny or my mother knew anything about birds. In some ways, I'm glad her wings weren't clipped. She flew around the kitchen while both of us tried to catch her to no avail. At one point she flew over the stove, which was on. I was frightened she would get burned. The screenless kitchen window was open to a beautiful sunny day, so I watched as she flew away. My first experience of loss had been when my friend Charlotte moved away, and this was another significant loss to me as a child. I was very unhappy about this. I don't remember going out to look for the parrot, but that is something I am sure I would have wanted to do. To this day, from time to time, I think about her and wonder what happened to her. Was she found by someone who loved and cared for her? I pray that she was.

My dog, who I named Lady, was medium sized with short, mostly black fur. A light-colored stripe on her underbelly ran up to her nose. She was my pal. Her home was the kitchen pantry with newspaper on the floor and a fence to keep her from getting out. My thinking is that Granny didn't want Lady doing her business all over the apartment. As an adult I feel that this wasn't right. However, as a kid I didn't know any better and wouldn't have been able to do anything about it anyway if I had.

Lady was never taken for walks. Every day Granny picked me up from a friend of hers who owned a store close to the school I attended. Granny would have me walk there to wait for her. She never had Lady with her. The woman who ran the store was nice, but she must not have known anything about kids. If she had, she wouldn't have given me goat milk to drink every day. Yuck, and yuck! She had a refrigerator case full of all kinds of milk, so why did she feed me goat milk? She probably thought it was good for me. I was very creative in finding ways to get rid of it every day.

In 1967 Granny found out she needed to move back to Memphis, Tennessee, to care for her mother and uncle. This was a huge turning point in my life. Most of the time adults don't understand the long-term ramifications of their decisions on children. Granny asked my mother if she could take me with her, and my mother said yes. I have a few ideas of why she said yes, but I don't know conclusively. For one thing, she trusted Granny; second, she had no clue how to raise a kid; and third, there was no one else to care for me. I think she also felt getting me away from Chicago would be a good idea. I'm sure she saw things there that she wouldn't have wanted me to experience. At the time, I was happy to be going with Granny. I loved her and didn't understand that this meant I wouldn't see my mother for a very long time.

When I look back, I know it was probably the best decision for me. If I had grown up in Chicago, I might not have survived. Or if I had survived, I am not sure that I would be the person I am today. Having a mother who didn't know how to parent and who was gone most of the time didn't bode well for my healthy survival into adulthood. I was a little kid who knew how to speak her mind, and I was not afraid of anyone or anything. I didn't pick fights, although one of my older cousins told me about an incident in which I beat up another older cousin. One of the cousins said or did something that caused me to fight with her, and I won. In my friendship with Charlotte, I was the dominant one and bossed her around. If I had been raised in Chicago, there is a distinct possibility that I would have gotten myself into a lot of trouble.

In astrology we talk about the planet Mars being the god of war. Under Mars there are only two options: eat or be eaten. I was a kid who wasn't about to be eaten. However, it seems to be a universal law that at some point someone bigger and stronger always comes along. My strength came from an inner source that I don't quite understand. By the time I was beginning to walk, I had to wear braces on my legs and feet to correct a problem. My feet and ankles were off kilter. I remember the braces but don't remember the specific problem with my feet. The braces came up my legs and stopped below the knee. They were cumbersome, but that never stopped me. I'm not sure how long I wore them, but I do know they were off by the time I began Head Start. I was also born with hand tremors. These were an inheritance from my mother, who inherited them from her mother. How I could be fearless considering the physical issues I was born with is beyond me. But kids learn to compensate for their challenges, and I was no exception.

My whole world was about to change. Everything up to this point had been a setup for what lay ahead. Psychologically, I was about to have my first real trauma. My world was going to be turned upside down, and the foundation I thought was secure was about to be jolted. Over the course of my life the psychological jolts would continue, and as each one happened, I learned to flow with them easier. This doesn't mean they weren't challenging. However, it was the only way I avoided being broken. I learned to adapt to the circumstances I faced while keeping my inner light alive—although sometimes that light was dim. And it is the only way I learned where my real foundation lay and what I was made of. Without the trauma, I never would have fought to change my circumstances. I am psychologically strong today because those jolts led me on the quest to discover who I am, and along the way I learned a few of the universal truths about life—one being that nothing is permanent. Knowing this goes a long way when it comes to accepting change, especially when we don't want the change.

In December Granny's son-in-law and one of her younger cousins drove a truck to Chicago, loaded up the furniture, Granny, Lady, and me, and we headed to the South. We were bound for Memphis, Tennessee. Little did I know, another reality had begun. The soil of my young life was about to change in profound ways. The trip to Memphis was pretty uneventful. As I recall we stopped once so Johnny Sr., Granny's son-in-law, could sleep for a couple of hours. I sat in the middle on the lap of the cousin. Lady was behind the cabin seat at times and sat in my lap at other times.

2

Move to Memphis

Memphis at that time was a hotbed of racial tension, but I didn't know anything about this then. For the most part the old adage "Children should be seen and not heard" was strictly enforced in the household I moved to. I also left the room when grown-ups were talking, as was expected in the culture at the time. I was faced with learning a new language, too—the language of the South. Everyone always says children adapt easily. I don't believe this statement. Of course, I only have myself as a reference. To the parent, it may look like the child is adapting when in fact they are just coping. If the parents were to look closely, they would see that the signs of trauma are there. The more drastic the change is, the deeper the child feels the shock, which means it takes longer for the child to adjust to new circumstances. In my case, the shocks kept coming one right after the other. Most of the shocks had nothing to do with being in Memphis, although there were some pretty significant events I was faced with as a six-year-old.

Granny's house was in southeast Memphis on the corner of Gill and Silver Streets. It sat on a narrow, long lot. The house was what was called a shotgun house. This meant you could stand at the front door and see through to the back of the house. I believe it was built in the '20s. It was painted white with a different color trim. I don't remember what the color of the trim was when I arrived because over the years Granny kept changing the color. But the primary color of the house was always white. Technically it was a three-bedroom house, although it began as a one-bedroom. Granny's daughter, Freddie Mae, added two bedrooms when she lived there. These rooms were on the side of the original structure, which made the house not really a shotgun.

Granny's daughter also put in a bathroom—thank the Lord! The bathroom was in between the two added bedrooms. There wasn't a shower, just a claw-foot tub. The entrance to the house was through the front porch, which had been enclosed to create another room. A big picture window was in this room. The living room, also known as the "front room," was next. It did double duty as a bedroom for Granny's mother, Cora Lee. There was a four-poster bed on one wall, a dresser on another, a couch on another, and a rocking chair by one of the two windows. This chair was Cora Lee's throne. She sat there most of the time rocking, looking out the window, smoking a pipe, dipping snuff, chewing tobacco, and spitting in a coffee can. There was also an armoire, or chifforobe, and a sewing machine. The sewing machine was the old-fashioned one, with a pedal and wheel.

The kitchen was next to the living room. It had a small table next the doorway as you entered from the living room. There was a gas stove, an old-fashioned refrigerator, a white sink with an area to dry dishes, and a cabinet to store everything in. There was no such thing as wall-to-wall cabinets, granite countertops, etc. All prep work for cooking was done on the little table. The floors throughout the house were covered with linoleum. They were so clean you could eat off them. From the kitchen, there were three doorways to choose from: one went back to the living room, the one on the right led to one of the added bedrooms, and the one straight ahead, which could be seen from the front door, led to a hallway, which led to another bedroom. In the hallway was a ringer washing machine and the bathroom. Granny would later add a second half bath in this small hall. The bathroom was your basic bath with a sink, tub (with a window above), toilet, mirror, and gas heater. There was no storage or shelves.

The hallway also led to a bedroom that was original to the house and that also could be seen from the front porch. This bedroom had a four-poster bed, chair, black-and-white TV, gas heater, and dresser. There was a window that overlooked the backyard and two doors. One door led outside and the other door led to the third bedroom, where Uncle Hayward, Cora Lee's brother and Granny's uncle, slept. He was called just Uncle Hayward. I don't think I ever knew his last name. His room was the smallest in the house. It had a twin bed, dresser, and another chifforobe. There was also a window that looked out onto the side yard and the house next door. This room was at the back of the house away from any activity.

The house really wasn't that large, maybe only 1,100 square feet, but to a kid it was a nice size. All of the furniture was old and kept polished. Just because a person is poor doesn't mean they are dirty. Every wall was painted white. Every year during my spring break, Granny and I washed the walls and applied a fresh coat of paint. We took down the curtains, washed them, and rehung them, as well as tore apart the kitchen, cleaned it, and put it back together. Granny taught me how to move a refrigerator without hurting my back. I am grateful for that. Going through life with back problems wouldn't be a good thing.

The front yard had grass and a huge tree that would drop what we used to call "stickers." The points of the stickers, which looked like points on a toothpick, could prick you if you weren't careful. There were red rose bushes against the house in the side yard, which faced Silver Street. There was also a row of hedge bushes on the same side. A dirt walkway separated the hedges from the roses. The walkway led to the backyard, where there was a chicken coop, chickens, a rooster, and a plum tree. The opposite side yard was clear of any vegetation. There was a fence that separated the property from the house next door. The land was a bit sloped, so the front of the house was level to the ground and as you walked to the rear, it gradually raised up on stilts to stay level. You couldn't see the stilts because the entire house was covered with wood-plank siding. There was an entrance to the underside of the house from the back. It was empty down there most of the time.

The first memory I have of living in that house was Christmas morning of 1967. My mom went all out for me that year. She must have bought my gifts before I moved and had Granny bring them with her on the moving truck, because no packages were delivered to the house. This was the year I received an Easy-Bake Oven. I loved that oven, and it came with real cake mix. There were other toys, but the oven is what sticks in my mind. I also remember one of the neighbor girls coming over to play. I took the oven out on the side steps and mixed up the batter for the cake and put the cake in the oven. Both of us were watching the cake cook when Granny called out to me telling me to go to the corner grocery store. The store was on South Parkway East, and I only had to cross one street. Yes, I know, I was only six and a half, but back then kids were older mentally because we had to be. Well, I asked Camilla—that was the name of the little girl who lived two doors down—to watch my cake while I went to the store. She watched it, all right. When I returned, she was gone and so was my cake. The only evidence that there had been a cake was the dirty pan. That obviously didn't sit well with me, but there wasn't anything I could do about it—the cake was gone. It was the only cake I got to bake in that oven. There was no way Granny was going to buy me more cake mix. For one thing, she didn't have much money, and for another, I knew not to ask.

Christmas is my favorite holiday, although when I look back on the holiday over the years, it really shouldn't be. As a kid I never received much in the form of presents. That first Christmas in Memphis was the best one. Each year I would take the money I earned doing things for the ladies in the neighborhood, head off to one of the stores on Elvis Presley Boulevard to buy presents for everyone in the family. Granny's daughter had five kids, all of whom were older than me. I would buy things like T-shirts, socks, hats—things a kid could afford.

Everyone would have something under the tree. Granny, Cora Lee, and I would go to Freddie Mae's house for Christmas dinner and to open presents every year. Uncle Hayward never went. I would sit on the couch waiting patiently for everyone to open the presents I had bought for them, which they did. And every year except one I received nothing in return. No presents for me. Every year I would be hurt and hide that pain. No one ever said anything about this. All I wanted was to belong, and it was clear that this would not happen. It took me many years to realize this. I guess I was just plain naïve. Every year I got to wash the dinner dishes, though, so that's something. Maybe I sound cynical, but I guess the family thought I should just be grateful for breathing. One year Freddie Mae bought me a Barbie doll, and this made me extremely happy. I still have a picture of myself sitting in between Granny and Cora Lee—everybody called her Little Mama—on the couch holding that doll. I must have some dog traits in me. That's not a very nice thing to say about myself, I know. It's just that I kept doing the same thing, year after year, hoping things would be different.

I'm embarrassed and ashamed of something I did as a kid, and I'm compelled to tell about it. It has haunted me for a very long time. First, I need to mention that I wasn't liked very much at school, which I'll tell about later. Because of that fact, none of the kids bought me presents for the Christmas exchanges the classes did. One year—I'm not sure which, although I know it was in elementary school—I received a present. Or so I thought. The name on the box said "Marie." Well, my name is Marie. What I didn't know was that my teacher's first name was Marie, too. I only knew her as Mrs. Pamplet.

I was so thrilled to get a present, so you can imagine my surprise when I opened the box to find a crystal punch bowl. What was I going to do with a punch bowl? I was a kid, for goodness' sake. Mrs. Pamplet had to have seen me open that box, and she never said a word. It didn't dawn on me until later that this must not have been meant for me. I gifted the bowl to Freddie Mae for Christmas. I was embarrassed that I had mistakenly taken a gift not meant for me, and I didn't want anyone to know. Mrs. Pamplet never said a thing to me about it. There have been a few times as an adult that I have looked for her so I could fess up and replace the bowl, but I've not been able to locate her. It doesn't matter to me that I was a kid. What I did was wrong, and I knew it before I regifted the bowl. Mrs. Pamplet was and still is my favorite teacher from school, not just because she never said anything to me about the punch bowl, but for all the kindness she showed me.

To this day, if someone is coming to my house for Christmas, they are going to receive a present—even if it's a box of candy. I always buy boxes of candy during the holidays just in case someone comes by unexpectedly, or, for that matter, if I have invited someone for dinner at the last minute. I hand out last-minute invitations because I'm chatty with people. If I find out someone I know doesn't have anything going on for Christmas, they get an invite. One of my close friends in Sequim used to say she never knew who was going to be at my house for dinner when she arrived because someone usually showed up who had been invited at the last minute. I wouldn't have it any other way. This rule goes for future Christmas dinners, too. If you don't want a Christmas dinner invitation from me, then don't tell me you are going to be alone that day. I won't force you to come if you don't want to, but I'll still extend you the invitation.

Granny rarely bought me presents, either. She simply didn't have the money to do so. Putting food on the table was enough of a challenge for her. I have no idea how much money was being brought into the household. Her mother, Little Mama, was over the age of 65 and was not working. I have no idea what she did for work before that age, and I don't know if she *ever* worked. Uncle Hayward was older than his sister, and he was the same.

I remember once when Granny used to get up at 3:00 a.m. to catch a bus that took her to pick cotton. I thought this was a fun thing to do. I'm not sure how old I was—maybe eight or nine—but I was young enough not to know what picking cotton was. And being from Chicago, how could I have known what it was? From my perspective I thought it was cool. She never really got in the bed to sleep at night. She would make a pallet on the floor in the kitchen. What I didn't know was that she was too tired to take a bath or to take her clothes off to get in bed. She would rise at Zero Dark Thirty and be out front waiting on the bus to pick her up. Well, I asked her if I could go with her. I wanted to pick cotton, too. This would have been in the summer. Otherwise, I would have been in school.

She said yes. I was so happy! It was going to be fun, I thought. I only went once. That was it for me. I was staying my tail in school. I'm sure she knew what she was doing by allowing me to accompany her to the cotton field. Jeez—now that's hard work. I was a little thing, closer to the ground than the adults were, and *I* was exhausted after one day. I can only imagine how they felt. What's that saying? "You do what you have to do to survive"—and Granny did exactly that. Granny was constantly looking for ways to bring in extra money. She never finished high school, either. When she was young, going to high school was optional, especially for Blacks. Remember, she was born in the Deep South in 1910. There weren't many opportunities available to her, which is why she ended up in Chicago. She went there to find work, make money, and send that money home to the family. Normally, it would have been the man who did this, but Granny wasn't married, and she had a child of her own to raise. I'm sure she had better prospects for work in Chicago. However, one of the problems with this decision was that she was away from her daughter, Freddie Mae. Freddie was raised by Cora Lee (Little Mama) while Granny earned money in Chicago. I don't know how long Granny was in Chicago, but I do know it was a while.

I had nothing to do with Granny's decision to leave her daughter and go to Chicago, and yet that choice would be the catalyst for part of my suffering during the years I lived in Memphis. Being an only child, I was so happy to have a big sister. It didn't matter to me that Freddie Mae was in her thirties and wasn't my blood kin. As I settled into the house in Memphis, I began to call Freddie Mae "Big Sister." I tried everything over the years to get her to love me, and it never worked.

Soon after Granny brought me to live with her in Memphis, I heard the two of them in the kitchen having a conversation. Big Sister was asking Granny why she had made the decision to bring me there. Didn't Granny know that I was only going to grow up, have babies, and bring them into the house for Granny to raise? Big Sister confronted her. At that time, I didn't know the full meaning of what she was saying. However, her tone was undeniable—she didn't want me there, and she made that fact very clear. Still, within my young mind and heart, I just *knew* she couldn't hate me.

But Big Sister's tone of voice stayed with me. It's still with me, all these years later, and I was six years old when those words were spoken. Big Sister; her husband, Johnny Sr.; and their five children had moved out long before I arrived and were living several streets away in a house they had purchased. That meant Granny's household consisted of Little Mama, Uncle Hayward, Granny, and me. When I first got there, I slept in the front room in the bed that Little Mama used to sleep in. I don't remember where Little Mama slept when I arrived because I had the bed.

In January 1968, I began school in Memphis at Hamilton Elementary. What a year that would turn out to be. The school wasn't that far away from the house—maybe half a mile. I'm not that good with distances, so it could have been a mile, but either way it wasn't far. When I started, there were two buildings on campus— one for the elementary kids and the other one for junior high and high school kids. A few years after I started attending, another school was built away from this campus to house grades ten through twelve. Junior high was grades seven, eight, and nine. When I started school, segregation was still in full swing. There weren't any kids of any other color than Black in attendance.

I was in junior high school when the school busing program began. That was a complete joke—an attempt at desegregation that did not integrate Black and white kids at all. We went to the same school, but we didn't mingle. The white kids hung out with each other, and the Black kids did the same. From my point of view, both groups were wary of each other, and as far as I remember, it stayed that way. Neither group of kids talked to the other group. That said, I applaud the adults' attempt. I didn't have to catch a bus to be shipped out of the neighborhood to another school. It might have been a good thing if I had been, but I stayed at Hamilton through twelfth grade. The reason I wasn't sent to another school was because of the street I lived on. My street wasn't bused, while the street next to mine was. The decision to choose who would be bused and who wouldn't be was based on the "every-two-street method," as I call it. This is because the neighborhood was broken down by streets, of course, and kids two streets away from me had to be bused, and kids two streets away from that street also had to be bused. I felt sorry for the white kids who were bused into our neighborhood. They clearly didn't want to be there. Why would they? For what it's worth, I've never had a prejudiced bone in my body, even though prejudice was all around me. I thought it was stupid then and still do. It's just plain dumb. This goes for all forms of prejudice.

Anyway, I have firsthand knowledge of how those kids must have felt being bused in because of my experience of entering a new school in another city in the middle of the school year. For the first time in my life, I felt fear, having to be in a class with kids I didn't know who talked and dressed differently than I did and who stared at me because they perceived me as different, too. What they saw was a kid from the North who dressed like a northerner, who talked like a northerner, and who wore thick Coke-bottle glasses. It went downhill from there. These kids had begun the school year together more than six months earlier. They had bonded already, and I was clearly out of my element—like a fish out of water. Granny warned me about fighting, too. She said that if I fought, she would whip me. I don't know why she felt she had to tell me this. I had never been in a fight before. Maybe she knew something that I didn't know. She had laid down the law, and I knew she meant it. She said, "Turn the other cheek." That's what the Bible said to do, and she was going to make sure I obeyed. With this rule, she basically tied my hands behind my back without me knowing it. New kids are usually tested, and boy, was I tested.

3

Neighborhood Elders

I never fit in, even though I tried. There was just something different about me and the kids knew it, albeit subconsciously. The spitballs started flying at me through their straws, and then the taunting started. None of this had ever happened to me before, and I didn't know how to respond. I was in perpetual shock the rest of that 1968 school year. Our class would sit in a circle on the classroom floor to read our books, and I can remember sitting in the reading circle with my head down reading a book silently when the little girl sitting next to me complained to the teacher that I was staring at her. In fact I wasn't—it just looked that way. I'm severely nearsighted, and one of my eyes is more severely nearsighted than the other. Because of this, when I focus on reading or anything else that requires close focus, my right eye sometimes becomes a lazy eye, which is what happened. The little girl thought I was staring, when that eye wasn't actually looking at anything.

I don't remember my first-grade teacher, and that's probably a good thing because in my opinion I didn't get any support from her. She told me to stop staring. In her defense, maybe she did try to support me, but I never felt it. To me, she never tried. She decided that I would have to repeat the first grade. I was held back, which essentially meant that I had failed. Who fails first grade? I was told that I was from Chicago and that the school systems were so different that it would be good for me. I could catch up. Catch up to what? I had gone through Head Start, kindergarten, and a half year of school before moving to Memphis. I wasn't a dumb kid. Well, the decision to hold me back a grade went over like a ton of bricks with Granny.

Granny was going to make sure this didn't happen again, so she came down hard on me from then on. She started with the ABCs, which I knew, but she wanted to make sure I knew them backwards, too. On the kitchen walls, she put pictures of alphabet letters that had an accompanying picture of something that began with that letter. I still remember the letter *H*. *H* had a picture of a horse. I sat at the kitchen table every day after school and Granny grilled me on those photos until I could demonstrate that I knew them by heart, in reverse order. Granny then moved on to times tables, which I also had to learn forwards and backwards. I think I was the only kid who could do this, and by the second grade, no less.

Granny told me not to ever bring home a grade lower than a B. Doing so would mean she would punish me with a whipping. Now, that's pressure. I definitely didn't want a whipping, and I also knew that I was a smart kid. So my grades became mostly A's, with a couple of Bs and no Cs for most of the 12 years of being in school. The pressure to achieve good grades was heightened even more by the ladies who lived in the neighborhood. I think of them as old ladies because all of them were over 50 or 60 when I moved to the neighborhood. I had to take my report card to them at the end of each term so that they could see it. Ms. Qualls, who lived across the street on Silver, would give me money for the grades I earned based on a sliding scale. I would receive so much for each A, another amount for Bs, and nothing for Cs. I'm not sure who instigated this ritual of taking my report card around to the ladies in the neighborhood, but one of the ladies did. They all knew each other and were friends. They used to meet each week at the Market Man's truck, which was parked next to our house on Silver

Street. Each week the Market Man, as he was called, would come with produce—vegetables and fruit—for the ladies to purchase. I can still hear his call: "Market Man! It's the Market Man! Market Man!" He had a loud voice, and everyone on the two streets could hear him. It was years before I ate vegetables or fruit purchased in a store.

As I recall, there weren't many men in the neighborhood—at least that I knew of. There was Mr. King, who was married to Mrs. King. They lived down the street in a duplex they owned, which was on the corner of Pillow and Silver Streets. I don't know their first names because I was a kid and not allowed to use first names with adults. If I did know their first name, it had to be prefaced with Miss, Mama, or Aunt. There was another man who lived at the opposite end of Silver, on the corner of Parkway and Silver. He rented a room, or apartment, from Mama Lou. I don't remember his name, but I do know he was drunk most of the time and would come to our house and talk to Granny. Sometimes he would come before I went to school for the day and be there in the same chair when I arrived home. Of course, that was normal for the time. People would visit each other and stay a while. They would be offered food, too. It was considered impolite not to offer a visitor food.

For some reason the ladies in the neighborhood took particular interest in me. I have no idea why. There were other kids around— not many, but they were there all the same. The personalities of the ladies were varied, of course, and all of them over the years acted as tribal elders for me. There was Mrs. King, the only housewife in the group, who I mentioned earlier. She made quilts and listened to gospel music most of the time. I used to make extra money cleaning her house on weekends. That lady had more knickknacks than anyone I've seen, and each of them had to be dusted. Cleaning for her cured me of wanting too many knickknacks.

Aunt Pat lived two doors down on Silver. She was raising her three grandchildren—Camellia, Terry, and Nicky. Camellia and I were the same age. Terry was the middle child, and Nicky was the youngest. Aunt Pat had her hands full, and she was alone.

Then there was Ms. Mandy, who lived across the street from us on Silver. In my opinion she was the curmudgeon in the neighborhood. She was also the only one who would send you to the store and give you a penny as payment. She wasn't mean. However, once she called Granny because I was eating unripe plums off the plum tree in our backyard. I wasn't supposed to be doing that, but she didn't need to get me in trouble.

Ms. Qualls also lived across the street from us on Silver, next door to Ms. Mandy. Ms. Qualls was always laughing. I can still hear her laughter. She was one of the only women who wore makeup and smelled of perfume, too. She was always nice to me. I used to write Christmas cards for her each year. She was a retired maid for a white family. Her photo album was filled with pictures of the kids she raised and their kids. On occasion some of kids she raised would visit her. Judging from their behavior, I think she was loved.

Mrs. Carmichael was widowed and lived next door to us on Gill Avenue. The house she owned had been subdivided into three units. Her son, his wife, and three kids lived in the main part of the house, there was a renter who lived upstairs, and Mrs. Carmichael had her own apartment on the far side of the house. She walked everywhere. I'd see her walking by with a long stick for support if needed. She looked educated and smart. Her clothes were Pendleton like, and she never used improper English.

On the other side of Ms. Qualls' house on Silver Street lived Ms. Grace. She had been married twice and widowed twice. I used to hear Granny talking about her to one of the other ladies periodically. It was their opinion that Ms. Grace caused both of her husbands to die because she lacked enough red blood cells. She had too many white blood cells. I still wonder how they came to such an outrageous conclusion. Ms. Grace wore makeup and had a soft voice. She was always kind to me. I loved to listen to her talk. She only chewed Trident gum, which I knew about because I was the one going to the store to purchase it.

Next to Ms. Grace lived Cousin Pearl. She was a distant cousin of Granny's. I have no idea how they were related. In my opinion, she was a bit off in the mind. Of course, it could have just been her personality. She had a temper, and I never knew when it was going to flare up, or how. I remember the time she was looking after me when Granny had to be gone. Cousin Pearl wouldn't allow me to go to school until I mopped the kitchen floor. She also gave me the only whipping I received while running. One day she told me not to go out of the yard. She didn't say why, and I didn't see her as the boss of me, so I went two doors down the street to see Camellia. I saw Cousin Pearl coming after me with a long switch—a tree branch. She beat me with that switch all the way home while I was running to get away from her. It was the only time she touched me, though. This was because she drew blood. I had numerous welts on my body, and one of them bled. I remember running to the place where Granny worked to show her that I was bleeding. Ms. Gladys, the lady she worked for, saw this, too, and it didn't go over well. It was the only time during my stay in Memphis that Granny called my mother because of a beating I received. My mother was angry, but she didn't take any action, which I didn't understand.

One of the things I did for Cousin Pearl over the years was to go to the corner grocery store to purchase Kotex napkins. For years I thought those things were for her kitchen table. They were called napkins, so how was I supposed to know what they really were used for? It wasn't until I began my own menstrual cycle and Granny sent one of her grandsons to the store to get them for me that I figured it out. I was so naïve about things.

Last but not least, Ms. Sweetie Bee lived up the street in one of the duplexes on Silver. She loved her soap operas. *As the World Turns* was her favorite. I would run errands for her, too.

I ran errands for all of these ladies and even slept in their homes periodically. I didn't understand at the time why Granny would loan me out to them over the years, but I do now. There were periods in each of their lives when fear would arise, and they just wanted someone else in the house at night—I was that person. I'd come home from school, get homework and chores done, and then head over to spend the night at one of the ladies' houses. I didn't do this all the time, for sure. However, it was a few times a year. I never knew when it would happen. I'd walk through the door from school and be told that I had to go to so-and-so's house that evening. I'd stay with them for a few evenings in a row, and then it would be done, until the next time. There were only a couple of the ladies that I minded having to do this for—Mrs. King, whose husband died, and Ms. Mandy. This was because they didn't have a TV—not that I watched much TV, but it would have given me something to do until bedtime.

The other lady who was tremendously influential in my life was Ms. Gladys. She lived on South Parkway East in what I called the rich neighborhood. The homes were large and gorgeous. Granny worked for Ms. Gladys. In the beginning it was to take care of her mother, who was not well. Granny took this job a couple of years after moving back to Memphis. Ms. Gladys was a high school principal. I don't remember the name of the school, but it wasn't anywhere near the neighborhood I lived in. She was petite, light skinned, and had good hair. Good hair is a cultural term for someone who doesn't have nappy hair. Ms. Gladys' hair was long and straight with a bit of a wave, which she covered with a wig. I never understood that, either. Why would someone who had such pretty hair want to cover it up?

Because she was an educator, Ms. Gladys took particular interest in my education. She had numerous books, which included encyclopedias. I would sometimes go to her house to do book reports when I needed to do research. She made awesome waffles, too. When I would visit on Saturday, she would make me breakfast. Waffles are, to this day, my favorite breakfast food—with bacon, of course. They were thin, crispy, and loaded with melted butter. We never ate like this at home. Ms. Gladys didn't have children, and I don't think she had ever been married. Gladys Green was her name. She had a sister who lived in Washington, D.C., and who was also a high school principal. Granny worked for Ms. Gladys long after the death of Ms. Gladys' mother, who Granny took care of during the day. In fact, Granny continued working for her until Granny's health caused her to stop. This was well after I finished high school.

Except for Ms. Sweetie Bee and Ms. Qualls, all of the ladies owned their homes. Home ownership was a huge deal and preferable to renting. It was a mark of stability. Ms. Sweetie Bee and Ms. Qualls were long-term renters. Ms. Qualls lived in her house for well over 20 years, and Ms. Sweetie Bee was a close second. All of the ladies' homes had one thing in common. Hanging on their living room walls were three pictures all who entered saw—Jesus, Dr. Martin Luther King Jr., and President John F. Kennedy. All three of these men were revered in the Black community. I don't think there were many homes that didn't have the same photos prominently displayed.

It's worth noting my experience of being in Memphis during the shooting of Dr. King. I hadn't been living in Memphis very long when it happened. I remember being in school when the voice of the principal came over the intercom telling us of the event and that school would be closing for the day. Our parents had been called and would be picking us up, since none of us would be allowed to walk home. Later that day I learned why. There was a fear of rioting and of the Black Panthers. The school was responsible for keeping us safe, and that meant only letting us leave the premises with a responsible adult. Big Sister was the only one in the family with a car, so she picked me up along with her kids. I can remember climbing into the back seat of the station wagon and being taken home. The TV was on, and Granny and Little Mama were crying. As a kid, I didn't know the full ramifications of what had taken place, but I knew it wasn't good. I don't remember if there was any rioting in Memphis, although I don't think there was. What I do remember is the quiet, somber attitudes of the adults, which lasted for days.

Temperate Climate

The temperature is moderate, not extreme. There is regular rain. The lotus plant needs variability with no extremes in temperature. All four seasons are represented. The life cycle of the lotus through its growth in temperate climate symbolizes that human need to strive for moderation with some variability. We seek the middle of the road—everything in moderation. When life is cruel, harsh, and extreme, we instinctively seek to find the middle ground, which is moderate with variability.

4

My New Normal

The flowering lotus needs the right climate in which to grow. The air must be moderate and warm, so as not to destroy the delicate germination process happening within the seed. Memphis was muggy in the summer and wet in the winter, and the emotional climate of my childhood continued to be filled with turmoil. A week rarely passed when I wasn't being beaten up in elementary school. As a matter of fact, it was more like two or three times a week. Because of Granny's rule, I couldn't fight, and the kids pounced.

One girl, who was *not* little, had a name I will never forget: *Von-god-a-dese*. She decided she was going to beat me up after school, and she told me so. Whenever there was going to be a fight on the playground, all the kids would gather around to watch. This particular afternoon was no different. We would be let out of school at 3:15 p.m. to go home. On this day, my thought was to get to the junior high school because Big Sister's youngest child was there, and I thought he could protect me. Well, I never made it. The kids must have seen the direction I was headed and followed me. I was terrified of what would happen. This girl towered over me. Like the character Olive Oyl from Popeye, I was long and skinny. I weighed 60 pounds until seventh grade. Vongodade walked up to me and hit me in the mouth with her fist. I hit the ground. It was over with one knockout blow. She hit me so hard that my front tooth was damaged. Years later I ended up needing a root canal of that tooth and a crown.

Each of my elementary school teachers tried their best to stop the bullying I was receiving, but they were not successful. They would tell the students to be kind to me, and the kids would be nice for a day or so. Then they would go back to their old behavior. It was humiliating to go through this. The name-calling, fights, taunting, and plain-old meanness could have crushed me, but it didn't.

My saving grace in elementary school was the fact that I loved learning. In sixth grade I became a safety patrol girl and participated in the demo computer program. I was allowed to leave class a few minutes early to do my job of assisting other kids across the street. The school was also testing a new way of learning math via computer. I was selected to be one of the kids to test the program. Every day, I went to the computer lab to work on math problems using the computer. I absolutely loved this, and I thrived. I loved math so much that when I entered junior high school I joined the math club.

My years in elementary school were in some ways close to nightmarish for me. In addition to what was going on in school, my home environment wasn't much better. Shortly after moving to Memphis, the dog pound came and took my dog, Lady, away. Little Mama didn't allow dogs in the house, so Lady had to stay outside. Not only that, but because the chickens were in the backyard, Lady had to be kept under the house. The poor girl was tied up to a beam under the house all day, which she hated, so she barked incessantly. The woman who rented the upstairs apartment in the house next door worked at night and slept during the day. As you can imagine, having a barking dog next door kept her awake, so she called the dog pound. When I think about it, she must have called the police, but the people I saw coming to take Lady away were from the dog pound.

The vision of this day will stay with me for the rest of my life. I stood at the window in the back bedroom watching my dog being loaded into a truck and taken away. I didn't cry. Instead, my heart began to close. I do recall saying to myself that I would never have another dog. That dog was all I had in the way of comfort and joy, and she was taken from me. I heard Granny telling the dog pound man, "You can have the dog, but you can't have the chickens. We are going to eat those." So I learned to pluck chickens that day. I sat on the back stairs while Granny taught me how to defeather a chicken and get the little pen-like feathers out, too. This was after watching her catch a chicken, ring its neck, and cut it off.

In addition to losing Lady, there were the whippings Granny gave me. The whippings turned into beatings once I arrived in Memphis. Back then most kids got whippings, but there is—or should I say, was—a distinct difference between a whipping and a beating. Granny's belief, along with others', was taken loosely from Proverbs 13:24 in the Bible: "Spare the rod and spoil the child." Well, she didn't spare the rod, and I certainly wasn't spoiled. I began to get beaten several times a week for this or that reason. Usually, it was just me being a kid. I really don't remember what it was that I was doing that she thought was so bad. The slightest infraction would warrant her getting the belt to beat me. She said she didn't believe in whipping clothes, so I was stripped naked and made to get down on the floor while she beat me. Everyone on the street knew when I was being beaten, too. This is because noise travels, and I was a screamer. How could I not scream? It hurt. I learned to get through these beatings by telling myself that it would only hurt as long as she was hitting me and that at some point she had to stop.

I'd flail around on the floor writhing in pain from the licks of the belt. At one point, she said she was tired of whipping me so often, so she decided to add up the infractions and whip me all at once for them. This meant that when I had done five things that warranted being punished, then I would get whipped for those five things. The beatings seemed to last forever. She would talk to me about each infraction and then whip me for that particular thing. Then she would talk to me about the next infraction and whip me for that. It would continue this way until I had been punished for each occurrence. Because she kept a running tally, my stomach would be tied in knots waiting for the day when the beating would happen.

I remember once when I was being beaten for something I kicked her. This was not intentional on my part; it was because of the flailing around. From then onward she began to tie me up. First, it was to a chair. She would sit in the chair and beat me, while I was tied to that same chair. I guess that must have been awkward because she soon stopped. I was then stripped naked, and my hands and feet bound together for the beatings.

I used to sit on the toilet with my head on the edge of the bathtub crying after these beatings and beg God to send my father to get me. I knew my father would save me. I did this for years. I knew my mother wouldn't save me. She hadn't responded to any of my pleas. She would call me twice a year, once for my birthday and again at Christmas. Each time I would tell her what was happening and she never did anything about it. I don't think she thought it was as severe as it was. I wanted to be with her, even if she couldn't take care of me. Each time I asked, she would say, "You can come for a visit when you are 12." What was so special about getting to 12 years of age? The bottom line was she wanted to push my coming to Chicago into the future, and since I was little, 12 was a long way away. So my plea to God was for the father I had never known to save me. I didn't know any better. I just wanted to be rescued from that hell.

To add insult to injury, when Big Sister's eldest son was getting married, the little girl who lived next door to them was asked to be the flower girl. I wasn't asked because I wasn't perceived as pretty. I was ugly to them. I wasn't even allowed to attend the wedding, and I stayed at Big Sister's house while everyone else went to the church. It was so clear that the family didn't care for me. Still I persisted with trying to get their love.

Most people have nicknames when they are kids, and sometimes those names carry over into adulthood. As a kid my nickname was Pig. I'm not sure how I acquired the name, but I do know it began shortly after I moved to Memphis. It might have been because of my allergies and hay fever, which caused me to sneeze and sniff a lot. I also used to be pinned to the floor sometimes by one of Big Sister's kids and have my nose pushed in, which would cause me to go into a convulsion of sneezing. They thought it was funny. I didn't.

I just didn't fit in—at school or at home. Then there were the times I would call my mother to ask for money for a school function. Each time she would promise to send it, and each time it would never arrive, and I wouldn't be able to participate. I'd be left behind for most school outings. The one time I went on an outing, I managed to make the money to pay for the trip myself. It was during the holiday season, and the school trip was to attend *The Nutcracker* ballet. I was so excited to see it. I got sick a few days before the big event. This didn't deter me from going—I went anyway. I felt awful, but I sat through that performance. I've not seen *The Nutcracker* since then, even though I keep intending to go.

Whenever I was sick with a cold or flu, I would go to school anyway. I liked being at school even though it was challenging. It was the learning that I liked. I loved to study and learn about whatever was being taught. My second home was the bookmobile. The bookmobile would park on Gill next to the Methodist church every Thursday. I'm not sure if it came during the school year, but I know it was there in the summer. I would walk up the street to return the load of books from the prior week and check out another pile. I adored reading, and I read voraciously. Reading was my refuge. I got lost in stories from faraway places every day while sitting on the front porch. This is where I read.

Because there weren't many kids in the neighborhood, I didn't get to play much. Sometimes Camellia or Terry would come over, and we would play jacks, but that was it. Granny didn't believe in playing checkers or anything else—she considered it gambling. She was quite religious. Sundays were sacred, so there wasn't any cooking or washing or any type of work done on that day. I would go to Sunday school and then 11:00 a.m. church service, where I would sit, bored to tears, watching the minister preaching, jumping up and down, shouting, and telling us this or that about Jesus. The game every Sunday for the kids was to see whose wig was going to come off first in church. Most of the ladies wore wigs. Why they wore those things on their heads was beyond me—it was hot, and everyone was sweating. It would get even hotter when someone would start shouting, as it was called. The Spirit was moving through them, and it caused them to do things they would never do otherwise. I remember seeing a lady walk the pews while flailing around, and the way she moved her body left an impression on me. Well, I thought church was an excuse for people to dance and get their groove on. I know that sounds awful, but I was a kid, and my mind was quite active. The wigs would go flying, and the arms and feet would move faster than James Brown's.

Speaking of wigs, there was a period of time when I was little that Granny decided I should wear one. She saw this as a good option for my short, nappy hair. I think she was tired of pressing my hair weekly. She used to press my hair on Saturday and ply it with Murray's grease. This was to slick down my hair to the scalp. I'd sleep in a stocking cap to keep my hair in place at night. I think I was ahead of my time with that style, don't you? Anyway, Granny bought me a wig, and I wore it. I'm not sure how long I did this, but I know there is a school picture with me cheesing for the camera and the wig is on. I can understand Granny being tired of having to do my hair, but I still can't believe she would make a little girl wear a wig. And the way she began to dress me was embarrassing. She didn't want me to catch a cold or get sick, so I had to wear a dress *and* pants. Today this is the style, but back then it wasn't. Picture an Olive-Oyl-skinny little girl with short hair, Coke-bottle glasses, pointy-toed shoes from Goodwill wearing a dress and long pants. Yes, I was hip. Granny did not know how to dress a kid, and the word *style* was not in her vocabulary where I was concerned.

My relationship with Granny is and was a paradox. As strange as it may seem, I knew she loved me. There is no doubt in my mind about this. She pushed me hard in school, and she never interfered with any of the school activities I wanted to participate in. Just the fact that she wanted to take me with her to Memphis for my benefit says she cared deeply for me. On the other side of the coin, her beatings were over-the-top cruel. It was as though she was trying to beat the "me" out of me. I felt my spirit was in danger of being broken by her. The flame that is me began to dim but was never extinguished. I wasn't consciously trying to keep it lit—I didn't know anything about this at the time. There was just something within me that caused me to keep going. In hindsight, I know that Granny could sense something within me that scared her. I know this because of two occurrences I had with her as a kid.

The first happened one night about three years after moving to Memphis—I think I was approaching nine years of age—I was asleep in the front room and was awakened when I heard Uncle Hayward calling to Granny. Her name to him was Luzanna. He kept calling, and I thought Granny couldn't hear him. So I got up to go look for her. I found her sitting on the toilet. I stood by the door in the hallway entrance and told her, "Uncle Hayward is calling you." The look she gave me and the feeling I felt from her was fear. She told me, "Uncle Hayward isn't calling me. He is dead." He had died that night. I had slept through it. I didn't understand what she was telling me because I knew what I heard. As a kid I could sense when other deceased people were around. I couldn't talk about it with anyone, but Granny had to have known about this ability, especially with that incident. I'll get to the other incident later.

When Uncle Hayward died, I inherited his bedroom, along with the bed and mattress he died in. That was the beginning of my fear of dead people. I was moved into that room the very next day. How can I explain this in a way to convey the level of fear that arose in me? I was beyond terrified. I used to lie awake at night seeing all sorts of shadows on the walls and hearing sounds that I couldn't explain. I never said a word to Granny or anyone about it. I knew not to. One night when I was going to bed, Granny's youngest granddaughter was at the house. I asked her to tell me a bedtime story. I didn't really want a story. I just wanted her to sit with me until I fell asleep. Well, as soon as she began the story, Granny told her to come out of the room so that I could go to sleep. That was the end of that. I grew more and more fearful of being left alone in a house. This fear extended to funerals, too.

One of the little girls who lived on Pillow Street was killed by a relative. She and I were the same age. Her little body had been raped and stabbed numerous times. At the funeral, the casket was open, and I could see her lying there. She didn't look like herself. Her face was unrecognizable to me. After that, whenever I would go to the bathroom, I'd see her lying in the bathtub. For that matter, whoever had died, I'd see them in that bathtub if I attended their funeral. I hated funerals. Years later when Little Mama died, I said I wasn't going to her funeral. Granny threatened me with a punishment that was over-the-top harsh, so I went. But I was scared almost to death.

I knew what I would see and feel. Dead people were everywhere. I carried this fear into adulthood. I was 40 years old before I conquered that fear. If I was going to be left alone for any amount of time, I'd leave the house, or I'd have someone stay with me if it was going to be overnight. No one ever got it. They didn't understand what I was talking about when I said I was scared of seeing dead people. Most people thought I was referring to seeing a physical dead body in the flesh. That's not what I meant at all. These dead people weren't really dead. They walked and talked, and I could sense them around most of the time. Sometimes I could see them.

As a child there wasn't anyone to talk to about this, so I just kept it inside. I remember when Granny decided to rent out two of the rooms in the house for a short period of time. Granny was at the hospital with Little Mama, who was dying. I was left at home alone, with the exception of the tenant who was in her quarters. Granny moved me out of Uncle Hayward's room for a while and turned it into a kitchen. She gave up her bedroom to rent the two back rooms out. A door was hung to close that area off from the rest of the house. In any event, Granny wasn't there, and I was alone that night. I sat up all night in Little Mama's rocking chair on high alert. I knew the dead people were there, and I didn't want to see them. Well, the tenant got up to go to the bathroom in the middle of the night, and I mentioned it to her the next morning. Her reply to me was that she hadn't gotten up at all. But I know I saw her come out of the room and go down the hall. If it wasn't her, who was it?

I prayed to God a lot when I was a kid. He was, of course, a white dude with a long beard and long white robe. I knew he heard me, too. There was never any doubt about this. I couldn't see him, but for some reason I knew my prayers were being listened to. There was someone there listening. It had to be God. Who else could it have been? I lived in my inner world most of the time talking to God. It was safe. I didn't have imaginary friends. My inner world felt warm, loving, and encouraging. It is what I clung to. I was an adult before I realized the "it," or the God I was talking to, was my Spirit Guide. Everyone around me was exceedingly superstitious, so I can only imagine what would have happened to me if I had mentioned any of this to them. But Granny had to know on some level, and it probably scared her.

There is no excuse for her beating me the way she did, and I know she had her demons. I just need to convey what I feel it was all about as I look back on it. In addition to this, because of my relationship with the God I knew internally, there was a disconnect with what I was being taught in church and by Granny about hell, fire, and damnation. I didn't buy into what they were saying about the punishing aspect of God. It couldn't be true because that wasn't my experience with him. Even with the way I was being treated by others, I knew what unconditional love felt like. I didn't know about unconditional love back then, but that's what it was. How could someone who felt so warm and loving toward me punish me? Even when I made a mistake or did something wrong, the feeling I felt coming from him was love.

When I turned 12, Granny said that this was the age when Jesus took on his own sins. Before that, anything he did was taken on by his parents, and this was the same with everyone. Because of this, I was now taking on my own sins. She said it was time for me to decide which church I wanted to join. It didn't matter to her which one I chose, but I had to choose. With that, I began to explore other denominations of Christianity. I didn't know about any other faiths, or I would have explored them too. Being a Gemini, this was perfect for me. I loved research—and still do.

I began by going to church with Mr. and Mrs. King. They belonged to the Church of God and Christ. There was nothing wrong with their church, but it taught the same thing that I had been taught at the Baptist church, just in a different way. I then moved on to the Methodist church, staying there for a bit of time. After that, it was the Jehovah's Witnesses. I only had access to denominations from the neighborhood. I didn't know about Mormonism, Presbyterianism, Islam, Judaism, Buddhism, or any other faith. Granny gave me a wonderful gift by allowing me to choose for myself where I wanted to worship.

In the end, I chose to stay with the Baptist church. This meant having to be baptized after a long week of going to revival. I sat on the church pew every evening listening to the minister go on and on and on, and then came the time for me to be baptized. I was scared to death. I was afraid I would drown since I didn't know how to swim. Behind the pulpit and choir was a curtain that I had never looked behind before. On the day of my baptism, I got to see what was there: a big, deep, scary pool filled with water. When my turn came to get into the water, I was sure the minister would let go of me and I would sink to the bottom of the pool. I weighed 60 pounds, and it wouldn't take much for me to sink. He grabbed me from the stairs and before I knew it, he was dunking me under the water. He did this three times—once in the name of the Father, then in the name of the Son, and last in the name of the Holy Spirit. I had been saved.

I also got to visit my mother in Chicago when I was 12, just as she had promised. I hadn't seen her since the age of seven when she came through Memphis on her way to Bogalusa for her mother's funeral. She didn't take me with her on that trip, and I wasn't happy about it. After all, the funeral was for my real grandmother. I didn't know then that my mother hated her and didn't want her to have anything to do with me. For that matter, she didn't even want me to be raised in Bogalusa, but I didn't know that either. From my vantage point, if she didn't want to raise me, she could have at least sent me to live with family. Maybe I would have been treated better. But that wasn't to be.

I wasn't sure that my mother would send the money for the trip that summer. Up to that point, she had not done anything she had promised to do for me. I learned pretty early that if I wanted to do something that required money, I had to earn it. Granny didn't have any money to spare, and I knew not to ask her for any. She would just say, "Girl, do you think money grows on trees?"

I was so excited to be going to Chicago that summer. It was my first trip alone, and it was by train. I had my ticket, my luggage checked, and instructions for how to behave on the train and in Chicago. Ms. Grace had given me the instructions for behavior in Chicago. One day I was over at her house after running an errand for her. She was standing at the kitchen sink and said, "While you are in Chicago, keep your skirt down." I had no clue what she was talking about, but I said, "Yes, ma'am." That was as close as any of the ladies, including Granny, ever came to talking to me about sex. As a matter of fact, when one of the girls who lived next door got pregnant and I heard about it, I went to the front yard and looked up for the stork. As far as I knew, that's where babies came from.

5

Illusion and Reality

My mother lived on the South Side of Chicago on Michigan Avenue near Garfield. The apartment was not that far from where I had lived with Granny on 51st and Prairie. Mom lived in what is called a six-flat. There were three floors, with two spacious apartments on each floor. A stairwell separated the apartments. Back then, people would live in the same apartment for decades. And in that area of the city, each apartment had maid quarters at the back for live-in help. The original inhabitants of those buildings had moved away, probably to the suburbs. It was now an all-Black community.

My mother's apartment was on the first floor. When you entered the building from the street, there was a vestibule with a flight of stairs that led to a door where you had to be buzzed in. Once you entered through the second door, you were on the first floor. Her apartment was on the left. Upon my arrival, I immediately noticed an iron gate in front of the wooden door that led to my mother's apartment. The other apartment didn't have one. Mom also didn't live alone. She shared the apartment with her boyfriend, Gerald, and another man, Mr. Sampson. Mr. Sampson was a foot doctor working out of the apartment, and Gerald was an alcoholic who didn't work at all. To this day I don't understand what my mother saw in that man, but I'm getting ahead of myself.

Upon entry, the living room was to the left with huge bay windows that looked out onto Michigan Avenue. There was a wonderful fireplace that was never used as far as I know. The living room served two purposes: it was where Mr. Sampson saw his clients and where he slept. He had a queen-sized bed on the wall where the fireplace was, a couch where his clients sat waiting to be treated, a desk where he worked, and a few other pieces of furniture. One thing that stood out to me about the room was the windows. I fell in love with them. To this day, I still love windows. The other thing that stood out in the room was the laughing Buddha figurine Mr. Sampson had on the mantle. It was made out of white porcelain, and it enthralled me.

There was a long hallway that led from the front of the apartment to the back. Next to the living room, a few steps off the hall, was a bedroom. This was to be my room while I was visiting. It was a nicely appointed room in my opinion. I had my very own queen-sized bed, dresser, nightstand, and highboy—all in a matching mahogany-wood set. There was also another cabinet with dress-up dresses that belonged to my mother. There was a window with an iron security bar attached from the inside, a radiator, a closet that had Mr. Sampson's things inside, and another door that led to a bathroom. This was a shared bathroom with two entrances: one from my room and one from the hall. It was used by Mr. Sampson, his guests, and me. It had a claw-foot tub, toilet, sink, and mirror. The flooring was that black-and-white small checker-style tile that was so popular back in the '60s.

A little further down the hall was a dining room. There were huge windows in there too, but they were always closed off with heavy curtains, which made the room dark. Off the dining room was another small bedroom with an adjoining bathroom—these were the maid's quarters that I mentioned earlier, and it was where my mother and Gerald slept. The dining room also led to the kitchen, which had a walk-in pantry. The kitchen had the usual items plus a deep freezer. There were also other winter staples in the pantry. Two big metal garbage cans with lids were filled with flour and meal. The pantry shelves were stacked with canned goods, spices, powdered milk, and a host of other cooking items. At the back of the kitchen was the back door, which led to the back porch, which was never used. There were also stairs. You could climb them to the next floors or go down to the basement entrance, where the coal furnace was housed, or to the backyard—which was also never used.

My mother was still working in Skokie, which meant she still had the same commute as when I lived in Chicago before. By the time I got up in the mornings, she would be gone until 8:00 or so in the evening. Occasionally she would accompany a few friends to the horse track and get home much later. I didn't get to see her much that summer except on Sundays. She worked six days a week.

Every Sunday we would attend church. I'm not sure what denomination the church was. This was because the minister—psychic Reverend Morris, who I came to hate later—would give out lottery numbers to the congregation to play. I thought this odd, even at 12. Reverend Morris lived above the church with Johnny. I don't remember Johnny's last name, but he was nice. Reverend Morris never smiled and was always yelling and giving orders. I didn't like this and wondered why grown people would do what he was saying.

The name of the church was Israel Tabernacle. My mother loved that church, and she usually followed through with everything Reverend Morris told her to do. However, there was one exception. One Sunday he stood at the pulpit, in front of the congregation, and told her that I needed to know who my father was and that she should have me meet him. (He made a habit of talking about other people's personal business in front of the congregation. I never liked this about him.) Well, I still haven't met the man. My mother told me she looked for him but couldn't find him. I'll never know if she was telling the truth, just like I never knew when she was telling the truth about anything. Lying, to this day, is a pet peeve of mine. The only thing I ever got her to tell me was his name, and only because I once mentioned the wrong name to her and she immediately corrected me. We never talked about my father again after that summer.

I began to get to know some of the other church kids that summer, which was nice. There were a couple of girls around my age who lived on the third floor of the building I lived in. I would play with them; we would sometimes walk to Garfield Park to play, but most of the time we just hung around the building. There was an older boy who lived in the apartment across the hall. He never played with us, but I did get to know him, and he was nice. None of the other kids came to my apartment to play. There just wasn't anywhere for us to be in that apartment, other than my bedroom, and there couldn't be much noise since Mr. Sampson sometimes saw clients at the apartment. I was okay with this, because for once I felt free. I didn't have any chores to do, and I could just be a kid. Mom would leave money for me on my dresser so that I could buy lunch or whatever I wanted that day. I guess you could say I was getting an allowance for once.

My mother's boyfriend, Gerald, was a piece of work. I grew to hate him. Let me rephrase—I grew to loathe him, and I told him so. Once during that first summer, I tried to hit him with a cast-iron skillet. I'm sorry I missed. Really, I am. He never worked during any of the years I visited, and he was usually drunk. Although, you usually wouldn't be able to tell that he was drunk just by looking at him. He was a functioning alcoholic—that is, until he couldn't function anymore.

Because I was on summer vacation, I used to stay up late watching TV—usually old movies. I still love the classics. I'd sometimes leave my room and head to the kitchen for a snack. Everyone in the household was usually asleep. On one occasion, this wasn't the case. As I passed through the dining room, Gerald was on the floor outside the door to his and my mother's bedroom. I thought he was asleep. As I attempted to walk by, he reached out and grabbed the bottom of my robe, pulling me down on the floor. He was on top of me before I knew what had happened. For some reason I wasn't afraid; I got angry. His boozed breath was repugnant, and his mouth was all over me while his hands touched me in places he had no business touching. Thank goodness he was drunk, because he wasn't as strong as he would have been if he were sober. I managed to kick, push, and shove my way out from under him before he could rape me. It was the first time I felt a man's erection, and I instinctively knew what he wanted to do to me. I'm not sure how I knew; I just did. I didn't scream either, although it would have been well within reason for me to do so. My dislike for him had begun as soon as I laid eyes on him, and this occurrence deepened that hatred. I managed to get away from him as fast as I could and went back to my room.

I didn't know how to tell my mother what had happened, but I knew she had to find out. Her best friend, Carrie, was the person I turned to. Carrie and my mother had been friends for years. I didn't know this until that summer, because my mother never mentioned her to me when she called. But I knew she was the person I could tell. So the very next Sunday after church, I managed to ask her if we could talk. I told her everything that had happened a few days earlier. She said that she would tell my mother, which she did.

My mother came home from work a few days later and as usual came to see how I was doing. She sat down next to me on the side of the bed this time rather than just sticking her head through the door. She asked me about the incident, and I told her what happened. I'm not sure she knew what to do about it. My expectation was for her to kick Gerald out—tell him to pack his bags and leave. This, however, isn't what happened. I was the one packed off to stay with church-member friends of Mom's who had kids.

I spent most of my time after that event at other people's homes. This went on summer after summer after summer until I was an adult. And when I was home, I usually had a girlfriend staying with me. On the occasions when I was home without a friend and Mr. Sampson wasn't there, I would bolt my bedroom door and keep the door to the bathroom locked. I had to do this because Gerald would sometimes try to get into my room. He would bang on the door in a drunken state and demand that I open it. Once he did this when Mr. Sampson was home and Mr. Sampson made him stop. There was no protection from him other than my locked door, which was pretty heavy. The doors in those old buildings were tall, made of thick wood, and durable. My room had a deadbolt on it, and I used it.

I was usually pretty careful when I was exiting my room, which meant I would be headed out the front door only a few paces away. Gerald never tried anything with me when he was sober. One day I thought I heard him go out, so I went to the kitchen for something. He appeared at the doorway to the kitchen. He had been drinking, but he wasn't drunk. I was 15 or 16 years old. When I saw him, I picked up the cast-iron skillet from the stove and threatened him with it if he came near. By this time, just seeing him made me angry. He took a step toward me and I swung the skillet at him, intending to bash his head in. I missed. I was too far away to make contact—so I threw the skillet at him and ran past as he began to laugh. Thank the gods he didn't come after me, or I would have been in trouble.

That first summer with my mother didn't go as I thought it would. I thought we would spend time together, hanging out and doing things together. What happened instead was that what little trust and respect I had for my mother began to fade. I knew she wouldn't follow through with promises, but I hadn't realized she couldn't or wouldn't protect me. I had told her about the beatings Granny had been giving me and she had done nothing, but I never thought she wouldn't protect me from her own boyfriend. I guess in her mind, sending me to stay with friends was protection. As it turned out, it wasn't.

6

Fight for Self Begins

Junior high was a turning point for me. I was 13 years old, and it seemed that something snapped inside of me. I didn't know it at the time, but I was doing my best to get my personal power back. It was as though I had been in a long sleep since the moment I moved to Memphis.

The first thing I did after returning to Memphis from visiting my mother for the second summer was to stop answering to the nickname Pig. It was quite interesting how this came about. One day I just decided I was done with the name—just like that. I systematically advised everyone I knew in the community that I would no longer answer to that name. "My name is Marie, and this is the only name I will answer to," I told them. I even told Granny this, and I didn't get a backhand across the face or a beating. The people in my Memphis community were the only people who called me Pig. (My mother used my middle name, and because of this, so did everyone I knew in Chicago.) I was fed up with the nickname. I followed through with my plan. It took a while for everyone to catch on, but in time they all did.

The next thing that happened was that I fought back at school. One day I was visiting a new friend, and one of the neighbor kids who I also went to school with decided she was going to beat me up. As I said, I have never picked a fight in my life, and this was no exception. The only difference was that this time, I beat her up in return. I got angry—I was tired of being bullied. The fights stopped. I never got into another fight at school, or anywhere else for that matter.

The third incident caused Granny to stop beating me. At the time, I had no idea that this would happen, and what I did wasn't premeditated. One day Granny told me that I had lost the cap from the Visine eye-drop bottle, and I had better find it or she was going to give me a beating. (What would a 13-year-old need with eye drops anyway?) I hadn't touched the bottle. That said, I knew she would follow through with her threat if I didn't find the cap. I looked high and low for it with no luck. True to her word, Granny had me strip off my clothes. This time she didn't bind my hands to my feet for some reason. I got down on my knees while she stood over me with the belt. She started to beat me, and I just looked up at her and stared. I didn't blink and I didn't budge. Even in that moment, I knew that I couldn't stop her from beating me, but I also knew that I had control over how I responded. She kept hitting me harder and harder, saying that she was going to make me cry. I just kept staring at her. I never shed a tear. There was only a part of me there. The larger part of me had exited my body in Chicago that same summer, and I was fighting to survive. Granny didn't get the response from me that she was expecting. And by the look in her eyes, I think I must have scared her. Maybe she thought I was going to go mad or something—I don't know. She never beat me again after that. She moved on to other forms of severe punishment—groundings that lasted months.

What precipitated all of this was that during my second summer visit to see my mother, I was raped. It wasn't my mother's boyfriend who did it. My mother, I guess trying to protect me that summer, sent me to stay with a church member who had three kids. The youngest girl and I hit it off. She was a year younger than me. The middle sister was my age, and there was another sister who was

51

older. The older girls were hardened and promiscuous, and neither the younger girl nor I knew much about life or sex. I was certainly pretty naïve. My life had been sheltered.

The middle sister, Yolanda, had a 19-year-old boyfriend who lived on the street. He saw me one day and asked if he could talk to me about Yolanda. He said they were having problems and that he wanted to get my input. I agreed. I didn't see any harm in it. He asked me to come to his apartment the next day at a particular time. Again, I said okay. I went to his home at the appointed time and knocked on the door; he answered and asked me to come in. When I looked around the apartment, I saw that the living room was empty of furniture except for a mattress on the floor. The mattress was near the doorway between the living room and kitchen, which I could see from the living room. He asked me to sit down. The only place to sit was on the mattress, so I sat down. And before I knew what was happening, he was on top of me. There was no way for me to fight him off—he was too strong. So I just lay there and let him do to me what he wanted. I didn't fight. It was horribly painful. I didn't know what to do. He just kept ramming his penis into me. It felt as though I was being torn apart. I didn't cry or scream. When he was done, I got up, walked back to my friend's house, went into the bathroom, and cleaned myself up. I was still hurting down there, wet and bleeding. I didn't tell anyone. Who was I going to tell? There wasn't anyone to tell. No one was going to protect me or do anything about it—no one. So he got away with it. The part of me that is me—the real me, if you will—had begun to go dormant in Memphis. Now it was almost completely dormant.

Some people blame themselves for what happens to them. They buy into what others tell them, that it was all their fault. I never blamed myself for being raped. I knew I had not done anything wrong. From that point on, I was as vigilant as a young teen could be about protecting myself. I wasn't one of those girls who wanted to have sex. After all, I didn't know much about it, so how could I? I hadn't been around boys that much either. But after Yolanda's boyfriend raped me, it seemed as though the wolves were circling the hen house—and because one got in, the others smelled fresh meat.

I was around 15 when an older man came to Granny's front door. He had to have been in his 30s. I was in the front room sitting on the couch and could hear his conversation with Granny. I had seen him several times while running errands and had spoken to him. Nothing serious, just me being nice. Well, apparently, he had other ideas. He asked Granny if he could date me. At least he didn't feel the need to just take what he wanted. Still, was he out of his mind? I couldn't help but think so. Granny promptly told him no—not because he was too old, but because I was too young. Granny wouldn't allow me to date until I was 18, but it seems she didn't have a problem with this man's age. If he waited a couple of years, then he could date me. Yikes!

I'd like to be able to say junior high was wonderful, but I can't. However, I still really liked parts of it. I joined the math club, as I said earlier. I also joined the theater club. I loved acting. As a kid, an actor was all I wanted to be when I grew up. And I was good at it.

My grades remained high, which made the neighborhood ladies and Granny happy. There wasn't much Granny could do to help me with the work in junior high, thank goodness. Her limit was times tables. She hadn't gone very far in school.

I had a best friend, Gwen, who lived in another neighborhood. She was my only friend. Part of the reason for this was the tight rein Granny kept on me. By the time I arrived home from school, did chores, and completed my homework, there wasn't much time left to socialize. Saturdays were for cleaning, yard work, and washing. I'd get up, clean the house, cut the hedge bushes with hand sheers, cut what grass was in the front yard with a push mower, and help wash clothes. Thank goodness Granny wouldn't allow me to use the ringer washing machine. A cousin of hers had gotten a finger caught in one, and it was cut off.

My job was to scrub the whites in the bathtub using a scrub board. I'd get down on my knees, lean over the tub, and scrub the whites with lye soap until they were pristine. After the clothes were hung on the line and dried, I'd iron my clothes for the week ahead. There wasn't any getting up in the morning to decide what I would wear for the day. My clothes were hung in the cabinet in order of the days they would be worn. Monday's outfit was hung first, then Tuesday's, and so on. To this day, if you look at my closet, you will see all the pants hanging together, dresses together, and blouses together. I don't like looking for anything. Having an organized closet makes getting dressed so much easier. (But no, I don't know what I will wear for the week ahead of time. That is a bit extreme.)

There were some Saturdays when I would clean for Mrs. King to make extra money. I'd usually clean for her in the morning to get it out of the way. On those days I ran late with my own chores. Granny or Little Mama did all the cooking. Occasionally I'd chop something for Granny, but that was it. I never really learned to cook, which is odd, but that's the way it was. I can cook today if I have a recipe, but cooking really isn't high on my list of hobbies. And cleaning is definitely at the bottom of the list.

I'm not sure how old I was when Granny had me periodically help her with Ms. Gladys' house. Granny cleaned for her after Ms. Gladys' mother died. I'd clean the bathrooms, of which there were three. I remember one occasion when she had me clean one of the bathtubs three times—it wasn't up to her standards. She told me, "If you clean it right the first time, you won't have to do it again." Thank God I didn't have to clean anything else in that house.

Sometime between junior high and high school, Ms. Gladys lost her gardener and Granny decided she would take that job on, too. And yes—of course I had to help. Thank the gods again I didn't have to help every week. My job was to edge the grass using a handheld, nonelectric edger. The handle was short, which meant I had to get down on the ground to use it. I'd crawl along the driveway and sidewalk edging the grass. My other job was cutting the hedge bushes. Those bushes were high, which meant getting on a ladder to trim them. Granny taught me to use an electric handheld trimmer. Years later, I was in a store walking down an isle that had hedge trimmers. I picked one up and it felt really light. There was a man close by looking for something and I commented, "These are so light; they used to be heavier." He asked when I had last used one. I said, "when I was a teenager." What he said next brought it all home for me. He said, "You were a kid; of course it would have been heavy." Wow! He was right. His comment put it into perspective.

Remember earlier when I told you that I was as vigilant as a young teen could be about protecting myself? Well, I wasn't vigilant enough, because I almost got raped again. One morning as I was headed to the junior high campus, a young man, standing at the front door of one of the houses I passed every day, called out to me. He asked me to come over to him. Stupid me—I went. He looked like he was in his early 20s. He opened the screen door and pulled me in. There was a bed in the living room, which wasn't odd; there was one in my house, too. I was scared, which was to be expected. What happened next wasn't. I talked my way out of being raped. He told me to lie down, and I wouldn't. I said I was on my way to school and that I was late. I promised him that I would come back later, after school. I just kept talking and promising him that I would return. He let me leave with a promise that I would return. I took another route home that day and every day after that.

Muddy Water

Water is a feminine element and represents our emotions.
Water is the source of life. For the lotus to evolve and
grow, the water must be deep and still. As the lotus
grows toward the surface, the water becomes
clearer. As we experience our emotions and
evolve the muddy water of our emotions,
they too become clearer. In the same
manner as the lotus evolves,
so do we.

7

Meeting My Family

The same summer when I turned 13 was also the summer I met my grandfather—C. B., as he was affectionately called. The letters were the initials of his name, Cleotha Burrell. He was named after his father, who was my great-grandfather. He was tall, big—yet not fat—and very kind to me. His wife, Ms. Mime as she was called, was very sweet. She had a soft voice that was never raised. For some reason my mother decided to take me to Bogalusa to see the family that summer. We stayed for a week. I learned later that she did this at my grandfather's request. One of my cousins told me years later that whenever someone would ask about me, my mother would say that I was in school and this was why they rarely got to see me. They didn't know what was going on in Memphis.

My grandfather had left his first wife, Lela (my grandmother), years earlier due to her behavior as an alcoholic and her temper. His second wife was the polar opposite. I liked her immediately. Grandfather was a quiet man. He observed everything that was happening around him in silence. When he did speak, everyone around him listened. By the time I met him, he had to have been in his late 60s or early 70s. His life had been spent working various jobs and raising his family. He worked on the railroad making the railroad tires. (I don't think the real name for them is tires, but that's what I heard them called. They were the wheels of the train.) He also owned a restaurant in New Orleans at some point. When I met him, he was retired and made extra money cutting grass for someone. He had five children by my grandmother Lela, of which my mother was the oldest. There were three other children that my grandmother had before marrying C. B. He raised them, too. And from what I could see, there was no distinction between which ones were his and which ones weren't—all of them were "his."

That summer I met one of my aunts and her husband, who lived in New Orleans. Uncle Hassie was a minister, and Aunt Alice cleaned house for a couple in the French Quarter. Two of my aunts lived in California, so I didn't get to meet them. I also met my uncles: Benny, Joe, Cleotha Jr., and Pete. Uncle Pete was blind. He'd had scarlet fever as a child and lost his sight due to this illness. He lived in the "home house" with Uncle Benny. The home house was the house where my grandmother and grandfather had raised the family. When C. B. left Lela, he moved only a few streets away. Cleotha Jr., aka Uncle Puna, didn't live that far away; neither did Uncle Joe. Uncle Joe owned a restaurant in town, which I frequented during that first visit, and Uncle Puna had an excavation company. Uncle Pete couldn't work much due to being blind, and I never knew what Uncle Benny did for a living. I do know he worked.

As it turned out, I was the youngest grandchild—which was kind of odd, since my mother had four younger siblings and three older. Neither Uncle Pete nor Aunt Alice, who were the youngest, ever had children, and the others had begun having children long before my mother had me. My grandmother had two sets of twins who died, along with I think several other pregnancies that didn't reach full term. In all, there would have been at least 12 children if all of them had lived. What's interesting is that none of my aunts or uncles had many children of their own. Uncle Puna and Aunt Lily had the most—three each. Aunt Lily was one of the aunts living in California.

At the time I visited, C. B. and Ms. Mime were raising another young lady, Lillian, who was around my age. I don't know what happened to her family, but she was truly a part of our family and accepted as a sibling by my other aunts and uncles. We got to hang out for a week, which was nice.

That summer I ate more rice than I had eaten in all my years up to that point. Rice was served with everything, including in rice pudding. Thank goodness I liked rice. The food was quite good; Ms. Mime was an excellent cook, and so was my grandfather. He liked to bake. Whenever I would visit for Christmas, which I began to do as an adult, he would make me a pecan cake. He liked baking his grandchildren's favorite desserts. Everyone would have their dessert eaten before the holiday was over. That is, everyone except me. I always took mine home. One of my cousins would ask, "Aren't you going to cut your cake?" The answer was no. "It's going home with me." It's not that I had a problem sharing, because that was never an issue for me. It was that I cherished his act of love and the feeling of being nurtured. Nurturing wasn't something I got as a child. That cake was it. And it made me feel good, so I refused to share. (A funny side note: My name is Marie Antoinette. One of my namesake's famous quotes is "Let them eat cake.")

My grandfather took me shopping for shoes in downtown Bogalusa one day. He couldn't drive, so he hired a friend to take us. I don't think my mother went with us. If she did, I don't remember. It was my grandfather who I remember sitting in the store watching and waiting for me to pick out the shoes I wanted. My mother had begun to buy my school clothes the summer before, but this was different. I could feel C. B.'s care and love for me. I've never felt that from my mother. I'm not saying she didn't love me, because I believe she did. I'm just saying I never felt it.

It was that level of love and caring that I longed for and needed. When my mother and I were getting ready to leave, C. B. slipped me some money. It wasn't much, but it was given with love—and I will never, ever forget it, nor the feeling I had receiving it. I can understand why my mother and her siblings adored their father. He never smiled. He seemed to contemplate and observe more than anyone I have ever known, and from my vantage point he was very wise. Just thinking about him and writing about who he was causes me to tear up with gratitude for him being my grandfather. He was the second man in my life who demonstrated unconditional love for me. He wanted nothing from me. He never took advantage of me in any way. He loved me just the way I was.

Many years after that visit to Bogalusa, one of my cousins told me about a conversation she overheard between my grandfather and my mother. My mother had gone home for Christmas, and I wasn't there. At the time I was living in Chicago and dating a white man. My mother never said a word about how she felt about this to me; she knew better than to interfere in my life at that point. What she did, though, was tell my grandfather. I don't know why she chose to do this. Maybe she thought my grandfather would step in and try to stop the relationship. She knew I loved and respected my grandfather and would listen to him.

From what I observed when in his presence, my grandfather was not an interfering man. He gave his opinion only when asked. My cousin said they were sitting in the living room, my mother on the couch and Grandfather in his favorite chair. My mother said, "Net"—that's short for Antionette, my middle name—"has stepped over the fence and gone on the other side." My grandfather asked a series of questions, none of them about the man's race. Every question was about how I was being treated. "Is he taking care of her?" "Is he kind to her?" "Is she happy?" Basically, was I being treated the way a woman should be treated by a man. My mother answered yes to his questions. She could see no fault in the way I was being treated. So my grandfather replied, "So what's your problem, then?" My cousin said there was silence after that.

I know my grandfather had to have faults—everybody does—I just didn't see any. I take that back; there was one. He didn't like salad. My cousin once wanted to put a green salad on the dining room table and my grandfather told her, "Don't you put that rabbit food on my table." Well, that was the end of that. I miss him.

8

Competition, Failure, and Rape

One year I decided to run for Miss Black Teenage Memphis. What possessed me to do it? Winning, of course! I had talent, which in my mind should have been enough.

At the ripe age of 16, I heard about an annual pageant for teens. I don't remember how I found out about it, but I decided to run. I had watched the Miss America pageant on TV previously, and I think that's where the idea came from. Big Sister and everyone else did their best to dissuade me. They said I wasn't pretty, that I was homely. Who did I think I was? Basically, I was laughed at.

None of their words could stop me. When I make up my mind about a course of action, only The Divine—aka God—can stop me. I have no problem working hard to reach a goal, and I'm very good at dismissing critiques. That doesn't mean I don't listen—if someone is giving me information to assist in reaching the goal, that is. This is my nature. If I fail, it won't be because of a lack of effort, and there will be no guilt on my part. Failure is okay with me. I'll just adjust the method used to reach my goal. Or, if the goal is no longer desirable, I'll move on with my head held high.

I had no money, no sponsor, no parental support, and—according to those around me—no beauty. None of it deterred me. I'll never forget that first evening, getting off the city bus, walking into the hotel and entering the room were all the other girls who were competing were assembled along with their parents. A few fathers were in the room, but mostly it was mothers. It was pretty loud in there with everyone talking. I was by myself and I have to admit, it was intimidating. I found a seat and began to relax; looking around the room, I didn't see any difference between me and the other girls. That evening, the pageant organizers went over the rules and procedures. They gave dates and locations of rehearsals. The competition would consist of several sections—evening gown, swimsuit, talent, and Q&A. I thought to myself, "I have the talent piece already, so that's good." My mind started working on how I could acquire the rest of the ensemble. In addition to needing an evening gown and swimsuit, I also needed a sporty outfit for the opening number that all of us would perform together. And I needed a male escort to walk me onto the stage. Oh, and of course the money to pay for the event. Where was I going to get the money to do this? I didn't know, but I knew I would get it somehow.

I went home that first evening full of energy, strategizing how to accomplish my goal. I don't remember how much time I had to gather all the things needed for the pageant—maybe two months. I started by asking the ladies in the neighborhood if I could do anything for them to make money. Thankfully, there was always something I could do. So I stepped up the work I had already been doing for a couple of the ladies by adding more cleaning jobs and errands.

The mother of my friend Gwen agreed to make my evening gown for a small fee. This was a good thing, because all I had to do was get a pattern and the material. Gwen and I went shopping at the fabric store and found a lovely Butterick pattern. It looked like the dress Marilyn Monroe wore in the movie where she was standing on a grate as a train went by. The difference was that this dress was long, and it had a sheer shawl attached to the back. I chose a lime green–colored fabric. It was pretty bright, but I liked it. The fabric was light in texture too, which meant the dress would move nicely as I walked. Over time I also earned the money to purchase the other outfits. The swimsuit was the hardest. I had never worn one, and trying them on, I felt naked. I ended up selecting a red one-piece that accentuated the V form of my body. I had begun to fill out by age 16. Although I was still skinny, I at least had some shape.

I asked Big Sister's youngest son if he would be my escort. He immediately said no. I then asked her other two sons, who also declined to do it. So I went to the brothers of my friend Gwen, of which she had many. One of them agreed to be my escort. I had to beg, but that was okay. I didn't mind. I didn't know who else to ask.

The pageant organizers found a sponsor for me. He was an insurance agent and would pay the pageant fee. He was also one of the judges, which was a conflict of interest, but that didn't cross my mind. For one thing, I didn't know that he was a judge until he told me. I was all set.

Rehearsals were a lot of work and fun. I had decided to recite a poem I learned years earlier for a church function. The title was "I'm Determined to Be Somebody Someday" by Herbert Brewster. It was my favorite poem, along with being the creed I lived by. The only thing that saddened me during rehearsal was that I was on my own. No one ever accompanied me to any of the events, including the pageant itself. I watched the support the other girls received from their parents. They were doted on and had their every need taken care of.

Even this was a fleeting sadness, though. I never wallowed in self-pity. Feeling sad is one thing, but self-pity is something else altogether. For some reason, I have rarely ever felt sorry for myself. I think it's because I have always known that it serves no purpose. Another reason is being so goal oriented. Self-pity takes energy away from achieving the goal, whatever it may be. That doesn't mean that I wasn't looking to be rescued back then. In fact, the shoes I bought for the pageant were reminiscent of Cinderella's glass slippers. It was love at first sight. The wedge heel was glass, and the part that covered the foot was clear.

One day I received a call from my sponsor. I don't remember his name, and it's probably best that way. He was a piece of work. He asked to see me, so I took the bus to his office. When I arrived, the office was empty. There was no one there except him. It may be obvious where this is going, but I'll lay it all out anyway.

We went into his office, which was in the back. The office was not well lit, and the curtains were drawn. The office had a desk with a couple of chairs in front of it, along with a couch that faced the desk and filing cabinets. He proceeded to ask me how things were going with preparations and if there was anything else I needed. He said he would be happy to help me in any way he could. This is also when I learned he was one of the judges. At 16, never having had any experience with pageants, I had no clue about what a conflict of interest was. Was that even something people thought about back then? I don't know.

In any case, he then asked me to show him my walk. He meant the walk everyone does in front of the judges and audience. I had been working on this walk and was eager to demonstrate it—so I did. He sat behind the desk and watched. When I finished the walk in front of his desk, he got up, walked around the desk, grabbed me, and stuck his tongue down my throat. I didn't fight. I felt deflated, defeated, and confused. So he raped me right there, in that office, on the couch. I didn't feel a thing. I was numb. Parts of me had begun to leave my body years earlier, and now more of me left.

Over the course of the pageant and months afterward, I had sex with him; on one occasion, he brought a friend and they both had sex with me. Why did I continued to go when he called? Because I had begun to feel that men just wanted to take what they wanted from me, and since it was my body they wanted, there was no point in fighting. Not fighting also meant I would at least not be hit. That was my logic.

66

The pageant though? I enjoyed that evening, even though Gwen's brother never showed up to be my escort. One of the escorts for another contestant walked me out on stage. I recited my poem flawlessly and performed well in the other areas—and I lost. I didn't even make the first cut. I was bummed about this but got over it pretty quickly. With the exception of my sponsor's horrid behavior, the pageant experience was positive. It was akin to going to finishing school for me. The year I participated in the pageant was the same year I entered high school. This meant going to a new campus. The high school was still considered fairly new and modern compared to the junior high and elementary schools. I loved the building and its modern design. There were also many more students coming from other schools. I felt a sense of freedom, too.

My usual way of achieving goals, even then, was to contemplate the goal, come up with a strategy to achieve the goal, and put the strategy into action. If the strategy needed tweaking, I tweaked it. The goal when I entered high school? Go to college. I knew I was going to college. It had been drummed into me for years by Granny, and my mother had been telling me for years that she was saving money for me—for college. Even without the two of them making these proclamations, I knew that I was college bound. It was a given.

The strategy for college? Join the military. One of the first things I did in high school was to join the junior ROTC. This was something that I had planned to do from the onset. Back then, the military paid for a four-year education. I knew that no matter how much money my mother saved, it wasn't going to be enough to get me through four years of college. I could use her money for extras. I would do military service for three years and then go to school. I also knew that by joining the junior ROTC and participating for three years, my starting rank in the military would be higher—E3, if I remember correctly. This rank translated into higher pay and quicker movement up the ranks. I had put this plan together a year in advance and was therefore able to implement it without much ado.

Not only did I join the JROTC, but I also joined the drill team. Being a part of this group was wonderful. We practiced drills most days and competed in high school competitions—winning most of them. Our colors were blue and white. Gwen's mom made my drill team outfit, which was a two-piece—pants and jacket. We were really good, if I do say so myself. And we carried rifles. Not real ones, just painted wood. I learned to twirl them, throw them in the air, and catch them—even throw mine to a teammate while they did the same. Our routines were polished through practice, and it showed.

The school had two drill teams. The other one was a dancing drill team—they were awesome, too. I went to a few of their meetings to see if I wanted to participate but decided I didn't. The schedule for the JROTC was going to be rigorous, and with everything else I was doing, I wouldn't be able to pull off being a part of another team.

The other group I belonged to was the theater group. I adored acting, as I said earlier. We had one big school performance each year, and I acted in two out of the three while I attended high school. My senior year, I had to take the role of stage manager. This was because I also took on a full-time job—working at night. That will come into play later.

Oh, here's another funny story: In my junior year, we had someone from a professional dance troupe come to the school to choreograph a show in which anyone could participate. Well, I'm sure it's no surprise that yours truly signed up.

The morning of one of the rehearsals, I realized I didn't have any clean underwear. Granny had always taught me to make sure my underwear was always clean. She'd say, "You never know what you will encounter in the day, and at least you will have clean underwear on." As luck would have it, Granny had clean underwear available for me to wear—HERS! Now, Granny was not small, which meant her underwear wasn't small. I was Ms. Olive Oyl the Second. I had a little shape, but I was still skinny, weighing in at 135 pounds at 5' 10". But what was I to do? Go without underwear? That would have been shameful, and uncomfortable to boot. So I dawned Granny's pristine white bloomers and went to school.

That afternoon was a dress rehearsal, which meant a full run-through of the show. Our costume was a black leotard with a short, red wrap-around skirt. Our legs and feet were bare. Picture this: I'm on stage dancing. My arms and legs are going everywhere. There are lots of jumps, swirling, and kicks. One part of the dance number required us to jump in the air while spreading our arms and legs out in a splayed position. While I was jumping and splaying, my skirt came undone, so I was using one of my hands to hold the skirt up. The dance teacher, who was sitting in the wings, yelled for me to let it drop. So I let the skirt fall to the floor and continued to do full jumps while splaying my arms and legs. Well, the kids in the audience—including my best friend, Gwen, and another friend, Paula—began to laugh uncontrollably. The pianist, who was quite large, was also laughing. He was laughing so hard that he stopped playing the piano and lay over it while convulsing with laughter. I wondered what was so funny. I don't know how I caught a glimpse of my legs, but I did. And what did I see? Granny's bloomers hanging halfway down the sides of my legs. The only thing keeping them on was the leotard. Now, perhaps a normal person would have run from the stage in embarrassment. That is not what I did—I kept dancing. After all, the creed of an actor is "The show must go on." I was embarrassed, but I didn't feel humiliation. To run from the stage would have been humiliating for me. I was going to be teased about this anyway, so why add humiliation to it? Well, the kids didn't tease me much about it, probably because I didn't run away. Later performances turned out really well—and I had my own underwear on.

9

Betrayal and Illusion of Family

As usual, my plate was full of activities in school, but that didn't stop me from adding the job of working in the assistant principal's office for one period each day. My job was to call the home of any student who didn't come to school that day and to hand out hall passes. I was well known in high school due to being involved in theater, the drill team, and the assistant principal's office. That said, I didn't know many kids personally, and of course I didn't date. Even with Granny prohibiting dating until I was 18, as a senior I could have dated one of the high school boys—but I didn't. They just didn't interest me, nor did I interest them. And it's no secret that by the time I was a senior, I was pretty confused and messed up sexually.

Upon turning 18 I went wild, as they say. I was no longer under Granny's control. She said her job was done and I was on my own. That didn't mean she wanted me to move or anything like that. She simply said she had raised me to the best of her ability, and now I was free to do what I wanted. There were no curfews to adhere to or

BETRAYAL AND ILLUSION OF FAMILY

rules to follow. In hindsight, I think her decision was a mistake—especially considering the tight control she held over me for so long. It's like when a person has been on a restrictive diet for a long time and it finally ends. I do believe I would have had more control over my sexual behavior if it had not been for the rapes, even with not being able to date until 18.

The coups de grace that pushed me overboard sexually was being raped by one of Granny's younger cousins. He was the same cousin who had accompanied Granny's son-in-law to Chicago years earlier to move Granny and me to Memphis. I had sat in his lap for the entire ride to Memphis. He was much older than me, and I wasn't around him much while growing up. He would sometimes come over to the house to see Granny and have a meal. Occasionally he would take me for a ride as a kid and have me sit in his lap and hold the steering wheel while he drove. I liked pretending to drive. He was Granny's favorite cousin, and he walked on water in her eyes. He's the only one in the family to whom Granny sent a drum set from Chicago. This was not an easy thing to do back then, and it was expensive.

I considered Granny's family as my family. I longed to belong, so in my mind they were my family. It didn't matter that they didn't reciprocate the love. I even wrote their names on the genealogy page of the St. James Bible my mother gave me when I was 12.

I was 17 when it happened. In fact, it happened during the time I performed the dance I mentioned earlier. I was a junior in high school. He and his significant other wanted me to babysit their three kids. Both of them worked the graveyard shift. His significant other worked at the hospital, and he was a welder. One of them would pick me up at home around 10:00 or so in the evenings and take me to their house to stay with the kids.

The kids would either be in bed or going to bed by the time I arrived, so I didn't have to do much for them except be there if something happened. I usually cleaned up the dishes or read a book until I got tired and went to sleep on the couch. Both parents worked midnight to 7:00 a.m., which meant one of them had to take me home in the morning so that I could get to school. I was fine with this arrangement, and I didn't mind babysitting—at first.

One night he came back home not too long after he had originally left. I was surprised and asked him, "What happened? Why are you home?" He said he hadn't been feeling well and decided to come home. He didn't look sick to me, but what would I know? Well, he wasn't too sick to come over and start groping me. I told him to stop and got angry. He was supposed to be family. I began to fight him, kicking and trying to push him away. He wouldn't stop. He seemed to get a thrill from my struggling to free myself from him. He was pulling me toward the hallway that led around the corner to his bedroom. I held onto the door frame of that hallway for dear life, trying to keep myself from being pulled around that corner. I cried, begged, and pleaded with him not to do this. He wouldn't stop. He threw me on the bed, stripped me, and raped me. When he was done, he put on his clothes and left the house. I just lay there, numb. By the time his significant other came home, I was up and dressed. I never said a word to her about it. She took me home.

That day I told my best friend, Gwen, about it. We talked about what to do. Should I tell, or not? And if I chose to tell, what might the consequences be? This was the late '70s, and women were often blamed for being raped. There was also the issue of Granny. Her favorite cousin had done this; what would she do? Would she believe me or take his side? We both knew the rest of the family would side with him. In the end, we both decided that I shouldn't say anything—that I would be the one punished. So I kept my mouth shut about it.

I continued to babysit, because I couldn't see a way out of it. Over the course of almost a year he would periodically come during the night and rape me. I grew to loathe him. He knew I wouldn't tell, and he began to say I wanted it. The only reason it stopped was that I got a full-time job and couldn't babysit anymore. I confronted him years later at Big Sister's house. He was in the dining room putting on a tie to go to Granny's funeral. I asked him why he had raped me. He said he didn't rape me—that I wanted it. This wasn't true, of course, but maybe in his sick mind it was.

So by the time I entered my senior year, I was way out of balance where men and sex were concerned. I began to sleep around with men. Never ones from high school, as I said earlier. I don't know how many men I slept with, but there were plenty. I couldn't feel a thing. I kept trying to feel, but it wasn't there. Once Big Sister's middle son mentioned to me that he had heard about my escapades with men. I didn't care what he was hearing about me; I was my own boss, and I was going to do exactly as I pleased.

Germinating Seed and Seedling

The germination of the seed gives life to the seedling and, just like the Soul, it comes in with an agenda. For the lotus plant, the agenda is to produce a beautiful flower. The lotus is a reflection of the human Soul coming in with its agenda. The agenda for the Soul includes the blueprint that will be used to reach the Soul's goal—which includes a level of strength, courage, and determination. This doesn't mean the agenda will be achieved. Not all seeds or humans bloom.

10

Trying to Stand on My Own

The summer just before my senior year began, I decided not to go to Chicago. Instead I put in an application to be a candy striper at John Gaston Hospital. I've always enjoyed helping people, and this would also keep me busy. Just before receiving the call from the hospital saying I was accepted, Gwen called and told me about another job at a factory called Shirlo. They were looking for people to work the assembly line, and it paid a decent wage. Gwen and I both took the factory job, and I turned down the job as a candy striper.

The factory was quite a distance from the house, so we had to find a ride to work every day. We worked the 4:30 p.m.–12:30 a.m. shift, Monday through Friday. Both of us would ask family members to take us to work. Gwen's mom took us a few times. We hitched rides for a while, too. Finally, we made a connection at work with two ladies who didn't live too far from us. They agreed to pick us up daily. This was a very good thing. The work wasn't difficult, but you had to move fast. We were the youngest girls there. Everyone else was in their 30s and 40s. The ladies would talk about their lives, which actually began to educate me more about life and how others lived it.

Getting that job allowed me to open my first savings account. I was so proud of myself. I went to the local credit union and opened the account. I went there because Gwen's mom had an account there. Granny never had a bank account. My first purchase was a Maytag washing machine for Granny—and I should also say for me. I was sick and tired of that scrub board. That machine was the talk of the neighborhood and the family. It was nice to be able to buy it for Granny. She worked harder than anyone I knew.

When the school year began, I kept the job. One of my teachers was furious with me for this. She said that this was the best year of my life and that I should be having fun, not working a full-time job in a factory. For a kid whose parents would support them financially, this was an option. But I needed to work. I needed money for all the things a high-school senior needed for graduation. I just looked at this teacher as though she were talking gibberish. Was she going to pay for my cap and gown, class ring, pictures, school trip, and other things for graduation? I thought not—so her words were blowing in the wind as far as I was concerned. Graduating from high school is expensive.

I also began to pay Granny rent: $100 a month plus buying some of the groceries. This might sound odd, but in a poor family everyone has to help. I had the money, and I didn't mind paying rent. It may have even been my idea in the first place.

Having a full-time job did put a crimp in my activities at school. That year I became captain of the drill team, which was a ton of work, and I was hardly ever there. I had to turn over control to my executive officer. Needless to say, the team didn't flourish that year. And, as I said before, I wasn't able to act in the school production. I took the role of stage manager.

It's sad to think that no one from the family ever came to see me perform in anything—ever. I never understood this. I was always doing something in school, especially high school, and they all knew it because I'd tell them. At my high school graduation, Big Daddy (Johnny Sr., Big Sister's husband) came and brought his youngest granddaughter; Granny was there, and so was my mother. It hurt me deeply that Big Sister didn't come. I decided to write her off as a sister because of it. I also decided that I wouldn't do it until Granny died—whenever that was. I didn't want to cause Granny any pain. So I waited, but I did follow through with this promise to myself. Weeks before graduation I had also told Granny that if my mother didn't show up for my graduation, I was writing her off as a mother—and I meant it. It's lucky for her and for me that she showed up. I was tired of her empty promises.

I graduated in the top 100 of my class of 444. My placement would have been at least in the top 50 if not for the job. I rarely had time to study. Fortunately for me, when I entered high school, I decided to load up on classes in the first two years so that I wouldn't have many in my senior year. We needed 18 credits to graduate, and I had 15 by the time senior year came. English was a mandatory class each year. ROTC was a given, and the third class I signed up for was music. My school day began at 7:30 a.m. and ended at 2:30 p.m. The three classes were not back to back, so I'd leave campus and go to Gwen's to watch soap operas or have lunch. Sometimes we would just walk around and talk, but mostly we hung out at her house.

We both decided to quit the factory job shortly before graduation. I would have continued working there, but I quit for two reasons: One reason was that Gwen was fed up with not having a dependable ride to work. The second reason was that she was my friend. We began the job together, so it was only fitting that we finish together. At least that's how I saw it. Both of us had purchased what we needed to graduate, and I had the money I needed for something else—contact lenses. They cost $300 in the late '70s and early '80s. I bought them in Chicago the summer after I graduated. Besides the washing machine, they were the best purchase of all.

The reason we didn't have a steady ride to work and had to quit was that the ladies we rode with told us that we couldn't ride with them anymore. I could blame Gwen for this, but in actuality it was both our faults. One day the ladies picked up Gwen and were on their way to pick me up, as usual. It was a nice, warm, sunny afternoon. I was walking home from school. My glasses were broken, so I couldn't see well. I'm legally blind without my glasses, but that never stopped me from doing what I wanted or needed to do when I couldn't wear them. I had learned to cope, so on this day I was going to work without seeing well. No problem.

Gwen and the ladies were driving down the street to my house, and I saw the outline of the car and its color, so I knew who it was. I went over and got in the car and we headed to work. Well, Gwen—knowing that I couldn't see two feet in front of me without my glasses—asked, "How did you know it was us?" I replied, "I saw a black spot and knew it had to be you guys." We cracked up laughing—both of us had tears, we were laughing so hard. (My comment was so funny because one of the ladies we rode with was really dark skinned—black as tar. I think this is a beautiful coloring, and I meant no disrespect. It's just that sometimes things pop out of my mouth, even today, that are not politically correct.)

The two ladies wanted to know what was funny. We said it was a private joke. We laughed all the way to work, and our laughter continued into the evening. Every time we looked at each other, we would laugh. Later on, one of the ladies approached Gwen to ask what the joke was that caused us to laugh so much. It's understandable that the ladies wanted to know what was so funny. Gwen decided to tell the lady what we had been laughing about. I don't know why. (She said she didn't think they would get that mad, but I find that hard to believe.) After that incident, no more rides for us.

Getting home at 12:30 a.m. was no fun. We sometimes hitchhiked, and at other times coworkers would take pity on us and take us as far as they were going, and we'd walk the rest of the way. Hitchhiking wasn't easy, and neither of us wanted to do it. We felt safer doing it together. But the writing was on the wall. Our days—or should I say, nights—at that job were numbered. It couldn't last, and that was okay.

High school overall was okay, but I was glad when it came to an end. I had learned a lot, including how to drive. Driver's ed was one of the other classes I took. I couldn't get Big Sister or her youngest son to teach me. Other than her eldest, they were the only two others in the family that I could ask. Big Daddy worked every day and wasn't around. I approached her youngest son first. He was three years older than me and had bought his first car. He said that he wasn't about to let me learn in his new car. I might damage it. I then approached Big Sister, who also said no. I have no idea what her reasoning was. Fortunately for me, the school had a driver's ed program, so I signed up and learned that way. As they say, "Where there's a will, there's a way."

Shortly before graduation, I went to the army recruiting office and signed up to go into the military. But sometimes even the best-laid plans can go awry. I failed the eye test. Yes, my eyesight was so bad that the recruitment officer told me, "If you lose your glasses in combat, you might shoot one of your own men." And just like that, the military wasn't an option.

The possibility of being turned down by the military due to my eyesight had never entered my mind. He was right, though. I could see myself in combat, scared to death and with a gun. God help anybody who I even heard moving about if I didn't have my glasses on. I don't know who I'd be today if I had gone to the military. Probably a five-star general. Why? Because I probably would have stayed in the military longer than originally planned, and people who are bullied as children often seek careers that give them real power in some part of society. It would have been only natural for me to go up the ranks as far as I could go.

Now I had to formulate a plan B. The first thing I did was call my mother to let her know that I would need the money she had been saving all these years for college. She said she would send it. Based on her track record of not telling me the truth, I should have known better than to believe her—but I did. I'm still waiting on the money for college that she said she was saving.

Thank goodness that part of my plan B included applying for a Pell Grant with the federal government. Because of my low income, this grant would pay for everything except room and board. When I took the factory job at the beginning of my senior year, I had informed my mother that she could no longer use me as a write-off on her taxes because I would be claiming myself. This made it much easier for me to fill out the paperwork myself for the grant—which I did. The only help I received was from the guidance counselor's office, learning about the grant and getting the paperwork to fill out.

I began to spend time in the guidance counselor's office poring over information on various schools around the country. Where was I going to go? I had asked my mother about going to Chicago to attend school, and she told me to wait a year. "What for?" I asked her. I don't remember what she told me. I do remember her telling me later that Chicago would eat me alive—that I was too kind and it wasn't a place that I should be. Really? And what had happened in Memphis?

My first choice was Pepperdine in California. I had always wanted to go to California. After all, it is home to Hollywood, and I was going to major in theater. I liked what Pepperdine offered. My issue was how I would pay for room and board. I was doing my best to think through everything and plan a course of action. I had two aunts in California, but I really didn't know them. Would they help me?

In the end, I decided to enroll in the community college in Memphis for the year my mother asked me to wait before going to Chicago. I chose Shelby State because of the cost and because Big Sister's youngest son had gotten his associate's degree there. I could stay at home, too. Memphis State was another option, but the cost was much higher, and if I remember correctly, the Pell Grant wouldn't cover the entire cost. As it was, I would have to work anyway, but I didn't want to worry about paying more than I had to. I stayed there a full year as planned. Before the school year was over, I had been accepted at Roosevelt University in Chicago. I had applied without my mother's knowledge. There wasn't anything she could do when she learned of this. She had told me to wait a year before coming to Chicago, and I had. I was going home, and there wasn't anything she could do about it.

My initial plan was to stay in Memphis that last summer. I had a job working at New Orleans Famous Fried Chicken on Elvis Presley Boulevard. It was a new business in the community, and I worked there for most of my first year in college. The job wasn't difficult, and it had perks in the form of chicken. I could eat all the chicken I wanted—which I did. After a while, my body started to reject the chicken. It was some time after leaving that job before I could eat chicken without digestive problems.

Another thing the job gave me was exposure to the strip club that was next door. Yep, that's right. I was 19, so it was legal for me to go into the club. Initially I didn't have any intention of going over there. However, my boss was dating one of the strippers. One night he asked me to take her a chicken dinner, so I did. When I walked in the door, I got more than an eyeful. I had never seen anything like it. Seeing a naked woman on stage didn't shock me—it was, after all, a strip joint. What I didn't expect was what she was doing. She was smoking a cigarette from her vagina! My mouth flew open and my eyes popped out of my head when I saw this. How was she doing this? How was this possible? All the men were sitting around watching and throwing money at her.

When I came to my senses, I asked the bartender for my manager's girlfriend. It turned out she was the one on stage. I watched a few minutes more, left the chicken with the bartender, and went back to the chicken place. My boss would send me over there periodically, and I had no problem with it. "Live and let live," as the saying goes. The girls had some pretty good moves, and I was sure they were making more money than I was.

One night I went in on my own, not at my boss's request. It was also the last night I ever stepped foot in the place. I was fascinated with how the girls could move their bodies, so I thought maybe I could learn a thing or two. By this time I was pretty promiscuous, too. The motto was "Love the one you're with." On this particular night—my last night—I was standing in the club watching one of the girls perform her act. This girl could do things with a knife that I didn't know were possible. Then an argument started with a couple of the men. I couldn't see them, but I knew what was happening because I could hear them over the music. And then a shot was fired. That was all I needed to hear. I ran out the front door and didn't stop running until I got to my front door. And I didn't look back while running, either. I was out of there, never to return. When my boss wanted me to take chicken to his girlfriend after that, I refused. He could take it himself—and he did.

What's funny about my visiting the strip club is that I wasn't of drinking age yet. The drinking age had been changed to 21 just before my 18th birthday. I remember being upset about this at the time, because I had been looking forward to that rite of passage and would now have to wait a few more years. I was carded when I first began going to night clubs. The bartenders started calling me the Coca-Cola girl, because that's all I would drink. But they were only teasing, and it was fun to be in the clubs all the same. I would dance and laugh and have a blast of a time. And I did it sober. I used to enter dance contests, and I usually won. If I didn't win, it was my friend and neighbor Faye who would win.

My party buddies were Faye and Big Sister's youngest daughter. Both of them were significantly older than me and had kids of their own. But they liked to party, and since I was 18 they took me along—thank the gods. They had another friend who would drive and go with us. I don't remember her name. We mostly just wanted to have fun, and we did. Faye and I even won an opportunity to compete for a chance to be on the show *Star Search*. We entered the contest at the club level. Both of us picked partners who could dance. We were out on the floor jamming. We won! We didn't win at the next level, but it was fun to go out on the stage and dance in front of judges and a crowd.

Once, at the club we frequented, I entered a swimsuit competition wearing the suit I had worn in the pageant—and won. My motivation for entering any competition was the money. The winner would usually get $100.

Another interesting thing about that time in my life is that I refused to smoke marijuana—go figure. I wanted to drink but not smoke. There were several reasons for this. First, I didn't like the way people acted when they were smoking, and I didn't want to act that way. I also cared about what I was putting in my body. Marijuana is a drug, and I didn't want to have anything to do with it. Looking back, the irony of this is clear. I wanted to drink alcohol but not smoke a joint. Brilliant thinking, wasn't it? But marijuana was also illegal. I didn't want to break the law. I stuck to my guns and didn't smoke. One time Big Sister's youngest daughter tried to pass a joint to me in the car and I wouldn't take it. She started calling me a square. I didn't care what I was being called; I wasn't about to smoke. So there was more for them. I'm sure I've received plenty of contact highs, though—just being in enclosed spaces with others who were smoking.

My lack of discernment about people coupled with promiscuity eventually caused me to bite off more than I could chew. Knowing who to trust was a challenge that began in childhood with my mother, and it caused me suffering for many years.

One day as I was walking down Elvis Presley Boulevard, a car pulled over alongside me. I think it was a Cadillac. I remember it had a big wheel on the back of the trunk. It was a pretty, green car with two men inside: one white and one Black. The white guy was older, and he was driving. They asked if I wanted a ride. I said okay. I couldn't see any harm in it. I had hitchhiked before, so I got in.

I'm not sure what had made them stop in the first place. I wasn't thumbing a ride. I suspect it had to do with the really tight, short denim overalls I was wearing. They took me where I was going, and I thanked them for the ride. The Black guy asked me for my number, so I gave it to him. Now this was 1981—the "love the one you're with" era. A day or so later, he called and wanted to get together. I don't remember his name. I met him at a park about a mile from my house. We had sex, and he went his way and I went mine. We got together a few more times before he asked if I wanted to go to a club with him and his friend—the guy who gave me the ride originally.

I was okay with it, so I went—they picked me up at my house and took me to a bar. It wasn't a club as I had thought it would be.

We sat at one of the tables and began to talk. At first the conversation was pretty benign and friendly. I noticed the white guy had a paper bag on the table, but I didn't ask what was inside—I figured it was none of my business. But I soon found out. Without saying a word, he opened the bag and pulled out a wig that had long, dark hair. I asked, "Who is that for?" He replied, "You." I laughed. He was out of his ever-loving mind if he thought I was going to wear a wig. I just knew he had to be joking. We sat there a bit longer. I finished drinking my Coke, and they took me home. I didn't think any more about it. You would think that I would have had a clue about what their intentions were—but I didn't. I was about to get myself caught in a trap.

A couple of days after going to the bar, I got a call from the Black guy. He and his friend wanted to take me someplace, so they picked me up. I never once asked either of them what they did for a living. It just wasn't important to me. They said they needed to stop by the apartment for something, which was fine with me, so that's where we went. They asked me to come in. Once inside, the demeanor of both men changed toward me. They said that I would be "turning tricks"—I was going to be a prostitute. Holy shit! How had I gotten myself into this? And more importantly, how would I get out of it? I knew these men could hurt me physically. It was two against one. There was nowhere for me to run, either. My mind was instantly clear and focused. The Black guy had been the bait used to catch me, I thought. And the white guy was the pimp. They had it all planned, and I walked right into it—no fuss, no hassle.

They told me to sit down, so I sat down. I didn't want to get hurt, so I did what I was told to do. Shortly after we got there, someone knocked on the door. When the door was opened, another man was standing there. He came in and stood there. I soon found out that he was a john (aka a client), and I was going to turn my first trick. I felt sick inside. I didn't want to do it, but I had no choice. We were taken to the bedroom, and I let him have sex with me. It didn't last long—maybe five minutes. He left, and I went to clean myself up. The two guys had to run an errand, so they locked me in the apartment. The lock was a deadbolt that needed a key to open it. I couldn't get out. I went to the windows and they were locked—plus we were on the second floor, so I could break my neck jumping. I needed to get out.

The apartment had a phone, which I don't think they thought about unplugging. I called the only person I knew to call for help—Granny's cousin. Even though he had raped me, I felt I had no one else to call. He had a car. I couldn't call Granny. For one thing, I didn't want her to know about this. Calling Big Sister's youngest son wasn't an option. Gwen didn't have a car, nor did anyone else who I thought would help me.

So I called the cousin, my former rapist. I told him what had happened, and he told me that I had gotten myself into this and I had to get myself out of it. He then hung up on me. I began to pray. I prayed harder than I have ever prayed in my life. I asked—no, begged—God for help. I pleaded with him to get me out of this mess. I didn't stop praying. I would go to the windows to see if there was some way I could get out and then to the door, trying to get it open. To this day, I'm not sure how I got out of that apartment—there is no memory—but I did. I only remember walking home. I can only say that I believe I got help from a higher power that day.

I remember making my way home and telling Granny that I was going to Chicago sooner than I had originally planned. I had been accepted at Roosevelt University. School began in August, and this was at the beginning of June. I felt that leaving Memphis quickly was the right thing to do—it was in my best interest. I didn't know what those men might do. They might come after me, and I couldn't have that. So within two weeks of that incident, I boarded a Greyhound for Chicago.

The day I left Memphis was hard. I needed to say goodbye to Granny. I couldn't get her to come out of the bathroom. I could hear her in there crying, and that was difficult to listen to. I loved her, but I knew I needed to go. I said goodbye through the door and left the house. My time living in Memphis had come to an end. I would only visit from then on.

A few years later Granny was diagnosed with Alzheimer's. The family tried to get me to come back to care for her. They argued that Granny had raised me, and therefore I owed her. This argument didn't fly with me. I hadn't asked to be raised by her—she chose to do it. I said, "There are five of you—her grandchildren, plus her daughter and son-in-law, who can take care of her. I'm one person, on my own, and I'm in school. I'm not coming back." This didn't go over well with them, but oh well. If there hadn't been anyone to take care of her, maybe I would have considered it—but that wasn't the case.

Big Sister ended up moving Granny into her house. She stayed there until Big Sister said it was too much for her to handle. Granny would walk off without anyone knowing where she had gone. Thank goodness most people in the neighborhood knew Granny and would call Big Sister to inform her of Granny's whereabouts. If she wasn't walking off, she was trying to light a fire on the kitchen stove with paper and a match. The gas stove in Granny's house had to be lit this way, but Big Sister's stove was different. The pilot would catch and the fire would come on without the use of a match. Granny would usually be found in the middle of the night trying light the stove. I'm sure this must have scared Big Sister. Granny could burn the house down. So Big Sister decided to put her in assisted living.

Granny stayed in assisted living until her death. She got dehydrated and was admitted to the hospital where she died. I happened to be visiting her at the time. It's interesting how this occurred, too. Once I moved away, I never visited Memphis for Christmas—that is, until 1990. I was living in Salt Lake City, Utah, and either went to Bogalusa for Christmas or stayed home. But that year I felt I needed to go to Memphis. I didn't know why. I knew it wouldn't be fun, and the memories of my Christmases there were painful, but I knew I had to go—so I did. No one told me that Granny was in the hospital. I learned of it only when I called Big

Sister to update her on my plans. Granny had been there for a few days when I arrived on Christmas Eve.

When I first began visiting Memphis, I stayed with Gwen and her family, but after a while I just booked myself a hotel—which I did on this occasion. Granny's house was usually either being rented out or used by one of her great-granddaughters. I went to see Granny as soon as I checked in to the hotel. Big Sister and her husband, Johnny Sr. (Big Daddy), were there. Granny recognized me and called me by name. Big Sister did not appreciate this—Granny didn't recognize her. There was that old jealousy rearing its head. But there wasn't anything I could do about it. If I could have had Granny say her daughter's name, I would have.

Granny was going to be in the hospital for a while. She looked emaciated, and her mind was someplace else, but she was hanging on. What I didn't know at the time was that she was waiting to see me one last time. She had somehow called to me through the ethers, compelling me to come to her, and I did. I was her child and she loved me. I loved her too.

Christmas Day I went back to the hospital for a visit and stayed a little while. I remember going over to Granny and stroking her head. She lay there just looking at me not saying a word. That afternoon I had dinner with Big Sister and the family. It was low key but nice. At least I didn't have to sit through watching everyone open presents. Big Sister gave me a bottle of Avon's Skin So Soft. I accepted it with a thank-you. I hadn't bought anyone any presents. Not that I hadn't thought about it before I flew down—I just wasn't in the mood to do it.

I had planned on staying until the day after New Year's. Gwen, a couple of her brothers, and I were going to go out for a New Year's Eve celebration. We hadn't decided on where yet, but we were going to go kick up our heels and party. Gwen's brothers were kind to me. I liked them. They were funny, too. They could always get me to laugh. Gwen's sister had died years earlier, so Gwen was the only girl in the family. At least her family was intact. Her mom and dad were still married—it was a family unit, and I loved being with them.

The day after Christmas I had decided not to go visit Granny. My intent was to just hang out and not do much. It was hard to see Granny just lying there, not doing anything or knowing anyone. It had also been a rough year for me; I needed a time-out. So I just vegged at Gwen's for the day.

That evening I picked up Big Sister's youngest granddaughter, who was now a teenager. Her parents had split up, and she was living with her mother. Her father had moved to Southern California with his significant other. We weren't planning on doing much, just cruising around and talking. At some point during the evening, she wanted to go see her great grandmother—Granny. I told her that I had been to see her the day before and didn't want to go that evening. She said she really wanted to see her, so I said I'd take her. How could I not? It was obvious that this meant a lot to her. When we got to the hospital, Big Sister and Big Daddy were there once again. Big Sister said she had been trying to reach me. "Sure," I thought. I want to be clear that Big Sister wasn't a bad person; she just didn't like me. I had usurped her in some way.

As usual, when I saw Granny I went to her bed and rubbed her head, telling her that I was there. Then I sat down. My intent was to wait until her great-granddaughter was ready to go. There wasn't anything I could do for Granny at this point. After about five minutes of us being in the room, Granny started throwing up this dark, bile-looking substance. That's when all hell broke loose. We were ushered out of the room. We waited for what felt like forever to hear any news. When the news came, it wasn't good—Granny had died. Just like that, she was gone. Sadly, one of the side effects of Granny's Alzheimer's was that she had been gone to me for a while. I had mourned the loss of her over the years. Now I couldn't conjure up any emotion around her death. I hated that it had happened, but I wasn't sad about it. She was free.

We started planning her funeral the next day, and for the most part that went smoothly. The only two issues were choosing the date and getting her favorite cousin, who had no money, back for the service. I was asked to pay for his ticket home. I adamantly refused.

There was no way I would spend a plug nickel on that man. As far as the date was concerned, Big Sister wanted to wait until after the new year, which would give the cousin and others time to get there. Again, I said absolutely not. I can be pretty determined at times, and this was one of those times. I wanted her buried before the new year. The new year needed to be free of this, in my opinion.

The funeral and burial were set for the 31st—perfect. The family found the money to get the cousin back to Memphis. I ended up having to pick him up at the bus station. I took Granny's great-granddaughter with me. There was no way I was going to be with that man alone ever again. It was a nice funeral, and I got to speak about Granny and her love. Afterwards, I promptly lost my voice. Amazing, isn't it? I went out that night for New Year's Eve and couldn't talk above a whisper. I had a good time all the same.

11

Move Back to Chicago

When I moved back to Chicago in 1981, I was excited to be living once again in my hometown. During my summer visits I hadn't gotten the opportunity to explore much of the city outside of the various neighborhoods on the South Side. Now I was an adult and could do as I pleased.

The first thing I did was get a job. I took a job with Marshall Field's department store downtown. I wanted to be in the middle of it all, and downtown Chicago was the hub. I worked in the grocery store, which was on the top floor of the department store, but not the top floor of the building. There were apartments above the store. I loved working there. The apartment tenants would come to the store to shop. Working there was the first time I saw caviar—what an education. I worked the evening shift because of school. The job was part time and paid minimum wage.

The next thing I did was join a modeling agency. I thought it would be nice to try my hand at modeling. I wasn't a beauty, but I wasn't ugly either. The first thing I was told was that I needed to lose weight. I was 145 pounds at 5′10″. I did my best to lose the weight, without any success. In fact, I gained weight—go figure. The agency did send me out on auditions, and I managed to get a runway job for a designer.

The show was being held at Marina City, which I think was called Twin Towers back then because there were two round, high-rise buildings together. The modeling agency Tondu Studios was also housed there. Doing the show was a lot of fun. I was chosen as one of the models because my curves and cleavage didn't matter. The clothes were flowy, thin, and very loose. I actually felt naked in them, but I was to wear whatever the designer put on me. The designer also didn't want us to have on underwear—no bra and no panties. Imagine what Granny would have thought of this! I complied, as did the other models.

I'll never forget walking out on the catwalk that night—it was thrilling. All eyes were on me. I was something. I walked the length of the catwalk and did my turn. Yep—I was hot. The cameras were flashing, and I was showing all my teeth. As I mentioned, the clothes were thin—which translated to sheer. And the outfit I had on had one fastener at the top of the open-front blouse.

I walked back up the catwalk and exited the stage. When I got backstage, one of the models asked me if I knew my boob had been out the entire time. Oh, holy shit! No—I had no idea. It must have happened during the turn I did at the end of the catwalk. There was no way for me to know. I felt naked in the clothes anyway, so I wouldn't have felt that anything was out of place. So *that's* why there was so much camera flashing. Oh, well. Onward and upward! There wasn't anything I could do about it.

That first summer in Chicago was nice. I also got a boyfriend. In Memphis I hadn't really dated. There were a couple of guys I sort of dated, but it wasn't exclusive by any means. This one in Chicago was exclusive. We had met shortly after I graduated high school, a year earlier. I was on one of my summer visits to Chicago. My mother had an old friend of hers, Doris, come for a visit. She conveniently brought her son, Kenny. I think it was a setup by the two women. When we first met, Kenny said he was planning to go to college. When I moved back to Chicago, we began to go out. He was my age. (Actually, I was two weeks older.) As it turns out, my mother and Doris had known each other when both women were pregnant more than 20 years earlier. That summer we spent a lot of time together, driving around and hanging out. We'd sometimes go downtown to the movies. I loved downtown, and that's really the only place I wanted to be. I even chose a college in the Loop. Roosevelt University was on Michigan Avenue across the street from Grant Park. Once school began my schedule was pretty tight, but we still saw each other as much as possible.

I had chosen theater as a major. What else could I have chosen? I was determined to be an actor, and this was a step in the right direction. While there, I also enrolled in the work-study program, which allowed me to work in the audiovisual department. This was fun, too. I learned how to operate some of the audio and video equipment and the studio soundboard.

I didn't have the structure that I'd had in Memphis, though. I was completely on my own, even in school. That first year I took the classes that interested me—theater, life drawing, anthropology—these are the classes I remember, but I know there were more. My grades were okay that first year, but by the second year they had begun to drop considerably. It was my fault, of course. I was playing, working, dating, and going to school.

By the time the second year came around, I had taken on two more part-time jobs. One of the girls from school worked at a company called Automation Academy. The boss was looking for a part-time receptionist to work Fridays. I applied for the job and got it. Then I added a third job working for the CETA program. Kenny's sister-in-law worked there as a secretary, and she told me they were looking for a runner who could work part time. So I applied for and got that job. It was one day a week. This left me only three days for classes, which I thought I could pull off. I worked at Marshall Field's part time too; but this was in the evening, so it didn't interfere with class time. Then there were the occasional modeling classes and auditions—though not much, because I rarely fit the type of person they were looking for.

I also managed to find a little bit of time to play; I went out when I could. The girl who got me the job at Automation Academy had a second job at a night club on the Gold Coast as a singer. Sometimes I'd go listen to her do a set; afterwards we'd go out to another club or go to breakfast before going home. She would usually take me home because she had a car. I remember one night she called me at midnight to ask if I wanted to go out. Of course, I said yes. So I got dressed, caught the train downtown, listened to her last set, and we went out.

Between occasional recreation and all of my other activities, I didn't have much time to study. I had to work, no two ways about it. My mother had lost her job, and even if she hadn't, I was used to taking care of myself financially. She had been working for a dry cleaner in Skokie, Illinois, for most of my life, and the owner decided to close. He wanted to retire—understandable. So my mother was out of a job and didn't want another one. I could understand that, too. But she needed money, and where was she going to get it? Certainly not from her alcoholic boyfriend, Gerald. The owner of the cleaner's offered to get her a job with another cleaner's, but she declined. I think part of the reason for this was that she was tired. After all, she had been working in a cleaner's since the late '40s when she first arrived in Chicago.

I didn't realize it at first, but my decision to leave Memphis meant I had no stability at all. In Memphis I never worried about where I would live or what I would eat. The basics were taken care of—Granny saw to that. She was never able to give me anything extra, but I knew where I was going to lay my head at night and that there was food in the fridge. I never once worried that the house would be taken away—the mortgage had been paid off long before I ever moved in.

Why am I saying this when all I ever wanted to do was to move back to Chicago to be with my mother? Because sometimes the grass looks greener on the other side.

One sunny morning in October 1982, I was lying on the bed watching something on TV. I didn't have class until the afternoon, so I was chilling out, doing nothing for a change. I heard someone knocking on the front door, and I heard Mr. Sampson going to answer it. I never answered the door because it was usually one of Mr. Sampson's clients. I also heard more than two voices, which piqued my attention. I couldn't hear what they were saying, but that would soon change.

Within a few minutes of the knock on the front door there was a knock on my bedroom door. Standing there was a man I didn't know—he told me that he was there to set our things out. I was confused about what he was saying, so I asked him for clarification. He said we were being evicted and that he was there to move our furniture out of the apartment. Standing behind him were other men and the police. It turned out my mother hadn't been paying the rent. Mr. Sampson gave her his portion, but she wasn't adding her nor Gerald's portion. Actually, I never knew if there was a Gerald's portion.

The man standing at my bedroom door wanted to get into my room to begin removing the furniture. I asked him if he could make my room last. He agreed and walked down the hall with his men to start in the rear of the apartment. I needed a minute to think about what to do. My mother was the only one not there. I had no idea where she was. The only emotion I could feel was urgency. I had to do something quick. I called Carrie, my mother's best friend, at work. She worked for the department of social services, and I needed to let her know what was happening. I didn't think she could do anything but offer moral support, which she did. She left work and came over. My next call was to my friend who lived in the building next door. I told her what was happening and asked if she could help me in some way. I didn't want to lose my bedroom furniture. At times like these you learn who your real friends are—and she wasn't one. She said she was tired and taking a nap. Her mother must have overheard the conversation and told her to let me know I could use their storage unit in the basement if I needed it—which I did. The sister of my so-called friend came over to help me move my bedroom furniture into her parents' storage locker. The third call I made was to my boyfriend, Kenny. I told him what was happening, and he came over to help. It took him a while to get there because he lived on the West Side of the city.

There was no time to think; I just had to act. Between the three of us, we moved all of my bedroom furniture and some of my mother's things—clothes, pots and pans, etc.—into the locker. It was small, so we couldn't fit much of her stuff. But I was grateful to my new friend Wanda's mother and father for allowing me to borrow their locker. Thank goodness it had been empty before that.

During the commotion, I managed to watch Gerald come out of the building, put his hat on, and walk up the street toward Garfield Avenue. I was outside with Kenny and Wanda moving a piece of furniture next door when the three of us saw him doing this. I never laid eyes on him again. And to paraphrase Clark Gable in *Gone with The Wind*: frankly, I didn't give a damn.

Mr. Sampson called a moving van to move his things into a storage unit someplace. It was awful seeing everything out on the sidewalk and lawn. All of Mr. Sampson's things were there, as well as most of my mother's things. I didn't want the movers touching any of my belongings, and they didn't. Somewhere toward the end of our moving my things I saw my mother outside. She looked dejected, and she should have. I was beginning to feel anger. How could she not have paid the rent? And if she wasn't going to pay it, why didn't she say something? I was working three part-time jobs; I could have helped. But she never said a word.

To be evicted back then meant she hadn't paid the rent in months. She had lived in that apartment with Gerald and Mr. Sampson since I was a little kid. I know she was living there when I was in elementary school, because she told me on one of our calls. I didn't understand, and I was too tired to contemplate it. My concern now was where I was going to sleep. I had no place to go. I really didn't care if my mother had a place to sleep. I know this sounds horrible—but it's the truth. She could sleep outside for all I cared. She had done this to me, and I wasn't about to show her any sympathy. Carrie was there with her, and I was sure she wouldn't let my mother sleep on the street. But what was *I* going to do?

When we were finished moving the furniture, the three of us were exhausted. We had worked hard, fast, and without any breaks, but it was done—mission accomplished. Kenny went home and Wanda's mother told me to come inside to eat. She had cooked a nice meal. So I went upstairs to Wanda's apartment to eat. I didn't know Wanda that well. She was the older sister of Jan—who was supposed to be my friend. Of course, Jan and I didn't hang out a lot because I didn't smoke pot and she did. But I had still thought we were friends until this incident. I'll never forget how Wanda and I were sitting in the dining room after eating, tired as heck. Jan came out of her bedroom with her boyfriend and asked us if we wanted to play Monopoly. Both Wanda and I just looked at her. I didn't have to say a word; Wanda flew into her sister with anger for not helping me. All I can say is that Wanda and her parents were angels that day. And I had a new friend.

My mother managed to get her things moved up the street into someone else's basement, and she slept on this person's couch. I didn't know who the lady was and I didn't care. For some reason Mom refused to stay with Carrie. I think it was her pride. I do know the church members would have helped her, but I don't know if they did or if she accepted any help from them. I didn't get any help from them. But then again, I got settled pretty quickly. Kenny's parents offered to let me stay with them, and I accepted their offer. Thus began my time of living with a boyfriend.

This was all so new for me. I was living in someone else's house— sleeping on a hide-a-bed couch in their dining room. I was grateful, and I adapted to my circumstances quickly. Kenny's mother's name was Doris, but she was called Dot. She was funny and pretty open minded about most things. It was odd to me to hear her talking about sex. I had never heard an elder talking about this subject so openly. There weren't any subjects as I recall that were off limits with Dot. She made extra money by baking cakes for people. She'd bake themed cakes that looked pretty good. Once while I lived there, I had her bake a coconut cake for Granny's birthday. I mailed it to Granny and it arrived undamaged, as I was told a few years later on one of my visits. Dot loved to cook and she spoiled her kids. In fact, this posed my first problem with Kenny. But I'll talk about that later. Rudolph was Dot's husband and Kenny's dad. Rudolph was pretty low key. He was tired most of the time because of his job as a garbage man. He would get up early and head off to work, coming home around 5:00 p.m. I still remember him coming in the front door and heading to his bedroom to take a nap.

Rudolph and Dot's home was a two-flat on the West Side of Chicago. They lived on the bottom floor, which also had a basement, and Dot's mother and daughter lived in the upstairs apartment.

Everybody called Dot's mother Nana. Nana was a very strong woman who was also kind. She was a minister and had a church, which I began to attend.

Dot and Rudolph had a daughter, Rita, and three sons. The eldest son, Jeffrey, was married and lived in another neighborhood on the West Side. It was Jeffrey's wife, Ella, who got me the job working for the CETA program, which was also on the West Side. Jeffrey was funny like his mother. He would joke around and basically take things as they came. His nickname for me became Flat Butt. He said I had nothing back there. Jeffrey was a garbage man like his dad. Both men took care of their families and owned homes. The youngest son, Rudolph Jr., who was called Junior, was in junior high and lived at home. He rarely came out of his room to do anything but go to school, get food, go to the bathroom, and—as I learned later—peek through the bathroom keyhole at me.

Rudolph's mentally challenged brother also lived on the first-floor apartment. He was pretty benign. Mostly he stayed in the house not doing much.

The two-flat was in a decent lower-middle-class neighborhood. It was a whole new world for me. I got to know a few of Kenny's friends, who were nice to me. I think they saw me as a good girl and therefore treated me with respect. This wasn't the case for other girls I saw them interacting with. One of Kenny's friends even painted my apartment for me when I moved out. I'll explain how this happened later. I moved in with Kenny's family in October 1982 and stayed with them a little over six months. I paid rent, which I was happy to do, and sometimes brought food home from Marshall Field's. I got into trouble at work for doing this, too. But at the time, I couldn't see throwing out food that was only a day old.

Each apartment had three bedrooms, a living room, a kitchen, and one bathroom. The first-floor apartment was pretty full—especially with me moving in. Nana kept her upstairs apartment spotless. Downstairs wasn't too bad, but it wasn't spotless. Dot and Rudolph's bedroom was in the back, off the kitchen. Rudolph's brother and Kenny slept in the front bedroom. There were two twin beds in there, and Junior had his own bedroom. When I moved in, Kenny began to sleep on the hide-a-bed with me.

12

Surviving on My Own

I was still working the three jobs but didn't attend any more college classes that fall. It was too late to cancel the classes, so I failed them. This, of course, caused my GPA to plummet. I didn't know it at the time, but I was beginning to suffer from depression. I was trying to keep my head above water, to just keep going. My life to that point wasn't what I thought it would be. I was grateful for the help and kindness shown by Kenny's family, but I didn't belong there. At that point, I didn't know where I belonged. I wasn't talking to my mother. I was still furious with her. The only information I got about her came through Carrie or Wanda.

I wrapped myself in my relationship and work. These were the only things I had to hold on to, other than my dreams. I wanted to be successful at something. Up to this point I hadn't experienced much in my life that demonstrated success. Life had been one big challenge after another. Even though I was around people, I felt alone—but not hopeless. No one knew how I felt, because I didn't talk about it—not even to Kenny. I had begun to see him more clearly before the eviction but had no intention of letting him go at that point. He had said he wanted to go to school, but I wasn't seeing any movement on his part in that direction. He had his parents' emotional and financial support, so what was the problem? I couldn't understand why he wasn't going to school. I had begun to contemplate the idea that he didn't want to go—that he was lazy. This wouldn't sit well with me because I was ambitious and saw no other way to succeed than having a college education. We didn't argue about this; however, he knew how I felt.

Kenny's not going to school wasn't the only issue we had. A few months before the eviction I learned he had been cheating on me. It was his mother who told me. I'll never forget standing in her living room having her tell me that he was having an affair with his ex-girlfriend. I'm not sure why she told me. After all, this was her son. Mothers usually protect their kids. Dot spoiled them, but this must have been a boundary she couldn't abide. And to top it off, she told me in front of him. My reaction was to go from calm to rage quicker than the blink of an eye. There wasn't an anger stage. It was raw rage. He was at least 6'2", and I pushed him into a corner with no way of getting around me and proceeded to use my knee to jab him in his balls. The only thing that hindered direct contact was his quick action of bringing his leg up to protect them. What's interesting is that I didn't break up with him—which I should have. I chose not to see him for a while, but I went back to him. That was idiocy on my part. The issue was that I loved him. He was my first real boyfriend. The trust was gone, and so was being monogamous, which spelled disaster for this relationship. I had other guys who were interested in me, but I hadn't taken any action with them. There wasn't an intention on my part to cheat—initially. That changed, not because Kenny cheated, but because of something else that happened a couple of months later—or should I say, didn't happen.

One night during the time I lived with Kenny, we were in bed having sex, and I told him—yet again—what I needed him to do to satisfy me. He refused; he said he wasn't going to do such a thing. He told me to go find some white guy who would do this for me, because no Black man would. He was wrong about this, but I didn't say anything. I was tired of not being sexually satisfied. It was good enough for me to please him, but not good enough for him to please me. I just got out of bed and made a phone call to one of the men I knew wanted to have sex with me. The man called a taxi for me, and I dressed while waiting for it to arrive. Of course, Kenny heard the call. He asked what I was doing. I told him that I was following his instructions. I was going to have someone else take care of my needs, because obviously he wouldn't. I got into the taxi and left him in bed. I had a good night and was pleasantly pleased—more than once. The next morning, I went home with a smile on my face. Kenny never said a word to me about it. That was the end of my being monogamous, and I didn't hide it.

One day Kenny, Rita, their cousin, and I piled into the car and went to O'Hare to apply for jobs. Someone heard that the Hilton was hiring. I needed and wanted a full-time job. I was only working two part-time jobs, and that wasn't enough. The job with Automation Academy had ended at the beginning of the year. I had only been working there on Fridays anyway and wasn't making that much money. Then they let me go. I was told the company was going through a re-organization and that I wasn't needed any longer. The Friday before they let me go, the manager had done his best to stick his tongue down my throat while pinning me against his office door. His advances were met with a refusal. I wasn't interested and told him so. Looking back on it, I don't think he took that well. But I needed work and thought it was a good idea to apply at the airport Hilton, which I did. I was hired on the spot as a waitress in the coffee shop. I had originally applied for the hostess job but was told they wanted me to be a waitress instead. I was concerned about whether I could do the job. I hadn't been a waitress before, but that wasn't what concerned me. It was the hand tremors. How was I going to carry a tray full of glasses filled with liquid without spilling it or an armful of plates without dropping them? I'd have to figure this out. None of the others were offered jobs. I thought this odd but was happy for myself. I would work the morning shift—6:00 a.m. to 2:00 p.m. That was early, especially since it meant leaving the house by 4:30 a.m.

The morning shift at a hotel coffee shop is fast and furious. People are going places, and they want to eat and get going. The coffee shop at a hotel connected to the airport by an underground walking tunnel was akin to a restaurant on steroids. It took me a couple of weeks to get up to speed, but I did. However, I wasn't fond of day shift and started working out how to get transferred to night shift. I didn't mind working fast, but this speed did not match my temperament, nor was the money good. People tipped less in the morning. I found this out quickly, and as a waitress you are working harder in the morning than the people who work night shift. This was the way it was at the Hilton. I didn't know how it was at other restaurants. I was working because I needed money, and I wanted to make the most money possible. Waitresses live on their tips, not the salary the restaurant pays. The waitress pay back then was $1.44 an hour—that's it. The tips you brought in determined whether the bills got paid that month. To this day, I tip more than is customary because I know this.

The crew was very nice to me. They taught me how to be an efficient waitress. There is a system to it, and I learned it quickly. I had to or I would make a lot of customers upset. I remember once the Green Bay Packers came in—all of them. They wanted their food to go, and they wanted it fast. I didn't know much about football or the men who played it. These guys were huge. They looked like warriors. They were nice, though, and polite. I still don't watch sports that much, but when I hear their name or see them on TV I think fondly of the team. I was working the counter when they came in and crowded around it. The counter was where to-go orders were taken. I hadn't been working there very long. Thank goodness I don't get intimidated easily, because the sheer size of them could have caused me to fear them. But I could see that they were nice, or at least that's how I perceived them. They waited for their orders to be filled by bantering with each other and talking to a few of the customers who knew who they were. I had no clue who they were until someone told me. When their burgers came, each of them tipped me and left.

One day Kenny's grandmother Nana wanted to have a talk with me, so I went upstairs. She was a strong, get-to-the-point woman who had a ready smile whenever I saw her. She liked me and I was grateful for that. I'll never forget the conversation we had that day. She was sitting in her kitchen and invited me to take a seat—which I did. She had a serious look on her face, and I wondered if I had done anything to upset her. She began by telling me that she didn't like what she was seeing in me. She said I was changing, and not in a good way. She told me that hanging around her grandkids wasn't good for me. She felt I was better than that and I needed to move before this change she saw became permanent. I listened to her advice because I knew she wanted the best for me. I hadn't seen the changes in myself—hadn't had time to even think about it. I was just trying to survive. But she saw it and told me so. She said the spark was going out in me and that she didn't like this. She had taken it upon herself to talk about me with a friend of hers who had a two-flat on the South Side. One of the apartments was vacant. Her friend lived in the upstairs apartment. She gave me the address and asked me if I would go and take a look, which I did.

What Nana didn't know was that I had already begun to look for an apartment. I began the search shortly after getting the job at the Hilton. Because I worked mornings, there was time for me to venture out during daylight hours to look at available places. My initial intention was to move to the North Side. I had nothing against the West or South Side. It's just that I wanted a new experience.

I had already looked at one apartment but didn't like it, plus it stretched my budget. I had also attempted to visit an apartment in one of the Latino neighborhoods. This didn't go well. For some reason I had Dot's car that day. I had probably asked to use her car for some other reason and made a side trip to see the apartment. I'm sure no one knew I was looking at apartments. When I arrived in the neighborhood, I began looking for the street. There were lots of people outside talking and hanging out. It was no different than any other neighborhood as far as I was concerned. The only difference was that everybody stopped talking and began staring at me as I drove by. The looks weren't welcoming, so I kept going and didn't get to see the apartment. I knew there were neighborhoods in

Chicago that I wasn't supposed to go into because of my race, but part of me is a rebel—plus I didn't know there was an issue between Blacks and Latinos. I was raised in the South and had no experience with the culture. It was years later when one of my Latino friends told me we weren't supposed to get along. I didn't understand what he was talking about, so he explained that Blacks and Latinos were supposed to be enemies. This was in the early '80s—I had no idea what the relationship was supposed to be like. His comment shocked me, but my mind went back to driving through that neighborhood. I've never understood prejudice and probably never will.

I went to see the apartment Nana asked me to see. It was a two-bedroom on Wells Street. One of the bedrooms had a full set of bedroom furniture in it. There was a large kitchen with a pantry, a nice-sized living room, and a bathroom. There was a small entryway to the apartment and a back porch. All in all, it was pretty nice. The yard also looked nice. I could tell the owner took care of the place. The price was also what I could afford—$400—so I said I would rent the apartment. All I needed to do was paint the walls and move in. I also wanted to get new carpet, which I mentioned to the landlord, who told me to do what I wanted to do.

I told Carrie about the apartment and received a lecture about my mother needing a place to stay. I didn't want to hear it. My mother had hurt me for the last time as far as I was concerned. I didn't hold back my feelings to Carrie. She was like my aunt. She listened but still implored me to let my mother live with me. She said she understood my point of view but that it was still my mother. In the end, I agreed to have her live with me as long as she paid rent. Carrie thought this was fair. I only wanted $100 per month.

I called my mother and told her about the apartment—offering her a place to live—and she accepted. I also told her that I would rent a truck to pick up the items she stored in the basement where she was living, along with my bedroom set that was in Dot's basement. I had moved my furniture from Wanda's parents' locker a few months earlier, at their request. They needed their locker for other items. I had been grateful to them for allowing me to store my things as long as they did. My mother had the couch and dining room furniture. She could use the bedroom set that was provided in one of the bedrooms, so I wouldn't have to buy anything. Kenny's friend painted the apartment for me. I chose an eggshell-white paint. It was clean and bright. Plus, I had always loved the idea of having an all-white room with varying shades and textures. I even ordered white carpet for the living room.

Moving day came, and I was happy to finally have my own place. It was the first time I had rented an apartment, and it felt nice. I had taken care of the business of having the lights, gas, and water turned on along with a phone service hooked up. After having my things moved into the apartment, I called my mother to let her know we were on our way to her place to get her and the furniture. I had rented a truck, and Kenny's friends were the movers. I would pay them for their time, which was only fair.

My mother informed me that she didn't have the furniture. She didn't say what had happened to it, but it wasn't in her possession anymore. I was upset. Why hadn't she told me this? I had rented a truck big enough to transport her furniture, and now she was telling me she didn't have it. I could have put my things in a pickup truck. I didn't yell or scream at her. Granny had trained me solidly on how to treat elders. I had to show respect—but my mom didn't deserve my respect. I did ask her why she hadn't communicated better, and she didn't answer, so I dropped it. Her clothes had been stored in the locker with my stuff. Thank goodness we had put them there, or she wouldn't have had clothes. She found a way to get them moved to the new apartment. I wasn't about to go get them. When I think back to that period in my mother's life, I think she must have felt defeated. Maybe she didn't care what happened anymore. Thank goodness the landlord had the bedroom furniture for her to sleep on and a kitchen table with chairs, along with all the appliances. The furniture was from the '60s, but I didn't care—it was usable, and use it we did.

I was rarely home except to sleep. Being on the South Side meant getting up at 3:00 a.m. to get to work. I would leave the house by 3:30 a.m. and walk to the 47th Street Dan Ryan train stop to catch the 4:00 a.m. train. I'd get up, shower, dress, and be out the door in a half hour. I wore a uniform, so there really wasn't much dressing involved. All I needed to do was put on a pair of jeans and a top.

I'd use the time on the train to apply makeup and finish my hair. I was teased about my hair at work. My coworkers never knew what style it would be in from week to week. Some weeks I'd put a fake ponytail on, and other weeks it might be curled or waved. (I never knew myself how I would wear it until the beautician was finished styling it. She had carte blanche with my hair, and I liked changing it up.) So by the time I needed to change trains downtown, I would be put together. The downtown train took me to River Road. At that time the train didn't go into O'Hare, so I would then take a bus the final leg of the journey. The bus stopped at the airport, not the hotel, which meant I walked into the airport, down the escalator, and through the tunnel that led to the hotel. Most of us who worked at the hotel were grateful for that tunnel in the winter.

The morning shift for me was over at 2:30. I'd change out of the lime-green dress that was the uniform and head home. The dress matched the color of the booths in the restaurant. Sometimes I'd stop downtown to go to the bank and deposit my tips. I liked having a savings account there. For one thing, the bank was downtown— my favorite place to be. The other reason was that I liked its name— the First National Bank of Chicago. I also enjoyed the kindness of the tellers, and the building fascinated me.

This was the second time in my life that I had a bank account, and it felt wonderful. I'd do my best to make it to the bank at least once a week. The only other place for me to put my tips was under the mattress, which wasn't safe. I'd only store tips there if I had been too tired to get to the bank. My route home was the same every day. Once I got off the train at 47th, I'd walk to Church's Chicken, pick up a chicken meal, walk home, eat, and collapse—sleeping until the next morning. There wasn't much time for any playing or dating or anything else.

I had to get myself off the morning shift—it just didn't suit my style. I was 22 years old and wanted to have fun, too. It didn't make any sense for me not to have some fun. So what did I do? I lied. I told the dayshift manager that I was going back to school and needed my days to attend class. (I really did want to go back to school but hadn't figured out when this would happen, and classes would be in the daytime.)

The dayshift manager was named Pari. She was from the Philippines. Pari ran a tight ship, meaning she was tough. She had also rubbed me the wrong way. Once I came to work with my hair in braids—the small single braids with hair extensions. It was a neat look, and it meant I didn't have to do anything to my hair in the morning, which was nice. I had sat on the floor an entire night having a friend braid my hair. It took at least six hours. The braids were small, and she braided my hair into a bob style. It was gorgeous. When I arrived at work, Pari told me I had to get rid of them—that they weren't professional and didn't fit the Hilton standard. There was no arguing with her—she wanted them gone. Obviously, she didn't know how much money I had spent to get my hair braided or why I had done it in the first place. The braids were done in a conservative style, but she didn't care. So I spent the next night taking them out.

Pari did, however, agree to me being transferred to nights—she couldn't argue with me saying I was going back to school. Night shift was wonderful. It began at 4:30 p.m. and ended at 12:30 a.m. This was a more laid-back shift because customers weren't rushing anywhere. Most of the customers were businessmen, too. They were staying in the hotel because of meetings, and because they were usually alone, they often came down to the coffee shop for dinner. All they wanted was to have a kind person take their order and serve them with a smile—which I did. Most of them were dog tired by the time they made it to dinner. I'd chat with them a bit sometimes—just asking them how they were or how their day had gone. All of them were nice to me and tipped well. But I wasn't being nice to them for the tips. I was being nice because I genuinely cared. I even had customers write nice comments about me in the comment book at the check-out counter and ask to be seated in my section when they returned.

Night shift felt so different than day shift. I had time to breathe and interact with my customers. Magdalena was the hostess. She had been a doctor in the Philippines before immigrating to the United States. Her intention was to become a doctor here, but in the meantime she needed to make a living. I liked Magdalena. She took care of the waitresses and was fair concerning where she seated customers. The hostess in any restaurant is a major part of whether or not the wait staff is happy. I more than doubled my income working nights and acquired a few friends as well.

Ramira was the other night-shift waitress. She was also from the Philippines. She and I didn't really talk that much. It wasn't that we didn't like each other, just that we didn't click well together. We were polite and talked a bit, but that was it. There were only the two of us on nights. Ramira had one side of the room, and I had the other—this made it easy. The cashier lived on the South Side and we started commuting together. She and my best friend in Memphis shared the same name: Gwen. It was safer being on a train with someone else at 1:00 a.m. Her stop was past mine, so I would get off first and walk home—at around 3:30 a.m.

Ramira and I each had our own busboy. Ricardo was mine. He was a hoot to work with, and I made sure to tip him well at the end of the evening. We would laugh and talk about our lives. Ricardo was dating a male doctor and was happy with his relationship. He and I hit it off so well that he invited me to a Halloween party at one of the clubs he frequented. I had never been to a gay club and was excited to party with Ricardo and his friends. I asked Gwen if she would go with me. She was apprehensive, but in the end I convinced her to accompany me. Neither of us dressed in a costume for the party. I kind of wish we had.

The party was in full swing by the time we arrived. Ricardo knew what time we were to arrive, so he and a couple of his friends were waiting for us outside. This is when I met Carmen Miranda. Wow—

that man was *fine*. It didn't matter to me that he had fruit on his head and wore a dress. I'll never forget looking up at him asking if he was sure he was gay. He laughed and assured me that he was. Ricardo's other friend was dressed as a nurse. He had on a white uniform with a nurse's hat. We went into the club and danced all night. I don't think Gwen was having much fun, but I sure was. These guys were fun and took very good care of us. I didn't buy a drink for myself all night—someone else would do it for me.

At the end of the evening Ricardo, Carmen Miranda, the nurse, Gwen, and I went to Denny's for breakfast. Denny's was 24 hours, so this was where we usually ended our evenings out—or should I say, mornings. It was around 4:00 or 5:00 a.m. The waitress serving us knew we had been to a Halloween party. She looked at me and said, "Oh—your makeup is so good, I would have sworn you were a woman." To which I replied, "You see these?" Pointing to my chest, I quipped, "Honey, these be real." Everybody roared with laughter, including the waitress. It had been a terrific evening—at least for me. Gwen was reserved the entire night. She was uncomfortable being there but did relax a bit after a libation or two.

Another reason I liked night shift was that the manager was hardly ever around. He managed more than one restaurant and tended to leave the coffee shop alone. We knew what we were doing and really didn't need much supervision anyway. However, when he would appear, we usually had been told he was coming. The information network from restaurant to restaurant was better than the internet. I don't remember his name, but he was pretty nice. I went to a party at one of the other employees' homes and he was there. He partied with all of us.

After working at the coffee shop for a bit, I applied to work as a stewardess with United Airlines. It was an easy fit as far as I was concerned. I would be a waitress in the sky and see the world.

There were several rounds of interviews, and I could be rejected at any point. It was easy for me to get to the interview since they were held at the airport. I took one of the airline buses out to the building where the interviews were being held. The bus was full of other young ladies applying with United for stewardess jobs. We were put in a large room with a circle of chairs. We were asked a couple of questions, and then we were weighed. This part made me nervous. I weighed 147 pounds and thought this might be too much. I was still skinny, but maybe not enough. Well, the interview ended and I went to work. I didn't make the cut. I was sad about this because I really had the travel bug and wanted to see the world. But there were other airlines, and I figured one of them would hire me.

My relationship with Kenny was on its last leg. He had gone off to college and been kicked out for selling drugs. I had suspected he sold drugs but wasn't sure. I had seen him smoke weed in his parents' basement with his friends, but smoking and selling were two very different things. I was fine with his smoking as long as he didn't try to get me to do it. My first suspicion arose when he once came up with a large quantity of money that I needed. This happened before I moved in with him and his family. I had inadvertently melted my $300 contact lenses and didn't have the money to replace them. Kenny left the house saying he had someplace to go, and when he returned he had the money. I asked him where he had gotten the money, and he said he borrowed it. Who had that kind of money to loan to someone who wasn't working? I had my suspicions, but not proof.

Kenny had decided to go to school in another state—I think Texas. I was proud of him for doing this. But when he was expelled, I knew we wouldn't last. I pretty much moved on but hadn't officially broken it off. I started going out with one of the cooks at the Hilton. He was the first white man I dated. And let me tell you, the only difference between a white man and a Black man is color. Everything else is the same. (Actually, the only real difference between any of us is our level of consciousness, but that's a topic for another time.)

I dated this guy for a while. He was fun and cooked for me at his apartment in Rosemont, which I liked. I would sometimes go to his place after work and then take his car home if it was too late for me to catch the train. It was nice of him to loan me his car. I remember once we had an argument about something, and I was so upset I told him that we were through and left his house. When I got home—almost three hours later—he called and said he was going to kill himself. I was still upset, so I told him to go ahead. I didn't think he would do such a thing. Being broken up with wasn't a reason to kill yourself, in my opinion. I called Gwen, the cashier at the Hilton, and told her what he had said. She advised me to call the police. She said, "That fool might do it; you know how he feels about you." I thought she was off her rocker, but I called the police as she had suggested and asked them to go check. When they got there, they looked through the basement window and saw him sitting on the floor with a paper bag over his head. He had gotten drunk and tried to commit suicide by suffocating himself. What I said to him the next day wasn't pretty, making the breakup official.

O'Hare rarely closes, but when it does, its pandemonium for everyone—including the Hilton coffee shop. Because of the coffee shop's location, stranded passengers could easily walk there from the airport without having to brave the elements. The winter of '83 was my first experience with this. Airlines were giving passengers food vouchers, and the coffee shop was packed most of the time. No one could get out for days, including the staff. We were given hotel rooms and worked 16-hour days. This went on for more than a week. The day shift couldn't get to work, so the night shift had to work both. Jeez, that was hard, but financially rewarding.

I somehow managed to get out one night after the coffee shop closed. The trains were still running, and the buses ran too—although behind schedule. I needed to get out to take my mother money for her trip to Bogalusa. She was going home for Christmas, and I knew she didn't have much money, so I took her some. I didn't know at the time that she had already borrowed money from someone else. I made it home, gave her the money, and went back to the airport. A few years later, when I would visit my mother, the people she had borrowed money from would sometimes approach me to pay them. I learned that she was only getting about $600 a month from Social Security once that began, and far less before that. To be honest, there was a part of me that didn't care. Once I lose respect for a person, they become a shadow in my world—and I had lost respect for my mother. I still did the right things by her, but that was as far as it went. My heart was closed to her.

After my mother lost her job with the dry cleaner's, she began working at the fish market her minister owned. The church and the market were on 73rd and Halsted. Earlier I mentioned Reverend Morris. He was a little man—in so many ways, including his height. Of course, this is only how I viewed him. The congregation loved him, including my mother. To me it seemed that they were taking care of him, doing everything from washing his clothes to working in his store for less than minimum wage. When I learned how little my mother was making working all day in that fish market, I fumed. He paid her a measly $40 a week. She could have made more than that anywhere else, but she wanted to be at that market. I thought all of the church members were mad for allowing the reverend to take advantage of them. But what did I know? In hindsight, I believe I was correct.

Years later, when my mother was dying from cancer, she called me to ask for $50. Reverend Morris wanted her to buy a special tea that would supposedly cure her cancer. This was the first time I ever lost my temper with my mother. I was angry at Reverend Morris for getting her hopes up and for having her pay for the tea. She had worked—no, slaved—for him for years, and he wanted to charge her for this. He could damn well pay for it himself. I yelled so much that she had to fight back, telling me that she was the mother and I wasn't to yell at her that way. I shut up, but I didn't send the money. I wasn't about to for any reason. I now regret acting that way. I should have sent the money even though I knew the tea was bogus. Over the years there have been a few situations that have gotten me riled up, and this was one of them.

Another instance that I got riled up was when a customer in the coffee shop walked in, sat down, and told me what I was going to do for her. She told me to get her a glass of wine. It was the tone of her voice that got me upset. I went to Gwen (the cashier) and informed her, "It's going to be a cold day in hell before I get that woman a glass of wine." I let her sit there and never went back to the table. She complained to Magdalena, who promptly brought her the wine and took her dinner order. Magdalena then came to me and told me that if I was not going to serve someone to at least let her know. I agreed to do this. I didn't know what had happened in that woman's life to cause her to be that way, but I was not her servant.

13

Dreaming of a Better Life

Having the job at O'Hare exposed me to people from all over the world. This fed my spirit and mind. It also gave me ideas about other ways of living, which I liked. I began a ritual of taking myself out to a high-end dinner once a month. I would pick a restaurant, usually one in the Loop, and eat there. It was expensive, but I didn't care. I wanted the experience. Going to these places was akin to finishing school. I watched how other people ate and sat, which utensil was used for which course, and other details of how to be in a high-end restaurant. I usually went alone, because no one in my circle had the money or the desire to do such a thing. Most of them thought I was throwing good money away. I did manage to get Ella, Kenny's sister-in-law, to accompany me once. We went to Maxim's at McCormick Place. I had been there before and thought it would be a nice place to take her. She was nervous but had a good time—that is, until the finger bowl. Ella thought it was for drinking, so that's what she began to do. When I saw her with the bowl up to her mouth, I told her what it was for. Both of us were embarrassed, but how would she know what it was for? She hadn't been to an expensive restaurant.

I caught a lot of flak in the neighborhood because of my choice to work at O'Hare. People I didn't even know would ask me, "What's wrong with working in the neighborhood? Who do you think you are? Why do you have to go all the way out there for work?" My answer was always "That's where I found a job; therefore that's where I am working." I wasn't uppity, as some people called me. The truth was that I wanted a better life, and I felt working at an airport would help me to get it. I wasn't happy with my life. I was sure an opportunity would come along if I worked in the middle of all the action. Nothing was happening in the neighborhoods. No one was coming around offering opportunities, and no one ever would. I had to go find the opportunities myself. I never expected opportunity to arise without planting seeds for it, and I was sure something would sprout.

My route home after work was the same. Gwen and I would take the bus to River Road for the train that took us downtown. We would then transfer to the southbound Dan Ryan. Most of the journey was uneventful. The trains during this time of the evening rarely had many passengers. So Gwen and I would just talk about our lives or work.

One evening I ended up going a stop further than I should have. This was because a group of young men on our train saw fit to harass us. Gwen kept quiet; I didn't. I don't remember what I said to them, but it wasn't nice. I knew I was in trouble by the look on their faces. I got out of my seat to exit the train at my stop. They also got up and went to the other exit to do the same. When the train stopped, they exited and I stayed on. The doors closed, so they couldn't get back on. That night I made my exit at the 55th Street stop. Because the trains ran every hour at that time of the evening, I ended up walking back to 47th—my normal exit. I knew I had dodged something horrible happening to me. I learned a lesson about opening my mouth when I couldn't back it up with action. I wasn't thinking when I made my comments to them.

On another occasion I was walking home from the train station when a guy decided he would mug me. That was scary. I was three blocks from the house, walking on a dimly lit street. It was the same street I had walked many times after work, which was one of the problems—I didn't alter my route; didn't think to do so. It was about 3:00 a.m. and the street was empty, so I noticed him right away. He was walking behind me—he had trailed me from the train stop. I thought about running but didn't think I could outrun him, so I just walked fast. He caught up with me and told me to give him my purse. And he said he had a gun, which I could see him holding in his coat pocket. I could tell he was nervous and I didn't want to be shot, so I handed him my purse. I started to talk to him. I told him to take the money but to please leave my ID—it would be too hard to replace it. I just kept talking while he rummaged through my purse, which was now on the ground with my things strewn all over the place. I really didn't want to lose my things. He could have the money. That night had been a light tip night—I only had $30. After he took the money, he decided he wanted more; he wanted to rape me, too. When he told me to get down on the ground, I started to scream and he ran off. I gathered my belongings and ran home. I began to alternate my route home after this.

A couple weeks later I was walking home from someplace during the day. As I passed the spot where the mugging took place, a middle-aged man leaned his head out of an upstairs window. He asked me what time I walked home in the evening. I told him. He then said, "You had better be careful, because a couple of weeks ago a girl was mugged right here." I thanked him and kept walking. He had seen me being mugged and did nothing to help. What kind of man was he? I really should have told him that it was me he saw being mugged, but I didn't. I didn't want him to feel uncomfortable. Yes—I was concerned about his feelings.

Fortunately, or unfortunately, depending on how you look at it, I was only mugged twice and stabbed once in Chicago. At least I wasn't killed. The other mugging happened more than a year earlier on my way to a photo shoot. I left the apartment on Michigan

Avenue with an outfit to wear for the shoot. The outfit happened to be my best suit. It was a cream two-piece—jacket and skirt. My clothes were in one of those plastic bags from the cleaner's, and it was hanging on my left arm. As I turned the corner onto Garfield, several people were standing at the bus stop waiting for the bus. I intended to walk to the 55th Street Dan Ryan train station to go downtown. Behind me I heard someone running. It sounded as though the person was jogging. In hindsight, it's silly that I thought that. Who would be jogging in the hood back in the early '80s? Whoever it was picked up speed as they got closer. I didn't turn to see who it was, but maybe I should have. It turned out to be a young man, who snatched my clothes. I never got a look at his face, but he was very tall and lean. Because the clothes were in plastic and I didn't have a tight grip on them, they made for an easy steal. When he grabbed the clothes, he kept running and headed for the State Street projects. It's interesting that there were men standing at that bus stop, and they just continued to stand there—not saying a word. They just looked at me. The only thing I could do was to go back home for another outfit, which I did.

The stabbing, which had happened years earlier, was a surreal experience. I was a teenager—I think 15 or 16. It was during the period of time when my mother would have me stay with some of the church families who had kids for me to hang out with. On this particular day, I wasn't staying with anyone. I had talked my mother into letting me come for Christmas. I had decided to go to the movies with Pam, one of the church girls that I knew. She was everyone's favorite—light skin, good hair, and a pleasing disposition. She was nice and I liked her. It didn't matter to me that she was favored.

We took the bus from her apartment on 73rd and Halsted to 63rd and transferred to the 63rd Street bus. This stop was the shopping district on the South Side where I got my school clothes every year. There was also a movie theater, which I attended frequently during the summer. Back then they had double features, and you could sit in the movie theater for hours. I saw most of the '70s Black movies in that theater. Bruce Lee movies were also a favorite of mine. After the movie I was supposed to go straight home, which meant going in the opposite direction from Pam's home. I'll never know where I got the idea that I needed to make sure Pam got home safe, but that was the truth of it—I wanted to make sure she was safe—never mind my own safety.

Pam's apartment was above the church we all attended. Reverend Morris owned the building. My intention was to make sure Pam got in her door and then catch the bus home. It was cold outside, which meant we were bundled up—thank goodness for this. I had on several layers of clothes underneath a warm coat. The entry for Pam's apartment was to the right of the church entrance. Once inside the door, there were stairs that led up to the apartment. To the right of her entry was a bar. As I stood behind Pam waiting for her to get her key out and open the door, a tall, skinny man came out of the bar. I looked at him as he came toward us. I thought he was just going to walk past, so I turned back to Pam, who was putting the key in the door. The next thing I felt was something hard on my back, just below the right scapula. Pam started screaming, and the man ran down the street. Everything happened in an instant. I went into shock and just stood motionless.

Pam's father must have heard her screaming and came running down the stairs. Pam told him what had happened, and he went running down the street to see if he could find the man—to no avail. In the meantime, Pam's mother came downstairs and ushered both of us upstairs and into the apartment, where she examined me for wounds. I didn't cry or scream when I was stabbed, but I did begin to cry when I saw my own blood. I had been stabbed with a Phillips-head screwdriver. Its imprint was on my back. As I said before, thank goodness I had on layers of clothes, or more damage would have been done. As it was, my skin had been pierced, but no real damage was done.

Around the time of the second mugging is when I bought my first car. Martha, one of the other hostesses at the coffee shop, had a '73 green AMC Hornet she was selling for $200. I needed wheels, so I bought her car. She said it was in good condition, but I had it checked out by the cook I was dating. He said it was fine. After I bought it, I found out from a real mechanic that (among other problems) the muffler had so many holes in it, it was like swiss cheese.

I began sinking money into the car to keep it running. There were a couple of things I didn't know about car ownership—one of them being that the car needed to be registered. I had no clue, as the police officer who pulled me over could tell. I was driving my new car one evening when flashing lights appeared in my rear-view mirror. I pulled over, and the officer walked up to the car and asked for my driver's license and registration. I looked at him, puzzled, while giving him my driver's license. He could tell I was naïve. A person can't fake this to a police officer. I told him that this was my first car and that I didn't know I needed to register it. I thought buying it was all that needed to be done. He was so nice. He told me where to go to get the car registered and gave me a ticket. But he said when I registered the car, I should go to the police station to let them know it had been done and the ticket would be torn up. I did as he asked.

I'm not a person who frequented police stations. As a matter of fact, I had never been inside of a police station. Usually, I'd walk on the opposite side of the street if I ever needed to walk past one. So going inside to let them know I had registered my car caused a wee bit of nervousness. I remember being asked to wait in one of the interrogation rooms you see on *L.A. Law*, or at least that's what it looked like to me. I sat and waited. After a bit, one of the officers came in and told me I could go. I will never forget that officer's kindness.

That car had its own temperament. It would operate when the weather was nice. If it was snowing, forget it—it wouldn't start. I began driving to work rather than taking the train. Gwen would catch the train to my place and ride with me. The novelty of having a car in the city wore off quickly, but I could get to work much faster than taking the train—that is, unless I was stuck in traffic. I can remember getting off the freeway, which was virtually stopped, winding my way through unfamiliar neighborhoods, and getting lost. There was no GPS—only maps, which I didn't have. We were late for work only once, and it was because I exited the freeway to find another route through the streets. Actually, we were late a second time, but it was not because of anything I did.

One day Gwen and I got into the car in front of my place to drive to work and it wouldn't start. I thought the battery was dead, so I called AAA—which I joined shortly after buying the car. I was on my own, and this way if there was a problem with the car, I had someone to call. I had learned the hard lesson of not depending on others to do anything for me. Well, the man from AAA came. When he opened the hood, he looked inside and then looked around the hood at me. I was sitting inside the car to turn the key on when he was ready. He told me that there was no battery to jump-start. Someone had stolen my battery. He told me what to buy and left. People in the neighborhood were peering out their windows or hanging out on stoops looking at me. I knew someone in my neighborhood had done this, but there was nothing I could do. At least they didn't steal the car. Of course, they probably thought it wasn't worth stealing. Gwen and I took the train to work that day. When the battery was replaced, I began the nightly ritual of taking the battery out, chaining the hood of the car, and taking the battery inside the house. I didn't want anything else to come up missing.

Little did I know that my life was about to change in ways I could never imagine. I have always prayed for guidance and help and have taken life as it comes. I also have always known that blessings come in different forms and that we never know what these will look like, and it is up to us to accept or reject them. I've known plenty of people who have rejected blessings because it didn't come in the form they thought acceptable—either by them, family, friends, or society. But that is not how I live my life. Sometimes I have no idea that a person who has entered my life is a blessing right away, but I don't reject them because they don't look like me or come from my world.

Underwater Tuber

The tuber forms the root structure of the lotus plant and
influences the health and growth of the plant. As
humans, our root structure determines how many
resources we have to reach the goal of the Soul.
Our memory bank forms our roots. Its growth
is determined by gaining more experience
from life and all other lifetimes. The
mind has to grow and expand with
each experience. It is the mind,
with all its memories and
foundation, that
anchors the Soul.

14

A Gift Offered and Accepted

One night at work—I'll never forget the date, December 3, 1983—it was a slow night and, as usual, the staff was bantering back and forth, just playing around talking about this and that. A man walked into the restaurant and Magdalena sat him in my station at his request. It wasn't my turn, and Ramira wasn't happy about this, but there wasn't anything she or I could do about it. Magdalena made it up to her by giving her the next two customers.

After a few minutes I went over to him to take his order. He had a medium-sized build with black, thick hair and an equally thick mustache; he was smartly dressed in slacks, shirt, and business jacket. I don't remember what he ordered, but he wasn't there to eat. Coming into the restaurant had been a ruse to talk to me. What I didn't know was that he had seen me earlier in the evening when he walked from the airport to the hotel. He said I looked exotic to him and that he wanted to get to know me. This was a new pickup line in my opinion, and I was intrigued.

What I didn't realize until much later was that he really meant it—I did look exotic to him. He said he had seen me as he was headed to the escalator to go up to registration. The escalators were in front of the coffee shop windows. He said he had to stop when he saw me and just watch me. "This guy is really good," I thought.

He continued by telling me he checked in to the hotel, put his bags in the room, and came down to meet me. What was I supposed to say to that? Well, he asked me for my number and I gave it to him. He seemed nice enough, so why not? His name was Bill, short for William, and he was of Irish-Welsh ancestry. He was clearly much older than me, but that wasn't an issue. His home was Salt Lake City, Utah, which I knew absolutely nothing about at that point and didn't care to. Bill said he was in Chicago on business and would be headed to Wisconsin in a couple of days. He took my number, paid for his meal after he had eaten, and said he would call me. I wasn't sure that he would, but it would be okay either way. It was nice to have someone talk to me the way he did.

Men eating at the restaurant had flirted with me before, but I never reciprocated. One reason was that I was dating the cook for a while, and another reason was Kenny. Although our relationship wasn't monogamous anymore, I still cared about him. It wasn't until I learned of his shenanigans at school that I began to put more distance between us. As I said earlier, I had little patience for anyone who didn't want a better life if they didn't already have it. And Kenny had proven to be lazy—giving me lip service about his dreams. I've always paid attention to whether a person's words match their actions. It may take me a while to see, but I always do—and Kenny's actions weren't matching his words. And, as I said earlier, once I lose respect for a person, the relationship is basically over.

A couple of days after I met Bill, all hell broke loose at the coffee shop. Bill had called me earlier in the day and asked me if I would fly to Wisconsin to meet him. I said I would. When I told my friends about it, they got upset and started talking about him possibly being an axe murderer or rapist. They said that I didn't know him and shouldn't go. I could understand their arguments, but I was going

126

to do it anyway. I was then told by one of the crew to ask him for his driver's license and tell him that a background check was going to be run. She had a friend who was a detective, and she was sure he would do her a favor. I was leaving in two days, so I called Bill that night and told him what my comrades wanted. He agreed and faxed a copy of his driver's license to me at the hotel. This man was serious—he really wanted me to come to Wisconsin. I didn't know why. What was so special about me? The background check came back clean, and my friends cleared me to go. Of course, they also gave me instructions to follow such as calling when I got there and giving them my room number. They already had Bill's information. I appreciated them doing this for me but didn't feel it was necessary. Actually, when you think about my history with men, it probably was necessary. But this felt different. He felt different. I had been cleared for takeoff, so I boarded my first airplane and headed for Appleton, Wisconsin.

Bill told me that he was a manufacturers' representative—selling custom furniture to institutions such as schools, churches, and office buildings. He was in Appleton to visit one of the institutional furniture companies he represented. He had been in the business since the early '60s. And yes—that meant he started his career when I was a mere babe. You could argue that when I met him, I was still a mere babe. He told me that he was 49; however, I learned later that he was 50. I still wonder what difference one year makes to a person. To him I guess it meant he could still pass for almost young—not yet middle aged. Maybe he thought I would reject him if I knew his real age—who knows? I did ask him later why he lied, which he didn't take well, so I let it go. I have a knack for asking questions that sometimes make others uncomfortable. The intention of the questions is to gather information so that I can gain clarity on a subject, not to put people on the spot.

My trip to Appleton wasn't exciting, but it was nice, especially since I was only there for one night. Bill and I went to dinner and then back to the hotel. At dinner we talked about our lives a bit. One thing I remember about being with him that first night was that he made a point of showing me checks he had received from the furniture company that were for large amounts. I couldn't figure out why he was doing this. I really didn't care that he had money. I looked at the checks blankly and then looked at him questioningly.

In any event, I had a nice evening, and the next morning he took me back to the airport for my return flight home. He said that he would call, but I never expected to hear from him again. He had gotten what he wanted, and that was that—in my opinion. At least that was how it had normally been with men who I slept with on the first date. My intention was to have the experience, not to get into a relationship. When I arrived back in Chicago I got in my car, went home, and slept until it was time to go to work. Bill called me two days later and asked if I would meet him again—this time I would fly to Salt Lake City and we would drive to Wyoming. I had never been west and was excited to see another part of the country. My coworkers were wary, but there wasn't much they could do. The background check hadn't turned up anything, so all they could say to me was to be careful. I told them that I would. I'd leave a couple of days after Christmas. This was a good thing, because within a few days of my having said yes, the airport was closed for days due to the snowstorm I mentioned earlier.

By the time of my flight to Salt Lake, O'Hare had reopened, which was wonderful since the Christmas holiday was in full swing. I left a couple of days before New Year's. I boarded the flight and we took off. It was the first time I saw the Rocky Mountains, and I remember being in awe of how majestic and beautiful they were. They didn't look the same as the Smoky Mountains, which are also gorgeous. The Rockies were covered with snow and very high. I couldn't stop looking at them. I even said to myself, "This must be where God lives." This was also the first time I felt an air pocket, and that sensation wasn't majestic.

Bill picked me up at the airport in his Suburban, and we headed straight to Wyoming. We didn't stop at his house, nor did I get a tour of the city. He wanted to get on the road, and I was fine with this. I don't remember if there was snow on the ground in Salt Lake City, but Wyoming had more snow than I had seen in my life. I was accustomed to Chicago snow, but this was different. For one thing, there was so much open space—no buildings. And this made the snow scene vast. You could see for miles, which was a first for me. It was also a different kind of snow—powdery.

We made our way to Jackson Hole, stopping along the way for me to see more vistas. Jackson Hole back then wasn't as big of a tourist destination as it is today, which meant there weren't so many people around. It looked like a town out of the Old West I had seen in movies, except there were sidewalks and people drove cars and wore modern clothes with cowboy hats. We checked in to a condo Bill had rented and the next morning went to the Silver Dollar restaurant for breakfast. I think everyone should go to the Silver Dollar at least once.

It was the first place I had visited where there weren't any people of color—that I saw, at least. Looking back on it, I wasn't concerned. On the drive from Utah to Wyoming we stopped at a café in Wyoming, and a scene unfolded that could have come straight out of Central Casting. As Bill and I approached the front door of the restaurant, we could hear people having lively conversation—typical for a restaurant. I walked through the door first, and as soon as I did the conversations began to cease. I literally saw people stop in their tracks with coffee cups to their mouths and stare at me. I wasn't expecting this. Why were they staring? Was there something on my pants? Or in my hair? It took me a minute—well, maybe two—to realize why all eyes were focused on me. A waitress came over and escorted us to a table. Conversations slowly started up again. What's funny is that I wasn't nervous, and I never thought the people were staring because they were prejudiced. I figured there was a distinct possibility they had never seen a Black person before. I had no idea what they were thinking, but as long as no one said the "N" word, I was fine. I do wonder if nobody said anything to me because Bill was there. He hailed from Wyoming originally and had that tough, "don't fuck with me" look.

I remember a conversation we had a couple of years after this incident in which he asked me why no one in my neighborhood bothered him when he came to see me on the South Side of Chicago. I told him it was because he looked like a mafia hit man, and if there's one group the gangs won't bother, it's the mafia. Bill had a thick mustache; thick, dark hair; dark sunglasses; he rarely smiled and walked with confidence. He wasn't a big man, but he had that bravado—that "I'm in charge" vibe. This should have been a blaring red flag, but I didn't see it. All I saw was someone who paid attention to me and treated me nicely. I also felt safe with him—this never changed. No one ever bothered me when we were together. I needed him. I needed him for so many reasons, but I wouldn't learn this until later in the relationship. I will say upfront that this was a deeply challenging relationship, yet it lasted 18 years.

Anyway, about every two weeks after my initial trip to Wyoming, I was on a plane headed someplace to meet Bill. As a salesperson he had a five-state territory and traveled extensively. Wyoming, New Mexico, Colorado, Utah, and Arizona were his stomping grounds. My first visit to California was because of him. We went to San Francisco, Monterey, and Carmel. I fell in love with the area. It felt like home to me. It was the ocean that did it for me. I absolutely loved the Pacific Ocean. Having spent my life in the South and Midwest, I had never seen an ocean. I remember just sitting on a rock looking out at the ocean with a feeling of peace that I had never felt before. Bill took me shopping for clothes in Monterey, which I also loved. I love boutiques. I'm not a mall person—I don't like seeing my clothes on other people. I like unique clothes, and boutiques might not have one-of-a-kind pieces, but they don't have hundreds-of-a-kind, either.

For Christmas that first year, Bill had asked me what I wanted, and I promptly told him a fur coat. So he took me to a furrier on Union Square in San Francisco, and I picked out a long, gray fox-fur coat. I was in heaven. What 22-year-old girl wouldn't be? Over the years we would make numerous trips to San Francisco and the Monterey Bay area. It was my favorite place to be, and Bill felt good there too.

I did spot another red flag on that trip—one that I recognized but ignored. It had to do with jealousy. I'm not an easily jealous person, and jealousy is dangerous to a relationship. We were staying at one of the hotels on Union Square. It had a disco club on the top floor. One night Bill asked me if I wanted to go up there, and of course I did. We went upstairs and found a table near the dance floor. I didn't know then that Bill didn't dance. So I just sat there while perfectly good music played. People were out on the dance floor having fun, and there I was—watching from the sidelines.

Pretty soon a guy came over and asked me to dance. I asked Bill if he minded. He said no. I asked again. He assured me that it was fine. So I went out on the dance floor and had fun. This was disco, so no one danced cheek to cheek unless it was a slow song, which this wasn't. I only danced through one song. I wanted to be respectful of my date. But when I arrived back at the table, he wasn't there. I looked for him without any success, so I went back to the room. He was there, and he was upset. I was confused. He had told me it was okay to dance with the guy when, in fact, it wasn't. This was new for me.

My nature is to talk about a problem, asking questions to get an understanding of the issue. This method didn't work with Bill. He just moped around. Even though I had nothing to apologize for, I apologized. I wanted to do anything to make him stop. I never went dancing with him again. That doesn't mean I didn't go—I just didn't go with him. He had other ideas that a 22-year-old would think odd. In his opinion, females who went to bars were going so that they could be picked up. I disagreed. Although it does happen, it was never my reason for going to bars. I went to hang out with friends and have a good time.

I never thought the relationship would last—it couldn't—we were too different. We were from two different worlds, not just by age. I was in it for the adventure. The adventure of having new experiences really does feed my soul. And by now I'm sure it's clear that some of my adventures have gotten me into places that I'd rather have not gone. This relationship was a huge adventure for me, and in hindsight, a blessing.

On my first trip to Salt Lake City I met Bill's son. We were close in age—two years apart—and I liked him. He seemed nice. He was attending the University of Utah. He had a slight build and an artistic flair. I could also tell that he was much more sensitive—softer—than his dad. He was kind to me, and I appreciated this. Of course, I had no idea where my relationship with Bill was going, but at least I got along with his son.

The weeks went by and Bill and I were still together, so I officially broke off my relationship with Kenny. We hadn't seen each other in several months. Kenny didn't fight me on this, thank goodness. Not that he could stop me from doing what I wanted to do anyway. We ended amicably. He acknowledged that his actions had caused the breakup in the first place. Kenny brought back the keys to my apartment, and I gave him the few items that were at my place. We didn't actually see each other to do this. Bill had asked me not to see Kenny face to face to make the trade, and I had agreed. I'm sure Bill must have thought I would end up not breaking it off. He didn't understand that once I make up my mind, I rarely change it. So I told Kenny to leave my keys on the front porch and that I would do the same with his things. That was it—the relationship was officially done. When Bill and I started going out, I had told him about Kenny. I was honest about the relationship—there was no need to hide it. Kenny and I hadn't slept together since his return from Texas, but I hadn't made the breakup official.

Somewhere around the end of March I decided to relocate to Salt Lake City. I don't think it was my idea, though I can't say for sure. Bill and I had been seeing each other several times a month, and the relationship was serious. My friends in Chicago were up in arms about this. One of my coworkers asked me if I knew anything about Utah and the people who lived there. Did I know the state was Mormon? I told her I didn't know anything about Utah or Mormons. I thought maybe they were like the Quakers. I had no problem with Quakers, so why would I have any issues with

Mormons? My coworker told me they had multiple wives and a little bit about the belief system based on her knowledge of the Book of Mormon. She did her best to dissuade me from moving to Utah—with no success. This was my first long-distance relationship, and I was tired of having to get on a plane to be with someone I cared about. We talked every night when I got home from work, which was fine—but that was getting old.

My only concern about moving was my mother. She was living with me, and I felt responsible for her. I remember telling Bill that if I moved to Salt Lake City he would have to pay all the expenses of the apartment for three months. This would give my mother enough time to save the money necessary to start paying the rent. I was leaving abruptly and wanted to be fair with her. Bill agreed to do this. Since I was quitting my job, I wouldn't have the money myself.

One of my old coworkers from the job I had with the CETA program had no problem with my moving to Salt Lake City. He was a gigolo by night and janitor by day. He was all about the money and advised me to have Bill buy me a condominium. I thought he was out of his mind. He said, "Girl, you've got to take care of yourself because no one else will." I agreed with the fact that I had to take care of myself, but I wasn't about to ask Bill to do this. I didn't need anyone to buy anything for me—I could do it myself.

That coworker was a hoot. He even invited me to his apartment a couple of times to hang out. A couple of us would go to his place on occasion. One of his friends was studying to be a massage therapist, and I was the guinea pig. It was all above board, nothing sexual. This coworker would tell me stories about the women he serviced. I found it fascinating that a woman would pay a man to sleep with her and that he would do it. He even told me who some of the women were—at least the ones at 10 S. Kedzie, where the CETA program was. I never saw him again after I moved and still wonder what happened to him.

In April of 1984 I quit my job, loaded up the truck, and moved to Beverly. Well, okay, that's not quite true—I've just always wanted to say that. I did quit my job and move, but I only took one suitcase of clothes. I left everything else for my mother.

About six months after I moved, my mother moved to a two-bedroom apartment on the third floor in one of the buildings Reverend Morris owned. The building was behind the church. Carrie told me that my mother had been offered a one-bedroom earlier but had refused it. She said she wanted to wait on a two-bedroom so that I would have my own room when I came to visit. When I came for a visit the next summer, I saw that she had taken the wall-to-wall carpet that I bought for the living room. She also had the refrigerator, table, and chairs, along with the extra bedroom set. She had even obtained a cream-colored living room set. I had never gotten around to buying one for the apartment. Anybody who came for a visit had to sit on the floor or in the kitchen.

The apartment my mother moved into was fixed up nicely. She did have a good eye for style. What I found interesting was that she never had any attachment to things. She just didn't care about stuff. She would loan or give anything she had to whoever wanted it. I remember one of her church friends telling me one summer that Mom had to go around and collect the things she had loaned out before I got there, because she knew I would get upset. In my defense, I was justified. I mean, she had loaned the living room lamp, for example—among other things.

Each summer I would rummage through Mom's dresser drawer for past-due bills that needed paying. She never asked me to pay them, nor did she tell me they were past due. I just knew they were. After fishing them out of the drawer, I'd pay them without saying a word to her. As a matter of fact, neither of us ever talked about it. My mother had a big heart, but she didn't know how to manage money. Most of the time I was just plain furious with her for one reason or another. I was never mean to her. I just didn't respect her—but I did love her.

15

Adapting to Salt Lake City

Salt Lake City, Utah—my new home. I didn't know what to expect. I had always been open to new experiences and was therefore excited to get to know this city. It was smaller than Chicago and lacked much hustle and bustle, but it was very clean and beautiful. The Wasatch Mountains were awe inspiring and still are.

My first action upon moving there was to get a job. I had always worked and had no intention to stop. Even though Bill would be responsible for the household bills, I didn't want to depend on him for everything. I also knew that our relationship might not last, and I needed to be able to take care of myself. I didn't want to get caught behind the eight ball, as the old folks used to say.

My first job was as a floater for JC Penney at Cottonwood Mall. I worked part time, which was fine with me. It was a good place to begin getting a pulse on the people of Salt Lake City, too. My job was to relieve cashiers for lunches and breaks—so I went from department to department constantly. I liked this, too.

Most of my coworkers were quite nice to me. I began to make friends with a few of them. Only two of my fellow coworkers weren't Mormon—Deloris and Susan. Deloris was from Cuba originally and had moved to Salt Lake City with her husband, who worked in the hospitality industry as a manager. He had been transferred to Salt Lake City. Susan hailed from Australia and had married an American who was a police officer in Salt Lake City. About seven or eight years after I met Susan, she was killed in an automobile accident. She was on her way to Provo, Utah, to work in one of the department stores. Susan was a wiz with makeup and worked for Clinique. On her way to work, a truck in front of her was carrying large pipes of some sort. Something happened, and the pipes came loose. One of them fell through Susan's windshield and decapitated her. It was such a tragedy.

There were two other ladies at JC Penny who I became friends with. I'll refer to them as Robin and Becky. Robin was a department manager. A couple of years after I met Robin, she got sick and died. This was also a tragedy. She was such a neat lady. On one occasion she came to my defense with my direct manager, who wasn't fond of me. One day about six months after I started working there, I was late to relieve a cashier and she yelled at me and berated me. This was too much, and I went into one of the changing rooms and cried. Robin saw this happen and promptly marched over and told my manager off. I quit. I had never been yelled at by any boss, and I wasn't going to hang around to have it happen to me again.

Except for my manager and the security person at JC Penney, it was a fun job. The security guard always seemed to be watching me. I was never quite sure why. One day he came over to me and asked if I had a used-car lot because I always drove different cars to work. I answered his question with a simple no. Bill had three cars: a Suburban, a Landcruiser, and a Mercedes Benz. I would drive either the Suburban or the Mercedes—never the Landcruiser, because I couldn't drive a stick shift.

As I said before, working at JC Penney helped me to get a grasp on the people of Salt Lake City. For one thing, this is where I learned about the Mormon temple garments. My education came with a bit of embarrassment on my part. I was working in the bridal department one day when a mother and daughter came in. The daughter was getting married and needed a gown. She was quite pretty and had a nice figure. I kept showing her gowns that I thought would look great on her. She and her mother said none of them would work. They found one that both of them liked, but I couldn't imagine why she would want to wear it. It covered her arms and had a high collar. But who was I to judge? I directed them to the dressing room and advised them that I would bring the gown—which I did.

When I walked into the dressing room, the young lady had taken off her dress and was standing there waiting. (Side note: I have a tendency to let what comes to my mind come out of my mouth. I'm still working to correct this flaw, and I'm making progress. At least I think I am.) I took one look at the young lady and said, "You must have gotten dressed fast this morning. You put your bra on the outside of your camisole." Both women turned beet red. I had no idea what had happened. The young lady politely responded, "No, I didn't. These are my garments." I wondered, "What type of garments would be worn underneath bra and panties?" But my reply was "Oh—I'm so sorry." I think they bought that dress, too. No one had schooled me about garments up to that point. I wasn't intending to be rude or disrespectful. People can wear whatever they want—its none of my business.

People from all walks of life came through that store. Another big shock was meeting my first polygamist family. It took a bit of time for me to figure out they were polygamists. Their style of dress and hair were different. Their hair was very long and braided, and none of them wore pants. Their dresses looked like the ones from *Little House on the Prairie*. All of them were polite and seemed to be attentive to one another. There were quite a few of them together the day I first encountered them. I was fascinated by them. I wondered how one man could have so many wives and why the women would agree to it. Many questions ran through my mind that were never answered. But if it worked for them, who was I to judge? Of course,

I wondered what would happen if the situation were reversed—that is, one woman had many husbands. How would society feel about this? What's good for the goose is good for the gander! (I hope you can tell by now that I am a bit of a rebel.)

There was one thing that stuck in my craw and caused me to grit my teeth. Some of the women who came into store would find wonderful items for themselves, only to say, "I don't know if my husband will like it." Or I would find an item that they would look adorable in and they would tell me that their husband wouldn't like it. I had never heard anyone say this. I for sure had never asked a man if he liked an article of clothing I was thinking of buying. If I like something and feel I look good in it—then by damn, I'm buying it. It's none of anyone else's business.

The first few years of being in Salt Lake City were quite challenging. I had jumped off the cliff into an environment that was alien to me. I didn't even realize such places existed. At the time I moved there, the Black population in Salt Lake City was less than one-tenth of 1 percent. I think my arrival brought the percentage to the one-tenth. I never got used to the stares I received wherever I went, including on the streets. I loved to walk, and on one occasion I saw a man driving by with (I assume) his wife and kids in the car. He was staring at me so intently that he almost wrecked his car.

I began to feel self-conscious. Bill made it worse. He was so worried that someone would see us together that we never went out. His house was also in an area that I would later learn was considered the upper-class area. To me, it was just a neighborhood that happened to be on the side of a mountain. The house wasn't special. It was in the Olympus Cove area. A friend of mine, years after I moved there, told me this house was actually in the lower Cove. I had no idea there was a demarcation of upper and lower Cove. It was all the same to me.

Because of Bill's concern over me being seen, he asked me to keep the curtains drawn during the day when he was at his office. No one was supposed to be home, and he didn't want any trouble from the neighbors. He said one of the Monsons lived across the street and that one of their family members was a part of the Mormon church leadership. And since one of Bill's furniture contracts was with the church, he didn't want to jeopardize his business. Why hadn't he thought about this before having me move to Salt Lake City? But I figured he knew what he was doing and there was no reason to question him about it. I just did what he asked. I didn't want him to be harmed because of me. I knew history and what some people were capable of.

I felt as though I had gone back in time to when my ancestors lived—when they had to hide in crawl spaces and rooms behind secret walls; being quiet when someone else was visiting the person who hid them away; fearful of being caught after running away and fearful for the person who had helped them. When I needed to leave the house, Bill would have me get on the floor in the back seat of the car in the garage, and either he or his son would drive the car to the parking lot of the neighborhood shopping center—where I could then drive to where I wanted. Whoever had driven me would walk back to the house. This was no way for me to live, and it got old pretty fast.

After I had been in Salt Lake City for a couple of months, Bill decided I needed my own apartment. I agreed. For one thing, only two of his family members knew I existed: Bill's son and middle brother. Bill had a large family and whenever someone visited, I had to go to a hotel. Bill's secretary, Christine, went apartment hunting with me. We found one in Holliday that I thought would work. I didn't want anything too expensive and I didn't want it too far away. It wasn't in the greatest area, but it served its purpose. Bill never put a limit on how much I should spend, which was nice. I furnished the place and moved in. I had always wanted to experience sleeping on a water bed—so I bought one. It was fun. I still spent considerable time at Bill's house when he was there, but I didn't feel as restricted.

The second action I took upon moving to Salt Lake City was enrolling in college, which would begin in August. This was another good reason for me to have my own place where I could come and go as I pleased, without having to be on the backseat floorboard of a car. My major in Memphis and Chicago had been theater. In Salt Lake City I changed it to speech language pathology. I realized that I needed to be able to take care of myself and at this juncture in my life, I didn't think a degree in theater would suffice. I needed a career that was stable, and in my mind speech pathology would be. After all, I was really good at speaking, so why not work with words and help others to do the same? I didn't do much research into the requirements to become a speech language pathologist—if I had, my choice might have been different.

The Pell Grant I had received a few years earlier in Memphis and Chicago was still in force, so I didn't have to apply again. This is how I would pay for college in Salt Lake City. I didn't, nor would I, ask Bill for any money for school. This I could do myself—and I did. He was providing the stability I desperately needed via room and board to be able to attend, which was a gift from the Divine in my opinion, and I wasn't going to let it slip away. When I mentioned to him that I would be going back to school, he was supportive. So in August of 1984, I began classes in the Health Sciences department at the University of Utah.

About the time I began school, Bill decided to purchase a different home. There were some very good reasons for this decision. One reason was the money he was spending. He was renting office space in Holliday and wanted to work from home, which would save money. Then there was the money he was spending on my place. It wasn't expensive, but it was still money going out. However, the biggest reason for the decision was his fear that one of his neighbors would see me. I was happy he wanted to move, but not for the same reasons. I hated his house. It had to be one of the ugliest houses I had seen. Yes, it was in a good neighborhood, but it hadn't been updated since the '60s. The other reason was that he had lived there with his former wife. I've never been a proponent of living under the same roof with a man whose previous wife had also lived there. Her ghost would still be there, and even at a young age I felt I was competing with it.

There was a dilemma, though. Bill wanted to stay in the Olympus Cove neighborhood—which was fine. The neighborhood was above Wasatch Boulevard and had beautiful views of the city, and if you were high enough, views of the Great Salt Lake as well. The dilemma was taking me to see houses. I'm not sure if this law is still on the books in Salt Lake City or if it ever was, because I never checked. But Bill told me that Blacks couldn't own homes in that neighborhood. So Bill decided to go with the realtor during the day to look at homes, and then in the evening he would take me to see the homes he had seen that day. I agreed—what choice did I have? My concern was that someone would call the police if they saw me creeping around empty houses and peering in windows.

Some of the houses were open, meaning a door had been left unlocked and we could get in; this was optimal. At other times I could only peer through windows. I didn't mind doing this, because it was what needed to be done to purchase a home. My mind was on the prize, not the temporary discomfort.

The house we both liked was on Covecrest Drive. I didn't know it was considered to be in a better area than the other house, but this house was much nicer. It was a split level with five bedrooms. Granted, having numerous bedrooms is the norm in Utah. Families there typically have lots of kids, and they need a place to sleep. It was on a quarter acre and totaled about 3,300 square feet. The downstairs, which had two bedrooms, a den, a bathroom, and a laundry room, would be used as the office space. The den would become the area for Christine, Bill's secretary. Bill would use one of the bedrooms for his brochure and Vydec room. (A Vydec was a huge computer that didn't have a hard drive. It had these big floppy discs that stored material.) The other bedroom would be his office. Access to the three-car heated garage was also from the lower level. Having a heated garage was a luxury that bordered on necessity. Utah has some pretty cold and snowy winters.

Upstairs was a formal dining room with sliding glass doors that led to the concrete patio. The living room was large and had a huge fireplace and a floor-to-ceiling, wall-to-railing window. The view of the city was gorgeous when I first saw it at night. The kitchen was next to the dining room, and it was also large. It had a double oven too, which I liked. The countertops were yellow Formica, and the cabinets were dark oak. The house had been built in '73, so it was 11 years old. There was a sliding glass door in the kitchen that led to the patio in the backyard. The master bedroom was down a hall on the left. It was nice size, with two hanging lamps where the bed would be. I wasn't thrilled about this. It meant I had no choice in where to put the bed. There was a sliding glass door in this room, too. It led to a separate patio in the backyard. The master bedroom had its own bathroom. I liked the layout but hated the blue shag carpet. The double sink and vanity could be seen from the bedroom, and there was a door on the other side of the bathroom where the shower and toilet were housed. To the left of the sink area was another door that led to the walk-in closet. There were two more bedrooms on the other side of the hall that had city views.

The house was on a hill, so the lot was slanted. The backyard had two distinct areas separated by stairs. There was a small fountain made out of stone on the lower part by the patio, and the upper part had a partial lawn. The entire yard was surrounded by trees. There were houses on both sides and in the back of the house, but they couldn't be seen in the summer. I loved this. I have always loved having privacy. The front yard had lots of oak trees and a small lawn area. Bill planned to fence the backyard and put a dog run in for Charlie. (Charlie was a collie Bill and his son found while camping. He had been abandoned, so they brought him home.) Bill bought the house, and we moved in on Halloween. I found this to be quite auspicious.

We then had to decide how we would explain my presence. This was Bill's idea, not mine. He was still very concerned about word getting back to the church officials that he was living with a Black woman, who he wasn't married to, and who wasn't Mormon. To make matters worse, he *was* Mormon—albeit a non-practicing Mormon, aka Jack Mormon. Being a Jack Mormon means you have been baptized in the church and are on its rolls but don't attend.

This was how he managed to get the church contract in the first place.

The church takes care of its own the same way most groups do. The problem was that Bill had begun to live a double life. He had gone down this road long before he met me, and getting involved with me complicated matters for him. For one thing, he smoked and drank. Both of these are "no-nos" in the Mormon church. I watched him for years go through the routine of showering and cleaning his nails to get any nicotine residue off of himself before going to visit one of the purchasing agents at the Church Office Building downtown. And because he smoked in the house, he kept his clothes in a bedroom that was rarely used. His clothes stayed in the bags from the dry cleaner's, behind a closed closet door, and the door to the room was kept closed. All of this was done to keep the smoke away from the suits and shirts he wore for his visits. I understood why he was taking such measures, and I supported him in doing it. So when he asked me not to tell anyone that we were dating, I agreed.

It's important to note that I am a bad—no, horrible—liar. For one thing, it's difficult for me to remember the lies I've told. For another thing, I always feel as though the lie is leaking through the pores of my skin and the person I'm lying to knows I'm lying. It's also in my eyes. All the same, I came up with a story that I hoped I could be consistent with and remember. I would become Bill's assistant. He was a single man who needed someone to help him with whatever he needed help with—that would be my job. Well, it was partially true. I didn't learn until years later what a toll this would take on the relationship, as well as the ultimate consequence for Bill of living his entire life as a lie.

While Bill and his siblings were growing up, their mother wanted all of them to fit in. They lived in a harsh environment— weather wise and otherwise. If you weren't a part of the group, you were ostracized. This was during the Depression in the '30s. So Bill's mom decided to have the kids baptized. I think Bill said he was eight years old when his time came to be baptized. He said he didn't want to be—he even ran but was caught. So he became an unwilling Mormon.

Bill was pretty smart in school—genius-level IQ is what he told me. When he was a kid, his father was usually away working for someone else—which left his mother as sole caretaker. By the time he was a teen, he said his father was back on the farm full time. His parents didn't have much money, but because of his grades he managed to get a scholarship to a college in Rochester, New York. He entered college earlier than most kids because of having skipped several grades in high school.

In college Bill still had to work to pay for extras. He was in medical school and used to keep cadaver arms or legs under his bed to work on at night. Now that's being a good Scorpio! I don't remember how long he stayed in school. What I do know is how he managed to get himself kicked out.

What he said was that he and a friend who needed money decided to rob a prostitution house. Bill called it a whore house. Their thinking was that it wouldn't be reported by the madame who ran the place. So they went for it. There were definite holes in this plan, as he told me. For one, you never know who the customers are in these places—it could even be the local sheriff. And if the sheriff *is* frequenting these places, they are definitely going to investigate. The second hole was the weather—it had been snowing. And the third hole was involving someone else in his plan. Bill had devised the plan and brought his friend into it. What's interesting is that his only regret was bringing a friend into the plan, rather than the fact that it was wrong to rob anyone in the first place. Anyway, they had decided that each of them would go back to their rooms after the heist and the money would be split between them.

Well, the plan wasn't successful—go figure. The madame called the sheriff, and the sheriff followed the footprints in the snow back to the apartment of Bill's accomplice, who immediately ratted on Bill. Thus there was a knock at Bill's door in the middle of the night—the same night of the robbery. Well, because Bill was liked by the dean of his school, they devised a plan to keep him out of prison—which is where he should have gone. Instead, he pled insanity and got to spend time in an insane asylum. Yes—he was declared crazy. I sure could pick 'em.

In the asylum Bill had to endure shock treatments. I had never heard of such a thing, but I guess this was customary treatment back then. Robbing the prostitution house wasn't his brightest move, but he wasn't crazy. "Why would they do that to you?" I asked him. He said there was no way to avoid it. It was just what was done. They strapped him down to a gurney, hooked his head up to electrodes, and shocked his brain. I truly wonder what affect that had on his behavior after the fact. His behavior was erratic, and the treatments could have caused it.

His actions had other consequences, too—in the family. His father was an honest person, which is a good thing. However, because Bill broke the law, his dad refused to visit him in the mental institution. Bill said this deeply hurt him and their relationship, which was already strained. His mother, on the other hand, did visit—which was a good thing.

When Bill was released from the asylum, he made his way to Salt Lake City and began working as a salesperson in an office furniture store. He eventually met his son's mom, got married, and moved to the house he was living in when we met. The marriage lasted seven years. I've heard his side of the story concerning the marriage—and I also know it was exceedingly skewed in his favor. I didn't know this at first; however, it was something I learned by living with him over the years.

16

Being an Ambassador for My Race

The first official action I took when Bill bought the new house was to change my voting district. This was an election year, and I wasn't going to miss an opportunity to do my civic duty. Being in a new voting district meant my voting location had changed. I would now go to the neighborhood high school to vote—Olympus High. On voting day, which was a week after moving into the house, I went to the high school to cast my vote. When I entered the school, there were tables set up with letters of the alphabet posted on the desks to direct people to the correct table based on their last name. The voting booths were set up on the other side of the hall, across from the tables. I found the table with the letter B and went over to give the lady my name and get a ballot.

As I approached the table, the lady sitting at the table looked up at me. She was probably in her 60s—gray hair, medium build. I'll never forget her nor what she said: "I know you. You live at 4433 South Covecrest Drive. When you moved in I thought you were the maid, but then I saw the maid coming to the house. Then I thought you must be the nanny—but there are no kids." She then glared at me for an explanation; I simply asked her for my ballot after giving my last name. She handed it to me and I walked away, dumbfounded. I had just moved into the new house, yet this woman knew not only my street, but my address. Coming from Chicago, this was a huge problem—and to top it off, she obviously didn't see anything wrong with what she said to me. I was shaken up by the experience.

I learned quickly not to tell Bill about any of the experiences I was having with other people. He didn't seem sympathetic—but it might have just been that he had no solution and didn't know how to respond. I'll never know. I remember telling him about an incident at school when one of the professors commented on the way I dressed. She would say, "You always look so nice." Under normal circumstances this would be taken as a compliment, but other students were dressing nicely too, and she wasn't commenting on how they dressed. I was singled out. Bill had no comment.

So when I was downtown and a middle-aged man came up to me and propositioned me, I didn't tell Bill about it. I had gone downtown to run an errand. I got out of the Mercedes and locked the door. As I turned to walk away from the car, a man was staring at me from the sidewalk in the direction I was headed. When I got to the sidewalk, he walked up to me and promptly offered me $50 to sleep with him. He actually thought I was a prostitute! I told him, "If that's all you have, you can't afford me," and kept walking. I didn't want him to see how hurt I was by his comment.

Once while standing in line at the post office, a little boy who was four or five years old was with his mother in line ahead of me. The little boy looked up at me and asked innocently, "Why is your skin so dirty?" His mother instantly turned red with embarrassment and apologized. I wasn't offended by the question. It was obvious the child had never seen a Black person. I answered his question by saying that it was the color of my skin and letting him touch me on the arm.

I used to run—or should I say, walk and jog—for exercise in the early days of being in Salt Lake City. I'd start out walking and then jog. Doing this was also a form of meditation. I could be with my thoughts without any interruption from Bill. Before moving to Salt Lake City I had never intentionally jogged in my life. I received plenty of exercise with the work I did and all the walking I did to get from point A to point B. But in Salt Lake City you had to drive most places. The transportation system wasn't efficient, nor was it plentiful.

I jogged most mornings before work or classes at 7:00 a.m. I had a five-mile route that weaved through the neighborhood to 33rd and Wasatch Boulevard, and depending on my energy level, to Highland Drive and back. I usually wore sweatpants and a matching top with a hood. Mornings were cool, so I would sometimes have the hood on my head. I liked yellow and blue, so I'm sure in a sea of beige and gray wearers this added to my oddness. On my route I would pass the same houses daily. There was a lady who lived on one of the streets I jogged down, who walked her dog at the same time I went jogging. Every morning when she saw me coming, she would cross the street. I thought this odd because her house wasn't across the street. I usually said good morning as I was passing and never got a reply.

One morning I decided that I would make her speak to me. I was tired of being ignored. So as I passed her that morning and said hello with no reply, I stopped, put my hands on my hips, and said loudly, "I said hello!" to which the frightened woman replied, "Hello," meekly. I realize now that my behavior wasn't appropriate. However, from then on, when she saw me, she said hello. Jeez— did she think I was going to assault her wearing a yellow hoodie? Probably.

A year or so after moving to Salt Lake City, I had my second encounter with police. This time it was a detective. I had gone home after anatomy class to do some work for Bill. (I had long stopped working for JC Penney and was working for Bill in his office.) His secretary informed me that a detective had called and that I needed to call him back. I thought she was joking. This secretary—her name was Julie—and I usually joked around. She and I were close to the same age and became friends. She was an open-minded Mormon, and I liked that. Well, I told her to stop pulling my leg. Only she wasn't joking. Bill came out of his office and said LaBelle's Jewelry Store in Ogden had been robbed that morning, and two Black women in a Suburban were the culprits. In Salt Lake City at that time, there were very few Black women—and even fewer who drove a Suburban. Bill said he had received a phone call from this detective asking about his Suburban and who had it.

"Fact: plenty of innocent people are in jail. And it is up to the accused to prove their innocence." This is what ran through my mind before returning the detective's call. I stayed calm on the surface, but fear was creeping in. Ogden is 40 miles north of Salt Lake City. At that time, I had only been through there a couple of times with Bill as we were headed to Idaho. I called the detective and answered his questions. Thank the gods that at the time of the robbery, I had been in class with my fellow speech therapy classmates and could prove it.

I sometimes picked up another friend to take her to school if the weather was bad and she thought the bus would be late. She was Black, too. And I had done this the day of the robbery. Obviously someone saw us together and turned that information in to the police. My friend Colleen was attending the same class as me, but I wondered if that would be enough. My mind went everywhere, through all sorts of ways I could be sent to prison for something I didn't do.

During my second semester at school, I took a class from the only Black professor on campus. He helped me to change my view of the situation I was in. Colleen and I would talk about incidents that happened to both of us; the difference is that she just shrugged them off. Her husband, who is white, had a similar attitude as I did about the situation. He was having problems with the stares from onlookers when he was out with Colleen. I don't know if he ever received any comments, but I do know he was uncomfortable.

I scheduled a meeting with the Black professor and went to see him. I told him that I didn't think I could stay there—that it was just too hard. I had never experienced such treatment, even while growing up in the Deep South. I didn't mention that I had no support at home, because no one knew the truth of my relationship with Bill. I felt alone and told the professor I was thinking of leaving. He listened intently to what I was saying without interrupting me. He allowed me to vent and get all of my feelings out. I wasn't crying or feeling sorry for myself, but there was a lot of passion in what I was saying. I just didn't want to put myself through this anymore. When I finished talking, he said simply: "If you leave, nothing will change. These people don't have much experience, if any at all, with Black people other than what they see on TV. They need you to show them reality." I didn't promise him that I would stay, but his words had struck a chord. I left his office that day with something to think about. In reality, he had convinced me to stay, but I needed to contemplate the conversation to be sure—which I did.

The people of Salt Lake City hadn't had much experience with Black people, if any. How would it be for them to go to an all-Black state or Africa and live there? Would their treatment be the same as mine? I didn't know the answer to these questions, but I thought I would give them the benefit of the doubt. I wasn't stupid—I knew I was being treated the way I was partially because of prejudice. But some of it was out of ignorance. (Well, I should clarify. Prejudice is ignorance too; it's just a different kind of ignorance.)

I decided to become an ambassador for my race. I didn't have to change my behavior or do anything special. I just had to be me. I now had a purpose, and that purpose was to help the people of Salt Lake City gain experience of another race. I would do my part to help the people I encountered shift their view of Black people. Changing my view of the people of Salt Lake City made it easier for me. That's not to say it was easy, because it wasn't. I found myself changing the clothes I wore. While I had previously worn bright colors, I began to wear beige, black, and gray. Occasionally a deep green color would creep into my wardrobe. I was trying to blend in and not be seen as much. But how could I not be? I didn't realize that this was what I was doing at the time. It's only as I looked back on that period in my life that this realization dawned.

A friend of mine in Memphis sent me a care package that included Black toiletries, because there were none in Salt Lake City. Back then women always wore stockings or pantyhose, and my shade wasn't represented. My hair products were also nowhere to be found. On my yearly visits to Chicago and Memphis I would stock up on toiletries to take back to Salt Lake City. Eventually, I began to see a shade of pantyhose that I could wear without looking pale.

Once, as a joke, I went to ZCMI, walked up to one of the makeup counters, and asked for a makeover to see the response of the salesperson. The look on her face was priceless. I know—that wasn't nice of me. As it turned out, it wasn't fun either. I felt bad. She had no clue how to give me a makeover. For one thing, she had no colors that would work for my skin tone. I never did that again. I did find a beautician, Melanie, who knew how to take care of my hair, and she was white. I don't remember where she learned to do Black hair, but she knew just what to do and could acquire the products. She was and still is Mormon. Melanie was a breath of fresh air. We became friends and still are. I could talk to her about anything, including my relationship with Bill. I told her the truth.

Actually, by the time Melanie began to be my hairdresser, I had come clean with a couple of new friends. As I said before, lying is not something I do well, and I hated being put in a position of having to lie about my relationship with Bill. The catalyst for my coming clean about it was a confusing conversation I had with Bill. It was during my second year at school. He asked me if any of my friends knew about him, and I said no. I had made a promise not to tell them about our relationship and had kept my word. Bill got upset that I hadn't told them. I was confused at his response and told him that I was just doing what he asked. He wasn't making sense to me, and I was tired of keeping up the charade.

I hung out with a group of three other people at school—that is, *only* at school. We rarely socialized together away from the campus. All of us were pretty busy—I think Colleen was the only one in the group not working. There was also a fourth person who I saw sometimes, Judy. She was an audiology student, so I didn't get to see her a lot due to our different classes. On top of attending school and most of us working, Colleen, Judy, and I were all in relationships. Colleen, Cindy, and I would occasionally do something outside of school—go to a movie or lunch. But between relationships, homework, and work, there wasn't much time for anything else.

Cindy and Linda were single. I used to tease Cindy about not dating or having sex. She was still a virgin at 30. She said she was waiting until she got married to have sex, which she did do. I told her she needed practice before marriage and should just start now. We would both laugh. On one hand, I admired her for waiting; on the other, I thought she was nuts for waiting.

Both Colleen and Cindy were understanding of my situation when I told them the truth. Cindy said she had suspected the truth but wasn't sure. I never told Linda or Judy. I didn't tell Linda because I didn't want to be judged and thought she might reject me. And I didn't say anything to Judy because we were just good acquaintances and didn't see each other a lot.

Stems

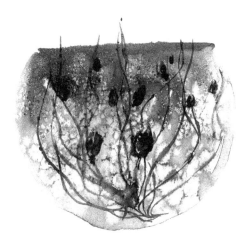

The stems are trying to get through the day-to-day murkiness
of the water; they mark the lotus's growth and are being fed
by the tuber. The stems are akin to a ruler put against
the wall to measure the growth of a child. And, like
the stems always stretching and growing upwards
toward the light, we humans are doing the
same trying to figure life out. We are in
the murkiness of life being fed by
our roots—our stored memories
and emotions.

17

My Strategy to Survive

I have always enjoyed learning, and being in college again quenched my thirst for knowledge and helped me settle into living in Salt Lake City. I got along with most of the other students, too. A few of us would get together to study for tests and drill each other with questions. I usually over-studied for tests—except for one test, which was a final exam. Bill had decided to take me to Hawaii, and he wanted to go a week before my final exam for an audiology class. This class was intense, because it was a subject I knew nothing about. Dr. Hansen was a no-nonsense professor, but I could tell he loved teaching. Well, I had this last-minute trip planned and would return two days before the exam. This meant I would need to take my books with me to study while in Hawaii. Why Bill decided to go to Hawaii during this time became clear much later. This was the beginning of a behavioral pattern regarding my education that took me a while to see.

I took my books on the trip but of course didn't crack open any of them. When I arrived home, I had to cram for the exam. Thank goodness I had a background in theater, which meant I was an excellent memorizer.

My adrenaline was flowing, and it flowed even more because of the No Doze (OTC "stay awake" medicine). I stayed up for two days memorizing notes from the class. I knew how Dr. Hansen would test. One of the things I had learned early was to use the first test to determine the structure of future tests. This applied to each class. So I already knew the format of the final exam, which meant I knew how to study for it. I took the test and got an A-plus.

Speaking of procrastination and adrenaline, when it came to writing reports and papers, I seemed to thrive on waiting until the last minute to type them up. This was a new phenomenon. In high school I had always worked steadily, doing research and hand-writing papers over time. They didn't need to be typed. In college, all papers had to be typed. The problem was that I didn't type—never learned. No one told me that I would need the skill in college and for the rest of my life. Fortunately for me, Bill typed at about 80 words a minute. I would ask him to type my papers, which he did. But the other problem was my procrastination. I would wait to hand-write papers until a day or so before they were due, which meant Bill was typing them and cursing me out for procrastinating at the same time. He never said he wouldn't type them, though, and I am grateful for that. I did eventually realize my error in not learning to type and took several college classes to pick up the skill. It took a bit of time for me to build my speed, but it came with time and practice. I was growing tired of Bill's behavior, and learning to type solved the problem of asking him to type my papers.

Living in Salt Lake City, I became more conservative in all aspects of my life. I think that was a natural outcome, since I was so young and impressionable. I had grown up in a household that voted Democrat, and now I lived in a household and a state that voted Republican. I was never very political—I'm still not—although I do follow what is happening in the world and the community I live in.

As a kid I remember watching Shirley Chisholm, the first Black congresswoman, on TV. Granny would watch her, so I also watched. I loved her voice and her eloquence, but that was as far as my political views went. After all, I was a kid. I didn't have much choice but to follow politics in Salt Lake City because Bill watched most of the evening news programs and the Sunday-morning news talk shows. I started calling them the talking heads, because you only ever saw the guests and moderator from the waist up. They all seemed to be talking in circles, saying the same things. I learned who was doing what in politics and when they were doing it—who the movers and shakers were. Basically, my life was inundated with politics for 18 years.

With the exception of Bill's son, Bill's entire family was Republican. It was quite an education for me to go from living in one extreme to another. I slowly got to know Bill's family, although they didn't come around much. Most of them lived in Idaho and Washington State. Bill didn't tell them the truth about my presence. He told them that I was there to help him with the house—in other words, his maid—in exchange for room and board while I was going to school. Fortunately for me, they were all courteous. I had no idea what they thought of me. The entire situation was a convoluted mess, to say the least. Here I was, a terrible liar, trying to keep on top of the lie about my presence in the household. I wonder if his family bought the story he told—I'll never know.

There were seven siblings including Bill. Bill was the oldest boy. Their mother had been married to someone else before Bill's father. She had four kids with the first husband: Mary, the oldest; the twins, Lois and Loah; and Iris. With Bill's father there was three boys: Bill, Clyde, and Don, in that order. During the years Bill and I were together, I spent the most time with Mary. I don't think most of Bill's family had any experience with minorities. Not that we are any different, really. But people have ideas and beliefs about cultures that may or may not be true. The only way to know the truth is to actually spend time in the culture. In Bill's family and in Utah in general, there wasn't much opportunity for cross-cultural experience.

It all goes back to a story I was told by a Mormon friend. It's a story that I had never heard—that is, I'd never heard the ending— Cain and Abel. Most of us have heard the Bible story, but here's the crux of it: Cain was jealous of his brother Abel and killed him.

Because of this, he was cursed by God. Now the part I hadn't heard was that he was cursed with black skin and wooly hair. As such, all of his descendants were cursed. This is honestly what the Mormon church was teaching. As hurtful as it was, it shined light on the problem I was facing being in Utah and with Bill's family. I was also told that Black men could jump so high playing basketball because they had an extra bone in each foot. How was I supposed to combat such beliefs? The answer: one person at a time. Fortunately for me, I am a friendly person and people feel comfortable talking to me. At the time I didn't think it was a fortunate trait.

One time I was in the kitchen with Mary and her husband, Glenn, along with Bill. They were sitting around the table talking and I was doing something else. Mary was referring to some flowers that were in bloom in Idaho by calling them "nigger toes." "What did you say?!" I asked. She looked at me strangely and said, "That's what they are called because that's what they look like." She didn't mean any harm with her words. I pointed out to her how such a term was perceived by a Black person. I don't think she understood my argument, and I had to be careful with how I approached Bill's family. I was the outsider, and he was protective of family. My ability to be open minded was consistently being put to the test, and I found myself closing down emotionally. This wasn't something I recognized at first, but I was going inward—living in my inner world.

Over time, I stopped expressing my thoughts and feelings to Bill. I had begun to observe the results of my being open with feelings to him. He would take the information and use it against me in an argument or to manipulate me. I had no experience with how to handle this, so I learned to withhold. It wasn't that I wasn't feeling my emotions—I just learned to control their outward expression. I didn't realize the cost of doing this at the time. My goal was to not fan the flames of his rage. But it didn't work. He just started calling me a cold bitch. I hate the word *bitch* and made the mistake of telling Bill this. Thus, he started using the word to describe me. His goal was to get a rise out of me. But that didn't work either—I would just stare at him with a straight face, watching him rage. I absolutely, unequivocally refused to show emotion.

However, there was one time when he pushed me to the edge. I don't remember what he was going on about—it could have been anything. The man could rage about the lack of salt in a salt shaker. Whatever it was, I had to walk away before I burst into tears in front of him. I went to the bathroom and cried silently. I couldn't let him hear me. The wall of protection that was already around me when we met got thicker. I couldn't trust him with my thoughts or feelings; they would just be used against me.

Over the years I would test Bill to see if he had changed and could be trusted. He failed the test every time. I would give him a bit of information—just a little—to see what he would do with it. Once, he grew so desperate to know what I was up to that he began to secretly tape my phone calls. He thought I was too naïve to catch on. Of course, I have no idea how long this went on before I actually did catch on, but I did.

The taping started because of Bill's unbridled jealousy. Once I obtained my master's degree, I wanted to work away from the home. I was tired of working for Bill and wanted another experience. This didn't sit well with him, but he had no power to stop me. I had actually been wanting to work someplace else for several years but felt it wise to wait until I finished school—which was grueling. In 1990 when I graduated, the country was in a recession. It took me a year to find a job. I was way overqualified for the job, but I wanted to work, so I took the job as a claims adjuster for a major insurance company.

Bill wanted to know what I was up to at work. Basically, was I cheating on him? The answer was no—I wasn't cheating. I went away to claims school in Illinois when I first got the job and came home to my things being rummaged through. I asked him about this, and he denied touching my things. But I always remember how I leave things, so I knew my belongings had been gone through. I also knew not to push the subject. At one point I began to notice him saying things to me about this or that—nothing important.

But they were things that I had not mentioned to him. He really thought I was stupid. My curiosity was piqued. How could he know? I wondered whether one of my friends had said something to him. The information was benign, but all the same, I grew concerned. I asked my friends if they had spoken to Bill, and each of them said no. This was perplexing. If they hadn't said anything, how was he getting his information?

The only explanation was taping. But how was he doing this? One day when he was away from the house, I went on a scavenger hunt—searching every room of that 3,300-square-foot house. There had to be a tape recorder someplace, plugged into a phone jack. And there was. It was under the bed in one of the guest bedrooms. He had set up a voice-activated recorder. He thought I would never find it there because I had long stopped cleaning the house since we had hired a housekeeper.

With the recording device located, the next question that needed to be answered was what to do about it? Would I confront him? What I decided to do was say nothing to him. I would leave the device in place and let him go on thinking I didn't know. I also told my friends to stop calling me at the house. I would talk to them from my work phone, either after the day was over or on weekends.

Periodically Bill would ask me why my friends weren't calling. I told him they were pretty busy. I know he never knew that I was on to him, because one day I came home unexpectedly from someplace. When I opened the door that led into the house from the garage, Bill was startled and quickly turned the recorder off—but not quickly enough for me not to hear what he was doing. He had been listening to old recordings of me. I never said a word. I just went upstairs like nothing had happened.

I'm sure the obvious question is why I stayed with this man. Why didn't I just leave? I had my education and a good job—I certainly could have left. Well, I did try to leave. One day I packed my bags and was walking out of the bedroom to get into my car when I ran into an invisible brick wall. It truly was a brick wall that I couldn't get past. I put my hand out and could feel it. Something was blocking me from leaving. I found out why that wall was there years later. At the time, I just wanted to scream. I remember sitting down on the bed, crying so hard I was heaving. I asked God why I couldn't leave this man. Why did I have to stay? I deserved to be treated better. There was silence—I heard nothing! Usually when I asked a question, I would get an answer—sometimes in the form of a knowing, sometimes a word or a phrase. But I got nothing. When I finished crying, I put my things away and carried on.

18

Focus on Goals While Being Bullied

Over the years, I watched Bill bully most of the people around him. This included the presidents of the companies he represented. He would be on the phone with them, telling them— not asking—what they were going to do for a client. I asked him how he could talk to them in such a way. His answer was simple. He said he always dealt from strength, not weakness. I would argue that you can catch more flies with honey than vinegar.

I thought I could show him by example how to act, but this thinking was flawed. For one thing, he was bullying me too; and for another, he didn't respect or honor my opinions. After all, I was much younger than him—what did I know? He never bullied his customers nor his secretary Chris. I liked Chris. She would tell him off and just keep on doing whatever she wanted to do.

When Bill bought the new house, he offered Chris and her kids the old house as a rental—and she accepted. I'd hang out with her and the kids when Bill was out of town, which was nice. I'd always been afraid to be in a house by myself. I could feel when someone from the other side was there, and I didn't like that feeling. Chris and I would watch VHS movies and talk until I got tired and went home. Everything was fine until Chris began to date a Black man. Then all hell broke loose. Bill thought he could control who she dated for some reason. On top of this, Chris got involved with a religious organization that Bill thought was a cult. He even spied on the organization. He told Chris she had to move, which also precipitated Chris' quitting. This left me on my own until he could find a replacement.

I think Bill's real issue was that Chris was dating a Black man. Bill was prejudiced, but he never admitted this. He used to tell me that I was different. But how different could I be? I am Black. There were several factors other than the incident with Chris that led me to believe he was prejudiced. For one, he never wanted to nor did he ever accompany me on any of my visits to family. He made excuses, so I went alone. This was okay with me because I never knew how he would behave anyway. The last thing I needed was for him to act out in front of my family or friends—not only would this be embarrassing, but it could cause an altercation in Bogalusa, especially with my male cousins. Plus, going alone meant I was free during my annual trips to Chicago, Memphis, and Bogalusa to see friends and family and basically play. Playing included going dancing until the wee hours of the morning. I wasn't doing anything wrong; I was just having fun. And I never told Bill about it.

On one occasion, a friend of mine from my mother's church was driving through Salt Lake City and wanted to stop by to see me. We hadn't grown up together, but we saw each other during the summer months on my annual visits to Chicago. He was a nice guy. There was never anything between us except friendship. He came by and we talked for a while. When he left, Bill informed me that he never wanted that man in his house again. I asked him why and he just said he didn't like him. I knew he was jealous, but there was more to it than that.

Then there was an incident with Big Sister's youngest son. He called me and said he wanted to come for a visit. The truth of it was that Big Sister wanted to know how I was living and what I was up to. Her son worked for DHL and could fly with them for free. I told him to come on out, which he did. Bill said he was going on a road trip. He didn't want to be there. Bill went to Idaho to visit Mary and Glenn while Big Sister's son visited me. We had a nice time, and I made excuses for Bill not being there.

As if that weren't enough, my best friend at the time, Gwen from Memphis, wanted to come out for a visit with her son, Omari. Gwen knew what the score was with Bill, because I had told her over the years what I was going through. She still wanted to come for a visit, so I told her fine. When I told Bill about this, he got upset. Didn't I have a right to invite people to visit me? Didn't I live there too? She was coming, and that was that. Bill once again conveniently went on a road trip. Gwen was there for a week, and I expected Bill to stay gone for that week. However, he came back after three days. I wondered why. He never spoke to Gwen or Omari the entire time they were there. I introduced them, but he didn't respond. Because of this I decided that Gwen, Omari, and I would leave the house every morning after breakfast and not return until it was bedtime. Gwen was uncomfortable and didn't like Bill—how could she? She would put a chair against her bedroom door to make sure he couldn't get in while she and Omari were asleep. I thought this was unnecessary but didn't try to dissuade her.

Gwen tried a second time to engage with Bill without success. He was outside raking leaves, and for some reason we had to come back to the house. Gwen went to the patio door and spoke to him— he still didn't respond.

On the morning Gwen and Omari were to fly home, I made sure my car was parked outside rather than in the garage. This was because I didn't want to wake Bill up and encounter him. I had Gwen and Omari go out the master bedroom patio door, walk around the side yard, and get in the car. Bill was sleeping downstairs rather than in the master bedroom while they were there. He would also sometimes sleep there whenever I was getting the silent treatment— which happened a few times a year.

I took Gwen and Omari to the airport that morning and went back home to find Bill in the kitchen. He told me someone had called for me and left a message. I knew this wasn't true, because I wasn't receiving calls at the house. So I ignored him asking me to play the message and went to bed. I wasn't upset, although I had every right to be. I also knew why he wanted me to play the messages on the answering machine. He was just a little too insistent on me listening to them, which told me he was up to something. I never listened to the message, but I heard him listen to it later that morning as he erased it. It was my voice talking to Gwen—one of the recordings he had made before I figured out what he was doing a few years earlier. I guess that since I wouldn't play the game, he lost interest and erased the message. I had to always be on my toes with him because I never knew what he was going to do.

Living this way took a drastic toll on me. I was fighting to not only keep my sanity but also some control over my life. Getting my education was a part of this. It couldn't be taken away, and it would prepare me to be able to take care of myself. I wanted out of the relationship but didn't know when it would actually happen.

When I had first moved to Salt Lake City, I drove Bill's cars, which was fine. However, if I was going someplace he didn't approve of or planning to have someone in his car who he didn't like, he would take the keys. Once when he did this, I told him, "I have feet; I can walk," and walked out the door, headed to wherever it was I was going. He promptly gave me the keys and said he was joking. I was tired of having to go through this, so I decided to purchase my very own car. That man had too much control over me, and I was determined to regain control of my life. (Having my own car was also the reason I was able to take Gwen and Omari to the airport.)

I had begun researching cars while in grad school, along with saving up for the down payment. Once I set my mind to achieve a goal, I steadily work until the goal is achieved. Bill never knew this about me, nor did he think I would achieve anything in life. He thought he had complete control over me. I had saved a percentage of every paycheck when I began working in Salt Lake City. I added to my savings until there was $10,000.

Once I had decided on the vehicle, including the color, I asked Bill to go with me to negotiate the deal. He was an excellent negotiator. I had watched him buy several vehicles over the years, so I thought it prudent to ask for his help. He said no, he wouldn't help, and he didn't. There was no internet back then, so I went to Utah CV Credit Union to ask for information on the vehicle and to apply for the loan. By the time I was ready to buy the car, I only had $5,000 as a down payment. I'll explain what happened to the other $5,000 later. I was pre-approved for a loan, plus they gave me the stats on what the car actually cost.

I had never negotiated anything and asked a friend to accompany me to the dealership for support. Joe was happy to help. She and I met in college and are still friends today. I can't say that I wasn't scared, but I stuck to my guns and got the vehicle I wanted—at the price I was willing to pay. After going to two dealerships, I got my brand-new 1991 Nissan Maxima. It was gorgeous—black leather seats, sporty model, a fire-red color. I loved that car. It was mine, and Bill could no longer dictate who I let ride in it nor where I went. He was furious but couldn't do anything about it.

When I drove the car home, Bill asked me where I was going to park it. The garage already had three cars. I told him that I would park it on the street—which I did. I think this must have gotten his ego churning. He relented and moved the Landcruiser to the driveway and then gave it to his son. I figured he didn't want to look bad in front of the neighbors. For someone who could be so mean, he was very concerned about his image in the community. He wasn't all bad; he just had a bullying/controlling streak several miles long.

19

College Graduation and Mother Dies

So, what happened to half the money I had saved for the down payment on the car? My mother was diagnosed with ovarian/colon cancer in 1989. The cancer had spread so far that the doctors couldn't say where it had begun. I remember getting a phone call from the hospital in Chicago. They wanted to take my mother into surgery immediately and for some reason needed my approval. I gave my consent. It was shocking news that she was even sick. I had gone to see her every year, and she had never said anything about feeling ill. Of course, she wouldn't. My mother never told me anything.

After Mom's surgery, the doctor called me to say the cancer was terminal. He gave her one year to live. She would be in intensive care for a while but would recover sufficiently to go home. I decided not to go to Chicago. I was in school, and it was finals week. I also didn't think that there was anything I could do, and I knew she wanted me to finish my education.

During the years I visited her from Salt Lake City, we had fallen into a bit more than a cordial relationship. I was still angry, and that anger would surface from time to time. But I did what society would expect a daughter to do. When Carrie would call to say my mother needed something, I would send the money. I bought her things like dentures, a TV, clothes, etc. I also paid for the annual church trips she took. I even went on a few of them. And I made sure her bills were paid up when I visited in the summer. That was as far as I could go. My heart was partially closed to her—had been since my teenage years. So when I found out she was dying, I had compassion for her condition, but I also felt empty.

I called the hospital daily to check on her. One of the nurses chewed me out because I wasn't there. She said, "This is your mother and you should be here." She called me a bad daughter. I guess maybe I was. But all the same, I wasn't traveling to Chicago until my school finals were done. My education was the primary focus for me. I did go for a visit that summer, and Mom and I went on one of the church trips. She had lost a lot of weight and looked gaunt, but she laughed a lot and seemed to have fun on the trip.

She had been taking chemotherapy but stopped after three treatments. To get to the treatments meant taking the bus, and she was dealing with nausea and other side effects, too. I couldn't help her with this. On top of this, someone actually broke into her apartment while she was gone for one of the treatments and stole her TV! Whoever it was went out the back door and down the stairs. He was seen by Johnny, Reverend Morris' friend, headed for the back fence. Johnny ran over and grabbed the guy by his pant leg but couldn't stop him from getting over the fence. The guy just dropped the TV on the other side of the fence so that he could pull himself over. Upon getting over the fence, he picked the TV up and ran. I replaced the TV.

I never had to physically take care of my mother while she was dying. The church members took care of her as much as they could. One of the younger members, DeDe, lived in the building and would help her with baths and doing whatever she needed. I was grateful to her for this—still am. Dede was in her early 20s and raising her little girl.

My mother began calling me weekly on Sunday nights at around 7:00 p.m. We didn't talk about much—there really wasn't much I could say. We didn't have many stories to reminisce about because she hadn't been in my life much. We talked about what she or I did that week. It was on one of these calls that I blew up at her for wanting money to buy Reverend Morris' "special tea" that I mentioned earlier. When that particular call ended, my body was shaking I was so mad. Looking back, I really should have sent her the money. I had no faith that the tea would do anything, and I was hostile about her minister. At the same time, she was dying and I refused the one thing she asked me for. I regretted that outburst and decision for years. I also regretted never apologizing for my behavior. After that, she wouldn't tell me anything about what she was doing. Not that she had told me much in the first place—but now a door was closed. She had been doing her best to make up for the past—at least that's what I thought at the time—and I had blown it. We still talked every week after my outburst, but our calls never lasted very long—maybe 15 or 20 minutes.

I graduated from Westminster in 1990 with an MBA. My mother and Carrie were going to attend graduation. Bill paid for the train tickets, since neither woman would fly. He purchased a sleeping car (a railway car with beds) for them. This was nice of him to do. Unfortunately, they didn't come. My mother was too ill to travel.

After graduation I went to Chicago for my annual visit close to the end of June. When I arrived, my mother was in the hospital. I went directly there. As I pulled into the parking lot, I saw Reverend Morris leaving, so I waited until he drove out of the parking lot before getting out of my car. I hated that my mother had made him her contact person at the hospital—not me, her only daughter. I could understand that I lived in another state, but damn—the knife of pain dug into my heart a little deeper upon learning this. The bottom line was that I felt she loved him more than she loved me. On occasion I even contemplated that he might be my father. She loved him so much, it didn't seem impossible. Of course, this couldn't be true. I didn't look anything like him—thank the heavens.

When I arrived at Mom's room, she was sitting up in bed and looked chipper. Of course she would—Reverend Morris had just visited. We talked about what had happened to put her in the hospital—or rather, I queried her and she answered my questions to the best of her ability. When I spoke to the doctor, he said she was having complications from the cancer. He said they would do what they could and that she would be there for a few days. I felt helpless and useless. I said goodbye to my mother and told her I would be back the next day. That evening I went by my friend Gwen's house. This was Gwen from the coffee shop, who I mentioned earlier.

When I arrived at Gwen's house, her older brother was there. We had not met before. He seemed like a nice person, and I could see the resemblance between him and his sister. I hung out for a few hours with them. We all joked around laughed and had a nice time. I could tell Gwen's older brother liked me. The next day, he called— Gwen had given him my number. He wanted to take me to dinner. I told him that wouldn't be a good idea, especially since I was in a relationship. He was okay with this and said he still would like to take me to dinner—no strings attached. I told him I'd think about it, so he gave me his number.

When I went to the hospital to see my mother that day, she had been moved to the intensive care unit. No one had informed me of this. I was in shock to see her there. Her breathing was labored, and she couldn't sit up. I had just seen her the day before sitting up, laughing, and looking fine. This was less than 24 hours later. I sat with her without saying much. I didn't know what to say. It felt surreal, and I was uncomfortable.

It never dawned on me that the end was so near. Here was the woman who birthed me all those years ago, lying in a hospital bed. She looked very small, but she still had her wits about her. I didn't ask any questions, stroke her cheek, or say "I love you." I just sat there and stared at her. I didn't have it in me to do those things. I can't say that I was numb—more dazed. I don't know how long I sat. At some point she told me that I didn't need to stay. I'm not sure if she really meant it, but I accepted the reprieve and said goodnight. That was the last time I saw my mother alive.

I went back to her apartment. I remember going to bed and not being able to sleep. A couple of hours later, the phone rang. It was the hospital telling me that my mother had just passed. It was 12:05 a.m. They asked if I wanted to come see her and get her things that night or wait until the morning. I didn't know what to do, so I told them I would call them back.

My first call was to Bill, to let him know that my mother had died. He picked up the phone and angrily asked me why I was waking him up. I gave him the news, and he said he was sorry to hear it. I then called Carrie and told her what had happened and asked her what to do. Her suggestion was to wait until the morning. I called the hospital and told them that I would come the next morning to collect my mother's belongings.

My next call was to one of Mom's sisters in Bogalusa. That call didn't go as planned. The first thing she asked me was what I was going to do with Mom's things. No "I'm sorry for your loss." No comforting words. I told her I didn't know; she had just died less than a half hour ago. My aunt didn't like my answer and decided to call Carrie's mother to ask her if she would go over and pack up my mother's things and send them to her. I had no idea my aunt even knew her. In any event, the hounds started to circle. My mother didn't have much, so what was there to take?

The next day, I made the decision to have one funeral in Chicago and one in Bogalusa. Chicago was really home for my mother, and she had lots of friends who wanted and needed to say goodbye. I decided to have the Chicago funeral three days after Mom's death rather than the customary week, as done in most Black families. I've never believed in waiting long to bury a person. And in this case, since there would be two funerals, Chicago would have to be quick.

The service would be held at her church, and her beloved Reverend Morris would preside. I had to move quickly to get everything arranged. I also had to pay for everything. My mother didn't have any money, so the cost was on my shoulders. Part of the funeral in Bogalusa would be paid for by the family, but it was up to me to take care of Chicago and get her to Bogalusa. I called Bill back the day after my mother died to ask him if he would go to Key Bank to pick up a check for me. I would call them and cash in my CD. I needed $5,000. Bill told me that I didn't have to do this. He would loan me the money, and I could pay him back when the CD came due—which I did. He didn't have to help me, but he did, which I appreciated.

At the end of the second day, I was spent and felt all alone. Bill wasn't coming to Chicago. He didn't offer and I didn't ask. He was loaning me the money, and that's all I could expect. That evening, I called Gwen's brother. I knew what I was doing. I wanted more than company. I wanted—no, needed—to be held in someone's arms. I wanted someone to say they cared about me, even if it was a lie. I needed to be touched and consoled. I wanted to bury my head in someone's arms and cry. I had never had the luxury of being able to do this. None of the men I had been with were into holding me when I felt insecure or just needed to be held. In their defense, I never asked them for it either. Maybe they saw me as strong and independent. But even someone who is strong needs someone they can lean on and feel supported by.

Well, I slept with Gwen's brother. He held me that night, all night. Honestly, I don't remember the sex; I only remember being held. I asked for what I needed, and he gave it to me. He stayed with me until he had to get up for work the next day. At the time, I didn't feel guilty for cheating on Bill. The guilt came later, and it ate me up inside.

Gwen's brother came to my mother's funeral and held my hand during the entire service. I am forever grateful to him for that and for being there for me when I was in desperate need of emotional support. For the first time in my life, I was receiving some form of emotional nurturing. Both of us knew what was going on—we had no illusions of a long-term relationship. Eyebrows were raised at the funeral. My friends—all except Gwen, that is—wondered who he was and why he was with me. Did this mean I was leaving Bill?

After I returned from burying my mother, Carrie had a chat with me about it. Wanda had gone to her concerned that I might leave Bill and go with this guy. She asked Carrie, who she knew I respected and valued, if she would intervene. I told Carrie that there was nothing to worry about. She didn't approve of what I had done and told me so. I understood her point of view. If I were her, I wouldn't approve either. Our affair didn't last long. Once I cleaned out my mother's apartment, gave the keys to Reverend Morris, and said goodbye to everyone, I was on a plane back to Salt Lake City.

No matter the reason or justification for my cheating, I knew it was wrong and I had to live with it. My dilemma was whether or not to tell Bill what I had done. It took me a while, but I eventually gathered the courage to tell him. Needless to say, his reaction wasn't pretty. He never forgave me for this and would bring it up periodically. I assume it was to punish me. He didn't have to do this; I was punishing myself enough. But even on his death bed he brought it up.

The day I told him about the infidelity, he asked me why I had done it, and I told him. He asked me if the guy was any good—i.e., was he better in bed than Bill? What did he expect me to say? I told him the guy was fine. He gave me what I needed, and that was to be held. Then I found myself talking to Bill again about my sexual issues and concerns. He wasn't a man who thought women could or should have sexual issues. I remember coming home one day to find my vibrator on a cabinet between two candles. He had gone through my things and found it. It appalled him that I had such a thing—go figure. He saw it as an insult to his manhood. I told him it had nothing to do with his performance; I just wanted to have fun on my own sometimes. In his mind, I shouldn't have been pleasing myself. But I kept my vibrator, thank you very much.

Anyway, on the day I confessed about cheating on him, I decided not to tell him about something else I had done. He was already over-the-top angry, and it would add insult to injury. I had on occasion expressed my concern that I couldn't have an orgasm through penetration, and this bothered me. I had also told him that I thought something was wrong with me. I didn't tell him that I

173

couldn't feel anything. I could orgasm through other means, but something was missing. I didn't know what that was.

Over the years I began to suspect that maybe I was a lesbian. Why else couldn't I feel anything when I had sex with a man? It didn't occur to me that the sexual assaults had affected me in this way. So I called a female friend of mine who I knew was bisexual. I told her what I suspected and that I wanted to test my theory. She promptly agreed to help me with the test. I slept with her and still didn't feel anything. We did it again, and still nothing. I did orgasm, but something was still missing. And on top of this, I realized that even without an orgasm through penetration, I still preferred men. The experiment had failed, and I was back to square one.

It was many years after my experiment that I eventually figured out what the problem was. It was after Bill had died. Part of the issue was my heart being closed and the protective armor I had erected around myself over the years to prevent me from getting hurt any more than I already had been. This was the reason I couldn't feel anything. It was what was missing, over and above the orgasm. My heart had been closed for many years but was beginning to open due to the psychological work I was doing. I hadn't developed intimacy with anyone I slept with. There was no bond, and for me—I learned that this is a must.

The other part of the issue was patience. One day I decided to see if I could cause myself to orgasm through penetration only. I took out my trusty red vibrator to see if I could please myself in this way. It took a while, but I achieved my goal. I could achieve orgasm through penetration. The problem was that guys were rushing to the finish line and not taking the time to let me orgasm first. And in their defense, I never told them to wait. I wanted to make sure it wasn't a fluke, so I did it again and again. It wasn't a fluke. After all those years, problem solved. I knew that there wasn't anything wrong with me. Back then, women didn't talk to each other about such things, so I never broached the subject with any of my friends. I know now that I wasn't the only one with this issue.

20

Getting an Abortion

During the tongue lashing I was receiving for having cheated, Bill decided to accuse me of something that wasn't true. And there was no way I could prove him wrong.

To tell this story, I must go back to my life at age 12 for context. My menstrual cycle began at 12—pretty normal. What wasn't normal was that my cycle would occur in three- to six-month intervals, so I never really knew when to expect my period. This went on until age 18.

At 18, Gwen from Memphis and I went to Planned Parenthood for birth control. Both of us chose the pill. This regulated my cycle. I was told that my body would need a rest from the pill after about five years. This meant at age 22 I needed to use another method. I had no intention of ever having an unwanted pregnancy. I had seen the way I came into the world and what other girls and women dealt with. Raising a kid on my own was OUT. Plus, I wanted my child to have a name. I was called a bastard, and no kid of mine would ever have that title.

I decided at 22 to use an intrauterine device—the Lippes loop. I had problems with it from the beginning and decided to have it removed. The other option was the copper-7—which I had heard was causing problems. This meant I would be without any form of birth control. I was in a committed relationship and figured if I got pregnant, we would just get married. I had broached the subject of condoms with Kenny, and he flat-out refused to use them. If I had been in my right mind, I would have said, "okay—then no sex." But that's not what I did.

My cycle went back to being irregular once I was off birth control. At some point I began to suspect that I couldn't get pregnant. So when I began to date Bill, I didn't use protection. I informed him of this, and he had no problem with it—at least that's what he said. And I was young and stupid, so I thought it wouldn't be a problem. We were together a little over three years when it happened—I got pregnant. I remember being extremely tired and having to lie on the couch a lot. Bill was the one who figured it out. I had no clue. It was confirmed with a visit to my OB-GYN.

When my doctor informed me that I was pregnant, I was surprised. After all these years of thinking I couldn't get pregnant, here I was—pregnant as a soon-to-be-26-year-old woman. At that age, I still didn't think of myself as a woman. I still saw myself as a girl. There was so much I didn't know.

I wasn't sure how I felt about being pregnant. My relationship with Bill wasn't healthy, and in 1987 I hadn't begun grad school yet. On the one hand, I was sort of okay with being pregnant—but on the other, my practical side kicked in. I wasn't married, my relationship wasn't good, this would blow the hat off Bill's lie to neighbors and family, etc. Bill also hadn't done a very good job raising his son, and I had no reason to believe he'd do any better with our child.

I went home to tell Bill the news. I still remember every moment of the conversation and how it felt. Bill was in his office, sitting at his desk when I got back. I went in and told him that I was pregnant. I had a bit of a smile on my face. I was beginning to feel okay about it. He looked at me and didn't say anything. I was perplexed by the lack of response. Later—that is, a few years later—I found out what he was thinking.

I went back to my desk in the den and began working. I wasn't sure what to make of Bill's reaction. So I just worked. A short while later, he came out to where I was sitting. Putting his hand on my shoulder, he asked, "What are you going to do about it?" In that moment I knew he didn't want it. I told him that I didn't know. What I did know was that I needed to think to figure this out. I'd had no expectation of what he would say, but at the same time it hurt to realize I was in this alone.

Gwen in Chicago thought I should have the baby. She didn't believe in abortion, and she also thought it would force Bill to make a commitment. I told her that would be entrapment and I would never do that to him. On top of that, the way he had reacted told me volumes about his character. You never really know someone until a crisis occurs. What I felt and knew in my heart was that if I chose to have the baby, I would be on my own. I'd be in a similar position as my mother was when she had me. The only difference was that I had my bachelor's degree but couldn't use it because I needed a master's degree to practice. I had always wanted kids, but I wanted them to be raised by both parents.

I decided to go south to have quiet time for contemplation. I went to my grandfather in Bogalusa. I couldn't tell him that I was pregnant, or at least I didn't think I could. For that matter, I couldn't tell anyone in the family. They would have a conniption if they thought I was even considering having an abortion. My grandfather and his wife, Ms. Mime, were glad to see me. I'd sit on the front porch with them shelling peas or peeling potatoes. I didn't have to cook. For some reason my elders in Bogalusa never thought I could cook, which in my mind was a good thing. As I mentioned earlier, cooking is not high on my list of hobbies.

I stayed with my grandfather for a week. I'm not sure if he ever knew why I came for a visit in the middle of summer. It was the end of June, and I had never visited him during that time of the year as an adult. He was a smart man, so he had to know there was something weighing on my mind. He never queried me about it. He just loved me and let me be. It was the most peace I had felt in a long time. I felt nurtured. I felt safe, too.

I took the time needed to contemplate my situation, and in the end, I decided it would be best to have an abortion. Bill didn't want the child, and I wasn't going to force this on him. I didn't want to take care of a kid on my own. Then there was grad school, which I would begin the next year. There were other reasons too, but the main one was my not wanting to have a kid without a father.

I went back to Salt Lake City and told Bill what I had decided. I found a clinic and went in for the initial interview—which was difficult. All the questions. The clinic wanted to make sure that I was sure about this—I was. Bill drove me to the clinic for the abortion and came back to pick me up after it was done. He didn't come in. I have never regretted my decision. I did the right thing for me at that time in my life.

Fast forward a few years later to the conversation—if you can call it that—in which Bill raked me over the coals for having cheated on him. He brought up the abortion and accused me of doing it because I had been cheating on him. In his mind, it had to be somebody else's kid. Why else would I have aborted it? But it was his child.

This is when he told me how he felt when I told him I was pregnant. For him, the smile on my face said that I had him trapped. For the rest of his life, I was never able to convince him that the child was his. He had never trusted me, and from that point on it didn't get any better.

Sunlight

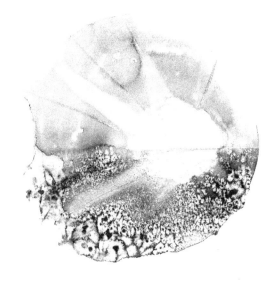

Sunlight helps to feed the plant. It causes the
photosynthesis to be pulled into the plant,
giving it strength to make the blossom.
This is the plant's circle of life. Like the
lotus, the human Soul knows it, too,
has to push toward the light. The
only way the Soul can grow and
bloom is through the gathering
of earthly experiences.

21

Filling in the Gaps

The year 1987 was pivotal for me, and not just because of the
pregnancy. I had graduated a year earlier from the University of
Utah with a bachelor's degree in speech language pathology and had
decided not to pursue a master's degree in the same field. The reason
for the decision came around 1985, after being in the program for a
year. Most of my electives had been fulfilled through the other two
colleges I attended. This meant I could focus on my major, which
was a good thing. I spent hours working as a student speech therapist
at the school's clinic and at the Veterans Hospital. I switched majors
because of the money. Back then, a speech therapist made around
$14,000 a year and had to have a master's degree. When I began the
program in 1984, I had no idea the salary was so low. I had chosen
the field not because I dreamed of being a speech therapist as my
friend Colleen had, but to earn a living. So I thought, if I needed
a master's degree to practice, why not obtain an MBA? I could still
work in a hospital or be an administrator. And if I had to spend
the money to get a master's degree, I figured I might as well get a
degree in something that gave me the potential to earn significantly
more. Besides, I had become accustomed to living a certain way

and wanted to make sure I could take care of myself at that same standard, too.

When I decided to switch majors, I also decided to complete the bachelor's in speech therapy. In my mind, it didn't make any sense to switch majors midstream. I would get the bachelor's and then move on.

I applied to the University of Utah's business school and was denied. My GPA at the university was around 3.5, but the problem was my grades from Roosevelt University in Chicago. My GPA there was hideously low. I was crestfallen by the denial but decided to apply to Westminster College. Westminster was a private college and had a wonderful MBA program. I was rejected there also, for the same reason. This time, however, with Bill's support, I appealed the decision. It was challenging for me to explain to strangers why my GPA had been so low in Chicago, but I did. I also explained that I had done well at Shelby State and the University of Utah—this they could see from the transcripts. My appeal was successful. I was accepted on the grounds that I raise my math score. Math was the one subject that I wasn't good at. I agreed. All of this happened in 1987. I would begin grad school in fall of 1988.

I used the year before starting grad school to earn the money to pay for the first year. The Pell Grant would not pay for graduate school, so I had to earn the money to attend. The year before starting grad school I also attended math classes at the University of Utah. To help me get up to speed, I hired a tutor. After each class I would go to the tutor's home to work on the formulas given in class. It was slow going, but I loved getting breakthroughs. The tutor would show me how a formula worked, over and over and over again, until the method clicked in my mind. Then she had me solve problem after problem using the formula until it was ingrained in my head. She would then send me home with more problems to solve. After a while, I began to like math again. The last time I had liked math was junior high. Now I was back on track with it.

In Memphis I had received the best education a Black girl in the South could receive at that time. Going to college meant I had to catch up on what I hadn't learned. There were no shortcuts—I buckled down, focused, and got the work done. And in the end, it paid off. Math was an integral element of getting the master's degree in business, and getting my foundation solid before I began school was a blessing. I would have struggled to keep up without it.

As it turned out, I loved grad school. The professors were great, and because the classes were small, each student received more attention. The most challenging classes for me were economics classes, because I knew nothing about it. My friend Joe was in these classes with me, and she never had to study. I, on the other hand, read the textbook, taped the classes, transcribed them as soon as I arrived home in the evening, and studied the transcribed notes for each test. I had learned early not to take notes in these classes; I wrote slowly due to my hand tremors, and trying to write notes while the professor was explaining a subject I knew nothing about would mean missing key points. Thus I got permission to tape the classes. I received an A-plus for both Economics 1 and 2. My friend Joe received an A-minus. I'm still proud of those grades. I worked my ass off, but I learned economics.

The classes I attended were held at night and were designed for professionals who were going back to school. Most of the professors also had day jobs in the field they were teaching, which meant we were taught business reality rather than theory. I also got to know people who worked in various industries and collaborated with them on school projects. I was only 27, so everyone was older than me.

Graduate school was one of the best experiences in my life. The only negative was the death of my grandfather shortly after I began classes in the fall of 1988. I received permission to miss several classes to fly to Bogalusa for his funeral. It was hard watching my mother and her siblings suffer at the loss of their father. I loved him but somehow felt he wasn't really gone. I think this is because of my experience with seeing ghosts. He was the first dead person I ever touched. Because I loved him and knew he loved me, it felt safe—well, almost safe—to go up and touch him in the casket. I wanted to rid myself of the fear of dead people and thought touching him might help. So when it was my turn to view him, I reached my hand into his coffin and lightly touched him. I didn't know what to expect. His body was cool and hard. I do believe touching him helped me in some way with my fear.

The beginning and ending of grad school were punctuated by death. My grandfather at the beginning and my mother and Granny at the end. Granny died six months—almost to the day—after my mother's death in 1990. I sometimes think both my mother and Granny felt their work was done once I received the MBA. They must have felt I could take care of myself at that point and didn't need them, so they left. I have to say, even though my relationship with both women was difficult, I felt completely alone when they died. I had no one. I didn't feel lost, but I felt abandoned. They had both left me so close behind one another. I still hadn't dealt with my mother's death, and Granny had to go and die, too. I didn't feel like an adult, although I was 29. I knew neither of them was a good parent, but they were all I had known. The only person I had in my life to hold onto was Bill, and our relationship wasn't healthy—to say the least.

Another example of the strife in mine and Bill's relationship pertained to my education. All during undergrad and grad school, whenever I had a test coming up, he would find a way to pick a fight. I knew he supported my education, yet it seemed as though he wanted to sabotage it. Because I was so determined to get my degrees, I didn't allow him to distract me. I'd use these times to go to the library or meet with study groups to prepare for tests rather than staying home listening to him or dealing with the silent treatment.

Our disagreements lasted for days, and during these times he'd give me the silent treatment, so we wouldn't speak to each other. I used this to my advantage even when I wasn't in school. I'd go to dinner with friends or watch a movie by myself. Sometimes it was just nice to be by myself.

The disagreements were always about something I said or did that Bill didn't agree with. One of them had to do with a man he wanted to hire as an associate. I didn't feel good about this guy and told Bill he shouldn't hire him. To Bill, I was interfering in his business. He got pretty upset with me about it and wouldn't speak to me for a day or so. Over time I stopped giving my opinion. He didn't want it, and I didn't share it—even when he began to ask. The guy he hired didn't work out and ended up stiffing Bill on a significant amount of money. Oh, well!

At some point Bill's family found out about our relationship. When Bill and I first moved into the new house, we slept in separate bedrooms when any of his family members came for a visit. At some point this stopped, though I don't remember when. We were together several years before it happened. The only family members who visited were his sister Mary and her husband, Glenn; his youngest brother; his sister Iris, along with one of her sons and his family; and his parents, who I liked. Bill really didn't get along well with most of his family, which was part of the reason so few visited.

Bill's parents moved into the house Bill owned in the lower Cove after Chris moved. They had moved out of their home in Wyoming, and Bill thought since he had the extra house it might be a good idea for them to live there. For the most part, I don't think they were happy there. It wasn't home, and I think they were lonely. They were on their own with the exception of Bill's visits or mine.

They didn't live in the house very long. I think it was less than a year. They decided to go to Idaho and stay with Iris for six months and then Mary for six months. They said they never wanted to be a burden on their kids. I don't remember when Bill's dad died, but after his death Bill's mother, Francis, began to live with us for four months a year. This took some of the pressure off the girls.

Bill would sometimes take me with him on his visits to see the family homestead in Sage, Wyoming, and to visit with Mary and Glenn in Idaho. The place where Bill was born was pretty desolate. There were only a few houses and a railroad in the town. The houses had long since been abandoned, and there was sagebrush everywhere. The house he grew up in seemed as though it might have been comfortable in the early twentieth century for people living as sheep herders. It was just so far away from any town. In Wyoming, land is king—not housing. The life Bill grew up in was hard. I couldn't imagine having to get up on a cold winter morning to stoke the kitchen stove to heat the house before the rest of the family got up or use an outhouse or drive a plow behind a horse. They lived without electricity or a phone for years, too.

Mary and Glenn lived in Pocatello and had a motor-home park in Lava Hot Springs, Idaho. Bill and I visited them frequently. Lava was a tourist town, and everyone loved to visit the hot springs. In the summer it would be bumper-to-bumper traffic and the motor-home park would be filled. It was the prettiest motor home park that I had seen. There was green grass and a stream in front. The place was immaculate. I don't know how Mary and Glenn did so much work, either. When I met them, they were in their late 60s or early 70s, and they kept that park looking pristine.

I enjoyed spending time with both of them. They were kind to me, and that was all that was required for me to like them. We would spend Thanksgivings together. Either Bill and I would go to Pocatello or Mary and Glenn would come to Salt Lake City. They visited for a few Christmases, too. I wasn't around for Christmas much because I'd be in Bogalusa. After my grandfather died in 1988, I went back once when my mother was visiting after her cancer diagnosis, and then I stopped going to Bogalusa for the holidays.

Because Christmas was my favorite holiday, I always wanted to go all out for it. I wanted the tree, the decorations, the presents, all of it. Bill wasn't much into Christmas and always asked me why I was doing so much just for two people. My answer was always "because I love Christmas." Bill would tell me not to get him anything and that Christmas didn't mean anything to him. And every year I would put a present for him under the tree. Everybody needs something under the tree in my opinion.

For years Bill would give me a check for my birthday and Christmas rather than go out and find a present. I put up with this until one year I told him that if he didn't care enough to go purchase a present, that was fine; but I wasn't going to accept any more checks. He replied that he didn't know what I wanted, but with a check I could buy what I liked. Maybe this was true. Maybe I was overreacting. But I didn't think so. Now, don't get me wrong—I like money. But there are a couple of times a year when money doesn't work as a present for me. Bill stopped giving me checks and bought presents from then on. Some of them I liked, and some of them I didn't. And that was fine—at least he made the effort.

22

Working to Gain Freedom

As I said before, the country was in a recession when I graduated in 1990. It took me a year to find a job, and it wasn't even a job I wanted. My master's was in marketing. All the aptitude tests I had taken put advertising and sales high on the list of careers that would be best for me. Plus, I knew I was not someone who should be sitting in a cubicle all day. Not to mention that I see myself as an equal to anyone I meet—including bosses. This doesn't sit well in the corporate environment.

I had been sending resumés all over the place, not just in Utah. I didn't tell Bill that I was applying to companies outside of Salt Lake City. Two companies replied: Novell in Salt Lake City and Pfizer Pharmaceuticals in Illinois. I went through several rounds of interviews with Novell in their marketing department. But in the end, they hired someone else. Pfizer wanted to interview me to be a representative for them. This sounded fine, but the person who was supposed to interview me kept changing the date. This posed a problem for me, because I would need to fly to Illinois for the interview and that cost money—especially at the last minute. After she changed the date the third time, I lost interest and told her I was done. I am flexible to a point, but once that point is reached, I don't budge.

My friend Joe and I were searching for jobs at the same time. Both of us had graduated in June of 1990, and here we were in spring of 1991 still looking for work. At least I still had a job working for Bill. Plus, I wasn't responsible for any of the household expenses. Bill never accepted any money from me. He even reimbursed me for groceries. On the one hand, this was a good thing. I didn't have much money, and it afforded me the luxury of spending my earnings any way I chose. On the other hand, his motive for this was not generosity. At the time, if you were living with someone in Utah and put yourselves forward into the community as husband and wife, there was the possibility of you becoming husband and wife legally after seven years. Without telling me, Bill contacted an attorney to find out what he needed to do to make sure this didn't occur. One of the suggestions was for him to pay for everything related to the house. He wasn't to accept any money from me for anything. Bill had no idea that I knew about his inquiry. (I think I must have found out through Chris.) The man really didn't know me very well. I never felt secure in the relationship nor in the house. It didn't belong to me, and I could be kicked out at any time.

Because I never felt like I belonged, I didn't take much of an interest in the house. I made sure it was clean and I planted flowers, but that's as far as I went. Periodically, Bill would mention that the house was his, especially when he wanted to get under my skin. Once, I went to an auction—I liked auctions. I rarely ever bought anything; I just liked to watch the process of people bidding on household goods and seeing beautiful furniture and accessories. At one of these auctions, I saw a beautiful mahogany wood table that would have been perfect for the entryway at the house. Without thinking, I bid on it and won the bid. I was elated for about a minute. Then my stomach started to churn. I was sure Bill would berate me for buying it—asking who I thought I was, buying it for his house. I felt an indescribable amount of fear. As the gods would have it, the lady who was bidding against me for the table came up to me and asked if she could purchase it. She offered me more than I had paid for it—I accepted. It was nice to make a profit, and I was glad to sell it. I couldn't accept the risk of what Bill would say.

I was trying to do what I could to support myself well and not be under Bill's thumb. Working for him afforded me the opportunity to study when I wanted, but it also meant being under his control for my income. He was a hard man to work for. Because of our relationship, I was treated differently than his other secretaries. He didn't yell at them—he would just talk about them behind their back. I knew I needed to find a job away from him, and that's what I did. He wasn't happy about it, but there wasn't anything he could do. He was fighting to keep control over me, and I was fighting to be released. When we met, I was 22; in the spring of 1991, I was about to turn 30. I was maturing, and he didn't like this.

Joe heard about a job fair being held at one of the hotels downtown, so we went together. I felt as though I was part of a flock of sheep willingly going to be castrated. The place was packed with people looking for work. Joe and I made the rounds. There was one company interested in me at the fair: an insurance company. The person at the fair was looking for claims adjusters. I was overqualified and told her so. She told me that I would be fast-tracked—that this was where everyone started. I agreed to be interviewed for the job and was offered a position. At my interview, I asked if I was being hired because of affirmative action. Although I understood the need for it, I wanted to be hired for my talent—not my race. I was told no. That answer, as it turned out, wasn't the truth.

Bill wasn't happy about my decision to work for the company. He said I wouldn't be successful—that I would be eaten alive. He told me that I didn't know how to play the corporate game. I told him that I would learn how to play it.

I accepted the job in April, bought my car in May, and visited my friend Deloris in Puerto Rico before starting my new job. Deloris and I had met while working for JC Penney. She and her husband had been transferred to Puerto Rico for his work. Deloris called me and said she was bored. I told her I would be right down to help her play. We both laughed, but we genuinely thought it a good idea for me to visit—so I did. Deloris and I spent days walking, talking, eating, hanging out on the beach, and basically having fun. She and her husband were gracious hosts and even took me for a day of sightseeing in San Juan. I had a really nice time.

When I got back to Salt Lake City, I began a new journey as a claims adjuster. What an ironic turn of events—I never wanted to work in an office in a cubicle nor in any corporate environment. I had my sights set on being an actor, being creative and free. And here I was, starting my first day of work in the complete antithesis of what my initial intent had been for most of my life to that point. Had I sold out on my dreams, or had I grown up? The jury was still out on this.

I met my new boss, Deni, who seemed nice enough. She led me to the cubicle that would be mine and introduced me to the unit—my coworkers. I would begin my journey with the team that handled car accidents only. The team I worked on consisted of about five people. One of the things I noticed right away was how much the phone rang in the departments. In my unit and one close to mine, the phones never seemed to stop ringing. Whereas in another nearby unit, they rarely rang.

Besides me, there was one other person of color in the office— actually in any of this insurance company's offices in Utah at the time. Ford had been recently hired as a supervisor for one of the other units. Since moving to Utah, I had become accustomed to being the only person of color for as far as the eye could see. Ford was a nice guy, and it was nice not to be the only person of color around for once.

My fellow unit members were fine. They were happy to have more help. Of course, I wouldn't be much help in the beginning, because I needed to be trained. It fell to the unit members to begin this process. I would also need to go to headquarters in the Midwest for three weeks' worth of training on how to read the policy. I found it interesting that I was sent to school for three weeks to learn how to read an insurance policy, yet the insureds—who are the recipients of said policy—are expected to know what's in it without any training. Just an observation.

It was slow going for me. I didn't know what I was doing, and the phones wouldn't stop ringing. The caseloads were horrific. Most adjusters had more than 100 cases at any given time. The only way to know which was which was by the claim number.

For the most part I was fine talking to people on the phone and helping them with their claims, but I had to learn to negotiate quickly. Diplomacy came naturally, but negotiation took time to develop. Most people are not happy with the amount of money they are offered for their car when it is damaged beyond its blue-book value, so customers would get upset. The issue is the value of the car versus the cost to replace it. The two are rarely the same due to depreciation. Getting a person who was already upset to understand this proved challenging. An adjuster never knows when they pick up the phone if they are going to be yelled at, cursed out, threatened . . . or if the person will be kind.

After going to the corporate office for training, I was given a full case load. It was trial by fire at that point. What I found difficult—in addition to being yelled at by people on the phone—was the sheer number of calls in a day and the amount of mail I received daily. I began not wanting to be on the phone at home nor open any of my personal mail. I must have a bit of residual PTSD from that job, because I still don't like opening mail. I hated seeing the mail person come to my cubicle to put a bundle of files, each with mail attached to it, in my inbox. Beth was the name of the first mail person I got to know. She was a lot of fun and we became friends.

I worked long hours at this job, which Bill wasn't too happy about. Even though the office closed at 5:00 p.m., which meant no calls got through, there was still paperwork to be done. Whatever was said to someone about a claim had to be logged in the file so that there was a record. I was told that if I said something to someone about a claim and didn't log it, it was like I didn't say it. Plus, I write slowly and methodically—meaning many words—so it took me a long time to write what had occurred for every call from the day. Sometimes I would still be at my desk at 8:00 p.m. Because we were salaried, it didn't matter how long it took to get the job done. A few of the adjusters would come in early in the morning to get the paperwork done before the phones began, while a few of us preferred to stay late. If I wasn't able to stay late, I would take the files home to work on them or go into the office on weekends. As I said, this began to be a problem for Bill—he wanted his dinner. Actually, what he wanted was control disguised as dinner. Once again, I didn't see this coming.

At one point early into my new job, Bill said he would take over cooking dinner. I was getting tired of his anger over dinner being late, and I thought he had come up with a good solution. I would cook on weekends. I thought this was a nice compromise, and it worked just fine for a short while. Then he began to call me at work daily around 5:00 to see when I would be home for dinner. This was a problem because I never knew when I would get to leave the office. If I was on the phone with someone at 5:00, I couldn't just say, "Got to go. It's 5:00." So I would tell him that I didn't know, to which he would push back with "I'm cooking; it's going to get cold," or "I need to know when to start cooking," or something else related to cooking. He would just push and push to get an answer. So I would try to give an answer, even though I wasn't sure I could get home at that time. The time was usually 6:00.

I would do my best to get home by 6:00. Sometimes I would almost make it. Sometimes traffic was heavy and I'd be a few minutes late; and at other times, like I said, something would delay me at work. In any event, Bill would be upset when I'd walk through the door. Over time I began to have anxiety about getting home on time for dinner. I'd be in the car trying to get there, my stomach tense, knowing that I might not make it through the door at or before 6:00. If I was even five minutes late, Bill got angry. He began to blame me for his getting drunk, too. He liked to have a glass or two of wine with dinner, and he would sit and drink while waiting on me; therefore it was "my fault." I knew better, but it still caused me distress.

I'm amazed that I didn't start drowning myself in alcohol. I did drink wine back then, but not a lot. Even a glass a month was a lot for me. My maternal grandmother had been an alcoholic, which always deterred me from drinking too much. Bill never seemed to have a "stop" switch. He would drink a whole bottle in one sitting. Even when I got home on time, I never knew what his mood would be. Sometimes he'd be happy about a new recipe or a job he was awarded that day, and other times he'd be upset about something. For example, maybe I forgot to buy something at the store, causing him to go out and get it, or I hadn't done the dishes and he had to do them before cooking.

Because of the mood swings, I stayed on edge most of the time. I also became very sensitive to anger. I never showed this outwardly, but it was there. I still can't handle other people's angry outbursts. I have no issue with a person getting angry—but using it to berate another human being is out of line and disrespectful. Bill's anger at me wasn't really about me, but that didn't matter. I felt it all the same. It took me back to childhood and the physical beatings. What's interesting is that I had been taught never to allow a man to hit me, and to this day that has never happened. But no one ever taught me about mental and emotional abuse. I didn't know how to handle that. When I first moved to Salt Lake City, Bill and I were in the kitchen of his old house having a disagreement. He raised his hand, and I thought he was planning on hitting me. I took evasive action and slapped him across the face, knocking his glasses off and breaking them. It was an instinctive move—no man was ever going to hit me. He said that his intention was to take his glasses off. Well, it sure didn't look like it. The point is, I wouldn't allow one form of abuse, but I allowed another.

Between Bill and work, I was in the middle of an emotional melee. The job was proving challenging due to the pressure from people who had wrecked their cars, paperwork, and being confined to a desk all day. I tried to alleviate some of the stress with plants.

Whoever walked into the office could immediately spot my desk by all the plants on top of the file cabinets. I love plants.

Periodically, people would come into the office unannounced. They were never allowed in the back-office space, so we had to go out to the lobby to see them. We'd take them into one of the offices designated for meetings, which were off the lobby area. Many times, someone would come to the office to see me, and upon actually seeing me, say, "You're Marie? You don't look like Marie. You're Black." These people had spoken to me on the phone and assumed that I was white. It was as if a bubble burst in their minds. It happened so often that I started joking to myself about it. The obvious question was, what did they expect a Black person to sound like?

There was one incident that truly scared me. A gentleman came in unannounced. I was in the middle of training another adjuster, who happened to be a Black man. (The company was trying to catch up with the times in Utah. I have to give them credit for it, because there really weren't that many Blacks in Utah in the first place, and I'm sure ones who wanted to be in the insurance industry were like needles in a haystack.) The trainee and I went out to greet this man. He was a tall, lean, mustached Caucasian who sported a cowboy hat and jeans with one of those large, shiny, cowboy-type belt buckles. He wasn't happy. I asked him to accompany me into one of the offices so that we could talk. I had his file in hand.

As I said, the man was angry, and I was having difficulty calming him down. My mode of operation is logic—not so much emotion. I went over the facts of the case, explaining why I had made a decision about his claim. What happened next was in slow motion in my mind, but it was actually very quick. The man stood up and came across the desk to grab me. The trainee acted fast—standing up and getting between us, holding the guy back. At that time, there were no security guards in the building, and if the trainee hadn't been there, I think the guy would have hurt me. There was no way I could have defended myself. Needless to say, I was shaken up but grateful that nothing happened. The guy left, and I went back to my desk to continue training the new guy. Being a claims adjuster was a stressful job.

23

Being Controlled by the Job

The insurance company I worked for had a few outreach programs that I participated in and enjoyed. A few of us worked with Habitat for Humanity, painting and repairing houses for people who couldn't afford to do it themselves. I'll never forget an incident at one house. Ford was cleaning out the gutters and I was painting a door. Suddenly, I saw Ford running for his life. He had disturbed a hornet's nest, and they were after him. I laughed so hard tears were running down my face. For him it wasn't funny, and it really shouldn't have been for me—but it was. There is nothing like seeing a grown man screaming while running to get away from hornets. I did get my payback for this years later when I disturbed a yellow-jacket nest in the ground. I ran faster than I had run in years.

The company had another program that I participated in for schools. A few of us would periodically go to elementary schools to teach the kids. I don't remember the subject I taught, but it was created by the company I worked for. The teachers loved having someone come to their class to work with the kids; it gave them an opportunity to do something else with that hour. It was something I also enjoyed being a part of.

One of the other groups I enjoyed being a part of was the CAT team—CAT being short for catastrophe. We would go wherever a storm or disaster had occurred. We were on a rotation schedule and only went out if extra help was needed, but I got to participate twice. I thrived in this role. For one thing, it was a nomadic job. Temporary offices were set up. For another, we adjusters were out of the office visiting homes and disaster sites rather than stuck in a cubicle all day. The only issue that arose was when a few customers wouldn't allow me to get on their roofs in Texas. I needed to see the damage a hailstorm had done to be able to judge how much it would cost to replace. Rather than cause more problems, my boss reassigned me to take care of the phones and handle paperwork. This wasn't ideal, but I had no choice if I wanted to stay in the field. What's interesting is that there were several other females on the team who didn't have that issue with homeowners. Oh, well—I have my suspicions, but I'll never know for sure why this happened.

During the seven years I worked as an adjuster, my performance reviews were never stellar. I did get consistent pay raises, though. I only thrived in the field and with one boss who seemed to know my temperament. She was great to work for. I wish she had remained my boss longer. She would give me extra research projects to do for her. I loved it. It broke up the monotony of the job. I still had a full load of claims to work, but the projects fed my being and lifted my vitality, which in turn helped me as a claims adjuster.

I had initially planned to work as an adjuster for five years. I thought that if I wasn't successful in that length of time, I would quit. One of the mistakes I made before taking the job was neglecting to do my due diligence in researching the company. Don't get me wrong—it's a good company. But the area I worked in wasn't the right fit for me. Plus, I wasn't being fast-tracked as I had been promised.

I would have worked well in human resources and sales. I'm good with people and know how to sell. Unfortunately, I was stuck as a claims adjuster. At about the five-year mark I heard a voice tell me, "Leave the job." This was in 1996. By that time I was making a decent salary and wasn't sure where else I could make that kind of money in Salt Lake City. A few years earlier the company had instituted a program to hire insurance agents from within. There would be a yearlong training process, which included spending a week out of every month at the regional office for intense study. Candidates had to be recommended for the program by their immediate management team. I applied and was accepted for the program. In my mind, this was the optimal solution to leaving the job as I had been instructed. The voice didn't say, "Leave the company." I liked the company as a whole.

Bill hated the idea of me being an agent for them. His reasoning was actually quite sound, but I didn't see any other way. For one thing, he felt I wouldn't be an independent agent if the company was providing everything they planned to give me as a new agent. Additionally, the company required to see the prospective agent's financial records. If I had been married to Bill, they would have wanted to see our joint records. Thank goodness we weren't married, because that would have put an end to my aspiration of becoming an insurance agent on the spot. I would never have been able to talk him into letting an outsider see his records. Another thing that got under his skin was the home visit the company wanted to do. They wanted to see the home environment. I had a problem with this too, but I had no power to refuse to comply. Bill said no at the outset, and I had a year to convince him to say yes. This wouldn't be easy, but I did have time on my side.

There was yet another reason Bill didn't want to cooperate with my becoming an agent for the company. It had to do with an incident in 1995. When that man had a grudge against a person or company, it was for life. There was no forgiveness. Early in 1995, Bill's mother was staying with us. It was our turn to care for her. Everything was fine until one weekend she got sick and died, just like that. Both of us were in shock—at least I know I was. Bill called me to come quick. I walked into her bedroom; her eyes were open, but she was gone. Losing a parent is one of the toughest things a person goes through emotionally, even if they don't like them. Bill loved his mother. They had issues, but he still loved her.

After the funeral, Bill, Mary, Glenn, and I were having a conversation about getting away. We wanted to take a trip someplace. We had traveled together a couple of times to California and Canada and thought it was time for another trip. The only issue was that I had a job that required me to ask for time off.

We decided to go to Europe. None of us had been there before, and we thought it might be nice. I hadn't taken any vacation that year, which meant I had three weeks available. Still, I would need to get permission. Even though I had the time, I also knew management frowned on taking it all at once. I asked my immediate supervisor and was given permission to take the full three weeks. This was great news.

We spent that summer planning for the trip. We intended to visit England, Ireland, Scotland, and France. The trip was booked and paid for, and we were within two weeks of our departure. We had even prepaid for our hotel stays. I had also paid my share of the trip and was fully invested—emotionally and financially.

What happened next sent me into a tailspin. My supervisor called me over to his desk two weeks before my departure and told me that I was two days short of the three weeks I had requested to be off. I wondered how this could be. I must have taken two days off and had forgotten about it. I told him I would just take it another way: sick days, without pay, or make it up somehow. He said I only had two options: I could leave for my trip two days later or come back two days earlier. That was impossible! The trip was paid for. I asked him why I couldn't have the days off as unpaid. He said these were the rules. I was crestfallen, but I wasn't going to just give up. I asked him why he hadn't given me this information when I put in my request months ago. He didn't have an answer.

My next move was to follow the chain of command up the ladder to ask for help. This was a horrible fix to be in. Every manager, including the person who ran the region, refused my request. I didn't understand why I couldn't just have the two days. I was willing to take them without pay. I was distraught, to say the least—so distraught, in fact, that I did the unthinkable: I burst into tears on the phone with the regional manager. I begged him for the days, and still he said no. I didn't know what to do. I felt as though I was in one of those rooms where the walls were closing in on me. I had no way out. This was the last rung of management. To this day, I don't know why I couldn't have the extra days off.

So what did I do? I went on the trip as planned and tried not to think about what to do about work. Needless to say, this put a bit of a damper on the trip for me. I still had a nice time until France. France was the last leg of the trip. We only had four days left before we would fly back to the States, and for me the tension of having to go home two days early was looming. In Paris, the four of us had rented a two-bedroom apartment in one of the hotels. We were all sitting at the dining-room table the morning after our arrival when Glenn asked what I was going to do. Glenn had worked in railroad management for years and knew the ropes of corporate thinking. He had retired years earlier, but he was sharp as a tack. I told him that I didn't know. He said, "Okay—we have to come up with a plan." So the four of us sat around the table and hatched a plan.

We knew that calling in sick was my only option since I wasn't planning on leaving Paris early. Glenn mentioned that under the circumstances, I would need a doctor's note. The company's policy was that if an employee was out sick for more than two days, a doctor's note was required. Even though I only needed two days, Glenn recommended I get a doctor's note just in case. The question then became how we would we get a doctor in Paris to write such a note and where we would find this doctor. The doctor would need to speak English, because my French was atrocious. On top if that, I would need to convince the doctor that I was ill. We decided the best place to begin our search was with the hotel concierge. It turned out there was a doctor on call for the hotel. The concierge said the doctor would be called and sent right up. Now I needed to feign being sick. This should have been easy—I'm an actor, right? The problem was three-fold—this was real life, I was nervous, and I don't lie very well. I had a little time to get into character, and I needed all the time I could get.

I lay down on the couch and started coughing when the doorbell rang. Mary opened the door and the doctor came in. He was ushered to the couch where I was and asked me what was wrong. I simply said, "I don't feel well." He narrowed his eyes and asked, "What is this all about? You're not sick." Holy shit—he saw right through my act! He didn't even take my temperature or put a stethoscope to my heart. I had no choice but to come clean to him. So all four of us told him what the issue was, along with our plan. The doctor was very sympathetic. He already had an opinion about American companies and how they work their employees. My story further solidified his opinion. He sat down and began to ponder what illness I could have that would keep me off an airplane for two days. The solution was a sinus infection. He wrote the doctor's note in French and gave me a prescription. He said I also needed to get the prescription filled and turn the receipt in to the company so that all bases were covered. I liked that doctor and owe him a debt of gratitude.

The next task was to call in sick—which I did on the day I was due to return to work. I made the long-distance call to my boss and told him I had a sinus infection and couldn't fly. He said okay, to take care of myself, and that he would see me when I returned. The only other thing left to do was to get the prescription filled, which I did. The last two days in Paris were wonderful, as would be expected, since my problem had been solved.

Upon my arrival at the office—fresh from three weeks in Europe—I went to my desk and began to work. An hour or so later, my boss came over to my cubicle and asked how the trip had gone and if I was feeling better. I told him, "The trip went well, and I am feeling much better. Thank you." He then laid the bombshell on me, or so he thought. He told me that under the circumstances of my illness, I would need to get a doctor's note to prove that I had been sick. He asked if I thought I could get one. I protested, spouting company policy. He just repeated his request in a sympathetic tone. Why hadn't he told me that I needed a doctor's note when I called him from Paris? It smelled like a trap to me, and I would have been caught if it had not been for the help and advice of people who were far older and smarter than me. I had no choice but to pull the doctor's note out of my purse and hand it to him, saying, "Yes, I think I can get a doctor's note. Here it is." I've never seen a man turn red in the face so quickly. He stared at the note and then glared at me. I glared back. There was nothing he could do. He couldn't read the note because it was in French, but he knew what it was. He just walked away from my cubicle and didn't say another word. I also went ahead and turned in the receipts for the prescriptions. I did get the prescriptions filled—I just didn't take them. Checkmate!

Given the context, it's easy to see why Bill didn't want to help me become an agent for this company. He wasn't pleased that I had gone through such trauma trying to get two days off work from them.

It was an intense year of training, but I loved it and did exceedingly well. I passed all the tests, met with other agents in the field, and was liked by management at the regional offices in Arizona, which was where all of the training took place. My performance in Salt Lake City was an entirely different matter. One of the requirements for becoming an agent was that the candidate had to keep up with their work on their current job. This proved to be quite a challenge. We would get three new claims a day and were required to contact the people involved within a 24-hour period. This was impossible, given that I was in Arizona one week out of every month. On top of this, I had a new boss who was hardnosed about it. She didn't allow any of the unit members to help me. I went to her to ask why she wouldn't allow me to have help. There were two other claims adjusters in the agency program with me from Salt Lake City whose units were pitching in to help. Why was I not getting the same type of help? My boss answered that they had different management and were in a different office. What they did was their business. It was as though she was trying to sabotage me—keep me from becoming an agent. Each month after spending a week away from the office, I found myself getting more and more behind at work. Plus, there were angry clients who had not been contacted. The unit had no choice but to take care of angry phone calls while I was away, but that was as far as they could go. The writing was on the wall, but I thought I could weather the storm. At the beginning of 1998 I was written up for not doing my job properly. I was also close to the end of the agency training program.

Around the same time I was written up, the home visit was to take place. I didn't know if Bill would allow the person to come to the house, but he said okay. On the day she was scheduled to come, she got lost on the west side of the city. She said that she thought I lived over there—even though she had my address. When she got there, she was in awe of my house. "It's so beautiful," she said. We were in the middle of remodeling the kitchen, and it didn't look beautiful to me.

The visit went well. She wanted to meet Bill, but he conveniently left the house before her arrival. He didn't want to have anything to do with this process. The only other person in the house was Bill's secretary. After the home visit, the company would let me know if I had been approved to become an agent. My boss threw a monkey wrench in my efforts by withdrawing her recommendation for me to be in the agency program. That was that—I received a rejection letter and, of course, another write-up. It was clear that my boss was trying to have me fired. I had caught up on my work, but that didn't matter. Something can always be found wrong with a file, no matter how diligent the person has been at logging activity.

Two weeks later, I was driving to work with a fellow claims adjuster. I had been picking him up in the mornings because his car was in the shop and his house was on my route to work. A black bird hit my windshield. We both looked at each other. I knew without having any symbology training what it meant. I was going to be fired soon.

At the end of that day, I was fired. Because I knew it was coming, I had already cleared out my desk and only had things on top that made it look like I hadn't emptied the drawers. So when my boss brought a box over for me to put my things in, I didn't have much to take. I didn't want to be humiliated anymore. I wanted out as quickly as possible, though to this day I don't think my being fired was justified. In hindsight, it was a blessing that I was fired. I would have made a very good agent—however, that's not the direction my Soul wished me to go in. I didn't know that back then.

I went into a small depression after being fired. Frankly, I had an identity crisis. For so many years I had identified myself with what I did to make a living and who I was in a relationship with. Now I didn't know who I was without my job. The bubble of my life was bursting, and in that bubble was an entire lifetime of sorrow. I hadn't analyzed my life too deeply when I was first fired—I just knew that I was hurt emotionally and mentally. I had put my hope in a company and had been rejected. Additionally, since moving to Salt Lake City I had carried the weight of being an ambassador for my race. I had failed at that, too. As a Black person, I had always been taught that I had to do better than what was expected of me to be considered even remotely equal to a white person. So now what did this say about me?

For the first three months after being fired, my days didn't boast much variety. I'd get up, go for a walk in Sugarhouse Park, go to McDonald's for breakfast, head over to the bookstore, and hang out for a few hours looking for books to read. If I already had books, I would just go back to the house, sit on the couch, and read. The books I read were light and fluffy—nothing deep. I couldn't handle anything that required depth of thought. After either coming home from the bookstore or reading, I'd watch Oprah. She had begun to do Change Your Life Television. It was timely because I really needed to change my life. After Oprah I'd think about what was for dinner and go cook, eat, clean up the kitchen, watch the news and then a movie, go to bed, and do it all over again the next day.

As it turned out, my being fired was timely. Sometime around the end of June, Bill was diagnosed with throat cancer. There is no way the company would have given me the time off that I needed to care for him. We weren't married, and there was no provision for our situation. His diagnosis was a shock to both of us. He smoked three packs a day, and it had caught up with him. Once he got his diagnosis, he decided to quit smoking cold turkey—no patch, no nothing, just a will to live.

I started going to his doctor's appointments with him, and all of the sudden he changed the way he was treating me. He was actually kind. And he said he wanted to get married—interesting. He ended up having surgery, which turned out well—he didn't have a tracheotomy, and that was a blessing. His doctors ran a scope to his lungs to see if there was any cancer there, and he was clean. Because of this, radiation was recommended rather than chemotherapy.

At about the same time he was getting radiation treatments, I heard about extras being needed for the TV show *Promised Land*. The show was filmed in Salt Lake City, and they were always looking for new faces. I thought it might be a good idea for me to apply to be an extra. I hadn't done any acting in years and thought it would be a great way to become involved in something fun. So I sent them a snapshot of me, along with a bit of information about myself, and was hired. I was now an extra on a TV show! This made me happy.

Bill finished his radiation treatments and only needed to have regular X-rays of his lungs to make sure the cancer hadn't spread. Both of us were happy about this. Of course, getting married was off now, and so was his kindness. He went back to his old ways since he knew he wasn't dying.

I started spending my days on the TV set. The days were long—12 hours—but I loved it. One of the extras told me about another show that was being filmed there, *Touched by an Angel*. I managed to get on that show as an extra, too. I didn't work on *Promised Land* for long because it was cancelled, but I did like it. On the set of *Promised Land* one of the extras also told me about a healer in town. I'll talk more about her later.

I got to meet some the stars of *Touched by an Angel*, along with a few of the guest stars. I even worked as a body double a few times for some of the guest stars and on one occasion for Della Reese. Della had a regular body double, but the director wanted me to take on the role for one of the episodes.

I still read constantly. There was plenty of time for reading while waiting for a scene to be shot on the set. One of the books I picked up changed the direction of my reading material. It was *The Celestine Prophecy*. I had never read anything like it before. I began to voraciously read other spiritual books.

One evening I was sitting on the couch reading when Bill came into the living room, snatched the book out of my hand, and asked angrily, "What are you looking for in these books?" In that instant I knew what I was looking for. I told him, "I'm looking for me." I don't think that was the answer he was looking for. He gave the book back to me and walked out of the room. I had lost "me" somewhere, and I had to find myself again. I was Dorothy on the yellow-brick road looking for home, and I had to get there. I knew that home wasn't a place—it was within me—but I needed help accessing that part of me.

I was searching for clues about who I was within the pages of spiritual books. It was as though the Universe was directing me to book after book. I managed to get Bill to leave me alone with my books. I knew he liked to read but never had the patience to scour bookshelves for the right book—I had that patience. I also had an ulterior motive: distraction. If he was reading, he wouldn't be bothering me. It worked. He loved history, and I learned the types of books he preferred to read through trial and error. I'd buy four or five books for him, and the ones he didn't want to read I would return to the bookstore. Over a short period of time, I didn't have to return any books. Problem solved. I made sure he had at least three books on his bedside table at all times.

I began working with a healer for the first time in my life in 1999. I had read a bit about them in my books but had not encountered any. I guess the Universe felt it was time for me to progress to the next step on the path to finding me. I had met a Native American and a friend of his on the set of *Touched by an Angel*. We would talk about our lives and laugh about our faux pas. One day I saw them on the set of *Promised Land*, and during our conversation the Native gentleman told me about a healer he had been using. If anyone needed a healer, I did. So I took down her contact information and made an appointment. Gillian was kind over the phone. I liked her instantly. She didn't live that far away either, which was nice. Gillian had been trained through the Barbara Brennan School of Healing. I didn't know anything about Barbara Brennan; I just knew I needed help.

When I arrived at my appointment, Gillian asked me what I wanted to occur. I told her I wanted to be healed. She chuckled and told me, "You know, no one can be healed with one session." What she said next took me by surprise. She told me that I had to be very careful what I asked for because when I changed, my relationships would change—I would be a different person.

That first session was quite interesting. Gillian told me I had a solid wall up around me for protection. This was definitely true—I knew the wall was there. I wasn't letting anyone in to hurt me ever again. I laugh about it now, but back then it wasn't funny. I saw her energetically use a chisel and hammer to attempt to get through the barrier I had erected. She couldn't get through. There was a lack of trust. Consciously I wanted to trust her, but my subconscious wasn't cooperating. We talked about what had occurred and knew it would take time for me to trust her enough to let her in.

In the meantime, Gillian worked on the areas she could reach. I'm not the same type of healer, so I'm not knowledgeable concerning the intricacies of how it works. What I do know is that it *does* work. Gillian became the first member of my team—helping me to find me again. She and I started working together every six weeks, and over time I began to notice a shift within myself. Gillian and I became friends and are still friends. I still work with her on an as-needed basis.

In spring of 2000, Bill came to me and said he thought we should sell the house. My name wasn't on the title, so I wondered why he was asking me. My guard was always up with him. He said simply that he thought if he didn't move soon, he would never get the opportunity to live anywhere else, and he had always wanted to experience living in another state. I didn't want to move. The house had been remodeled, and I had allowed myself to become attached to the place. But I told him, "Fine, sell it." I also suggested to him that we sell it ourselves and put a high price on it. My thinking was that it wouldn't sell—it couldn't. He agreed.

One interesting aspect of deciding to sell the house was that we officially put it on the market on my birthday. Plus, because Bill was out of town, I was the person who placed the for-sale sign in the yard that day. I see it all in retrospect, but back then I didn't get the message I was being sent by the Universe. I was supposed to move. My time in Salt Lake City had come to an end. The Universe had a plan, and even my stubbornness wasn't going to stop it. Of course, I didn't know there was a plan. If I had, I wouldn't have fought so hard to do the opposite.

The house sold and for close to the asking price. Yikes! My plan hadn't worked. I remember standing in the doorway of the bedroom, looking up to the sky. I said to God, "Obviously you want me to move!" I wasn't happy but had no choice in the matter.

"Now what?" I wondered. This was late July or early August, and we had to be out of the house by Halloween. Interesting—we had moved into the house on Halloween 16 years earlier.

We had no clue where we would go. We started revisiting the places we had vacationed. Bill refused to relocate anywhere east of Colorado—so that eliminated most of the country. I liked parts of Arizona, Colorado, New Mexico, and of course Northern California. I loved San Francisco. It was my favorite big city in the U.S. The first place we visited was Monterey—this was my top choice. The problem was the cost of housing. It would take every penny Bill had to purchase a tiny house—so there went Monterey. It was the same with Sedona, Scottsdale, and Jackson Hole.

Leaf Nodes and Leaves

The leaf nodes and leaves gather the food from the sun,
which is sent back down through the stems to the
tuber to maintain its life. When we get to a certain
point in development, we must reach out to
gather our own energy. Like the leaves and
leaf nodes, we reach out to gather food,
energy, and knowledge to sustain
and bring life force back
to ourselves.

24

Dealing with Sudden Change

By September, we still hadn't found a place. Bill went in for his routine X-ray, which revealed spots on his lungs. Further tests revealed stage-four lung cancer. The throat cancer had metastasized to his lungs. The doctors told him to go home and get his affairs in order—he had maybe six months. This was a shock for both of us. My idea was to tell the people who were buying the house that it couldn't be sold, give them money for inconveniencing them, and stay in the house. There was no point in moving. We had a battle on our hands, and moving would take energy away from the fight. Bill refused. He was determined to move and to fight the cancer.

Both of us began to research cancer hospitals and clinics. The top two choices were in Sacramento and Houston. We went to both for Bill to be examined. MD Anderson in Houston could begin treating him much sooner than the hospital in Sacramento, plus it had some possible cancer trials. The doctor told both of us that Bill's cancer couldn't be cured; the only thing they could do was prolong his life by maybe a year.

Treatment was to commence in January of 2001. We would need to travel to Houston every three weeks for treatment. The doctor told us that she could give the formula to Bill's doctor in Salt Lake City to avoid the need to travel so much. But Bill refused, saying his doctor in Salt Lake City didn't believe anything could be done, and therefore he didn't trust him to administer the treatment. I'm confident that Bill's Salt Lake City doctor would have performed the treatment if we had asked, but Bill thought otherwise.

Now I had the added task of finding a rental house in Salt Lake City for us to move into. Because of the cancer diagnosis, there was no way we could spend the time needed to travel all over the place looking for a city to move to, not to mention finding a house in that city. I didn't have much time. Bill, being who he was, rejected every place that I thought would be comfortable and nice. Place after place, he told me no. I was getting desperate because October 31st was approaching.

It was about a week before we needed to be out when I found a place that Bill finally said yes to. It was a house in a gated community. We went through the credit check and were accepted as renters. It was my credit rating that procured the place for us. Bill didn't have any credit because he paid his bills in full as soon as they arrived in the mail. I had purchased my vehicle with credit and had credit cards that I paid on—not off. It was an eye opener how things worked— he was the one with the money, not me.

We moved in and began to prepare for the journey of going to Houston every three weeks. One of the issues we talked about was my rights to make decisions for him—I had none. We weren't married, and therefore if he ever became incapacitated or couldn't make his own decisions, the responsibility would fall to his son as next of kin. Bill and his son hadn't gotten along over the years, plus it was me who would be with Bill in Houston.

Another issue also came up because we weren't married: the money. Over the years Bill had done everything he could do to protect his money from me. He never wanted me to be able to take a penny from him. And frankly, I didn't want any of his money. It was my opinion that he earned it—it was his, not mine. I had what I needed and could take care of myself. With an education I would always be able to work to support myself.

So the money talk commenced. He asked what I wanted, and I replied that I wanted nothing from him. He was concerned about inheritance taxes. This was the real reason he now wanted to marry me—protect the money to the end. I found it interesting that all the hard work he put into sheltering his money from me was for nothing. In the end it would, for the most part, come to me. His son told me later that it was combat pay. He had a point.

Bill and I decided to go to Vegas a couple of days before we needed to be in Houston to have the ceremony. Bill chose not to tell his family about this until it was over. I can only speculate his reasoning for this. It wasn't difficult having Christmas dinner with Mary and Glenn without telling them. I had been emotionally numb where Bill was concerned for years. I used only logic, or at least what logic I had at the time. This is how I earned the pet name Cold Bitch. Of course, I was neither cold nor a bitch, but that's how Bill saw me.

Another discussion we had turned out to be a trap—a way to control me from the grave. I didn't figure this out until I was released from the trap two years later. Bill knew that I had always wanted to have kids, so he said that he wanted to give me children. The only way this would work was if he froze his sperm. The chemotherapy would cause his sperm count to go way down. And it turned out his sperm count wasn't high to begin with, due to his excessive smoking. We would use in vitro fertilization. Time was of the essence with this. I was in my late 30s, and he was dying. I would begin taking shots about the time Bill began chemotherapy—crazy, I know. So at the beginning of January, we flew to Vegas, got married, flew to Houston for his first treatment, and shortly after I started giving myself hormone shots. When his family found out we had gotten married and I was going through in vitro, they were in shock. No one said anything to me about it, but they did give Bill an earful, some of which he shared with me. Mary was understandably hurt. I would have been hurt too if I were in her position.

The day I had the in vitro turned out to be the same day I had tickets to see His Holiness the Dalai Lama. He was in Salt Lake City giving a talk. I really wanted to see him but ended up giving my ticket to my hairdresser, Melanie, for her daughter. Melanie and I were planning to attend together, but now I had to be at the clinic. (With in vitro, you only have a small window of opportunity to implant fertilized eggs.)

I went to the clinic and had the eggs implanted. Bill was getting weaker with each chemo session. I was taking care of him plus going through my daily routine of shots. The in vitro didn't take. I wasn't pregnant. We talked about going through it again, but I had my hands full taking care of him and making all the arrangements for our trips to Houston. I would start making plans for the next trip to Houston while he was getting treatments—scheduling his next appointments, calling the airlines for the best prices, getting the hotel lined up. And at home, the only thing I didn't do was clean the house. I had refused to let go of the housekeeper when I lost my job. I couldn't do it all. Taking care of someone who is ill is a full-time job in itself. I said I would go through another session, but it would have to wait awhile.

The next thing Bill did was send a letter to the landlord telling him that he was dying and that if he didn't want his tenant to die in the house, he needed to let him out of the lease. I didn't know anything about this letter at first. Bill only showed me the letter when he received the reply from the landlord letting us out of the lease. This was in May or June of 2001. The letter gave us until September 30 to leave. I was furious. I could have bitch-slapped him on the spot. He had done this behind my back; and besides, why did he want to be let out of the lease? We had no place to go. We hadn't been able to look for other cities to live in, plus he was dying. Additionally, moving would take me away from my support system. I was also finally seeing progress as an actor, having had small roles in a couple of movies. And now this.

The only comment Bill made after I read the letter and glared at him was "I guess you will now get up off your ass and find us a place to move." These were his exact words. He had me backed into a corner. He had out-witted me. For some reason he wanted to move, but I wouldn't learn the reason until after his death. Bill taught me to be discerning about people's motives the hard way, through trial and error.

Bill had blamed me for us not having found a place to relocate to. He never ceased to amaze me by the way he thought. I didn't want to move, and he knew this. Now he was forcing the move. But I kept wondering, "Why? Doesn't he know he is going to die?" The doctors had been very clear about what could and couldn't be done to prolong his life. At that time, the tumors had shrunk due to the chemotherapy, but we knew that wouldn't last. They would grow again. Maybe Bill saw a window of opportunity to move and just wanted to get going to make it happen. As I said, I wouldn't be told the truth until after his death. (For the record, I hate that Spirit Guides sometimes have to give us the silent treatment when we are going through a test or working out a serious problem. I understand that if they helped it would be akin to giving us the answers to the test, but I still don't like it.)

So finding a place to move became a priority. Because the tumors shrank and Bill told the doctor we were looking for a place to move, she gave him the summer off. He wouldn't need to be back in Houston until the end of September. This gave us three months to find *the* city and buy a house. I needed a miracle.

We began by going back over the places we had visited the previous summer and narrowed the search to three states: Washington, Wyoming, and Arizona. Each state had towns that both of us liked. We took trips back to these places and ruled out Arizona and Wyoming. Washington would be the state. Now all we had to do was find the city or town. I liked Seattle, Whidbey Island, and Bellingham. Bellingham was my first choice because of its proximity to Vancouver, Canada. Vancouver was a city both of us loved, and I felt I might be able to get acting jobs there. I didn't mention the latter reason to Bill. I had a hunch about why he wanted to move me away from Salt Lake City, but I wasn't sure, so I kept my mouth shut.

We went to realtors on Whidbey Island first. Bill didn't want to be in Seattle, so that was out. I liked Whidbey but was concerned about being so far away from the city. This, of course, was ideal for Bill; he didn't want to be anywhere near the city. We looked at houses there and found several that we liked. We then went to Bellingham and got listings of homes for sale in the area. We spent considerable time driving by homes.

One day we were having a meal in a restaurant in Bellingham. The person sitting next to us overheard our conversation about the area. We were talking about the rain and whether we could handle it. Neither of us had lived anyplace where it rained so much. The gentleman sitting next to us leaned over and said, "You should look at Sequim. It doesn't rain as much there. It's in the rain shadow." He went on to say that airline pilots used it sometimes when flying into Seattle because the weather was nicer and they could see clearer. I had never heard of the place, but both Bill and I thought it would be worth an exploratory trip.

The next morning, we set out for Sequim, Washington. I wasn't impressed with the town. For one thing, it was way too small. The population was a little over 5,000, and downtown was one street. It was a cute downtown, but still—too small for my taste. There were, I think, two stoplights in the town. The gentleman who recommended we take a look at Sequim was, however, correct about the weather. The sky was clear. We went to one of the local realtors to get a few listings to see. They put us on the mailing list. This meant we would get information about listings in our price range as they were put on the market. I was hoping we would find something in Bellingham.

We went back to Salt Lake City and began actively searching the online listings for houses in the Bellingham area. I did not want to move to Sequim. It was just too isolated for me—too far away from the city. Plus, it was a retirement community, and I wasn't retired. Bill had sold his business and was retired, but he wouldn't be there—I would. I needed to have access to what cities offer— theater, shopping, restaurant variety, etc. And I just knew I was a city girl. I like the vibe of city life.

Alas, in August Bill decided we should take a second look at Sequim. I wasn't pleased, but by that time I was worn out and knew I wouldn't win a fight about it anyway. We went back to Sequim. This time the realtor took us to see four houses that were in our price range. Bill was determined to move to Sequim, though I didn't know why. At that point, I didn't have any more fight in me—I had lost. Bill was dictating where we lived. My attitude shifted to "Okay, when he dies, I'll just sell the place and move someplace else."

What I didn't realize at the time was that a war was raging between Bill and me. It was between his continued need to control, even after his death, and my desire for freedom. I wouldn't learn of this war until he died. It was like a war between dark and light, and so far, dark was winning. I had always prayed, but during my years with Bill my prayers intensified. I knew that I was being watched over, but I felt I was about to drown. My head was barely above the water. I had to surrender any control I thought I had to The Divine to take care of me, because I couldn't take care of myself anymore.

We decided to purchase one of the four houses in Sequim. It was a nice house, but it really wasn't me. I balked at various things in the house—fixtures, countertops, molding, lighting. I kept comparing this house to the remodeled Salt Lake City house.

There were two floors: the main floor and a daylight basement. On the main floor was the master bedroom suite, office, living room, kitchen with eating area, laundry room, garage, and two and a half bathrooms. The garage also had a bathroom. The downstairs had two guest bedrooms, a den with a wood-burning stove, a large storage area, and a full bathroom. There was a wraparound wood deck on the back of both floors. The house was about 3,400 square feet and was on a little more than an acre.

Bill fell in love with the house as soon as he walked through the front door. He was enamored with the view out the living room window. There was a wall-to-wall, floor-to-ceiling window that looked out onto wide views of the backyard with a dairy farm in the distance and the Juan de Fuca Strait, which leads in and out of Seattle, beyond it. He was in heaven. I liked seeing the water too, but I didn't want it to sidetrack us from whether or not the house was right. Bill's response to my complaints about the house was "Who the hell do you think you are, a fucking queen?" He said this in front of the realtor. The realtor tried to appease me by saying the things that bothered me could be changed but that the bones of the house were solid. I wasn't going to win, and even though Bill was being a dick, I still had compassion for the fact that he was dying. I could move after he died.

I conceded and we bought the house. Our closing date would be September 14, 2001. We flew back to Salt Lake City and began planning for the move to Sequim, Washington. The plan was for me to drive back to Sequim in my car to drop it off, pick up the keys to the house, and fly back to Salt Lake City to help Bill drive the other car up. His strength was back, but he tired easier. I was supposed to take off on September 11, 2001. Considering the historic event that occurred in the U.S. on that date, the decision for me to take off on a road trip alone that day was in hindsight an omen. At least I think it was.

25

Move to Sequim and Death

I had planned on leaving Salt Lake City around 8:00 a.m.; since my car was already packed, I only needed to dress, eat, and take off. When I went into the kitchen that morning, Bill was watching TV. He always had it on in the morning to catch the news. I glanced at the TV and thought the scene was a movie trailer. Bill told me what was happening, and in one moment my world shifted. I couldn't believe what my eyes were showing me, and at the same time I knew it was real. But I didn't have time to process what I was seeing—I had to get going.

I drove away from Salt Lake City that day, on my own, with a heavy heart. It took me two days to get to Sequim, and I have never felt more connected to my fellow Americans than during that time. Everywhere I stopped, the World Trade Center attack was all people talked about. I entered into conversation with people in restaurants and gas stations. There was a kinship between us. There was no differentiation of race, sex, or anything that had a few hours earlier separated us. We were all in the same boat.

When I made it to Sequim, the people who had sold us the house wanted to meet me and show me around the place. I was fine with this. They also wanted to introduce me to the next-door neighbors, Marilyn and Wayne. They took me to the neighbors' house and we sat around, talked, and had coffee. I liked Marilyn and Wayne. They were an older couple, in their 70s. They had lived in Switzerland for a time due to Wayne's work. He was a scientist for Dupont and had been transferred many times over the years. Marilyn had been a stay-at-home mom but had worked to put Wayne through college.

The previous owners of the house wanted to get going. They were moving back to Alaska to be near their son and grandson. They wanted to give me the keys a day early, which they did. I took possession of the house on the 13th, which was a good thing. It gave me plenty of time to decide where I wanted the movers to put the furniture. There was no way I would be able to move big pieces of furniture on my own, and Bill didn't have the strength to help. So I took a piece of paper and made notes to guide the movers.

The next day, I parked my car in the garage and took the shuttle to the Sea-Tac Airport. I wasn't sure I would be able to fly out on the 14th, because all flights had been grounded since the 11th. Luckily for me, the day I needed to fly out was the first day flights were allowed to depart. I arrived at the airport to organized chaos. The lines were unbelievable, but no one was upset or yelling. I felt for the airport and airline employees. They were trying to get everyone where they needed to be. Since I was scheduled on a flight that left that day, I was able to board my scheduled flight back to Salt Lake City.

I had gone back to Salt Lake City to help Bill drive the SUV. The movers came and picked up the furniture, and we took off for Sequim. Bill was driving. He refused to let me relieve him. I didn't understand this. If he intended to drive the whole way himself, why had I come back to help him? I could have either stayed in Sequim or we could have driven up together, each of us driving a car.

Two days after we arrived in Sequim, we got on a plane for Houston. Bill had an appointment with his doctor and to have his lungs scanned. The doctor informed us that the tumors were growing again, so Bill went through another treatment on that visit. The doctor didn't think further treatment would help, but she wanted to try anyway, as did we. The treatments over time were wearing on Bill. Each one made him weaker, and to receive chemotherapy, the patient has to be at a certain level of health. The doctor would see us one more time and then release Bill to go home. There was nothing more that could be done. I remember watching tears running down her face as she released Bill. She was deeply affected. I really liked her. She had tremendous compassion for her patients.

Having Bill be released to go home and prepare for death was a blow to every part of my being. I wanted to be free, but I didn't want him to die. It was a very difficult pill to swallow. I can only imagine what was going through his head. We were at the end of the road.

Christmas that year was pretty subdued. I still went through the motions—putting up a tree and what not. Neither of us knew anyone in Sequim, and I didn't feel as though I belonged there.

The neighbors had tried to be nice. On the day we moved in, one of them came over to say hello. Her name was Virginia, and she lived next door to the east of us. I liked Virginia right away—she had a compassionate heart. However, we wouldn't be able to get to know each other until Bill died. This was partly because I didn't have a lot of extra time, but mostly it was because I never knew what harmful thing Bill would say.

I guess at this point in Bill's life he didn't have the energy to keep up the pretense of being nice to people who didn't know him. In our new home, he wasn't just rude to me, and I didn't want to give him the opportunity to be rude to the neighbors. I knew that one day he would say something to one of them and we would be shunned. One day I was outside having a conversation with another couple of new neighbors. They were out for a walk and saw me in the yard, so they stopped to say hello. We hadn't met yet. While we were talking, Bill banged on the window by the front door, yelling that he was late for the doctor and I was "outside squawking." The neighbors heard this and promptly left. I went into the house and asked him why he had done this—he still had two hours before his appointment. His response? "Oh—I forgot." No apology, no nothing. Thus I knew not to give him any opportunities to be rude to the neighbors or to me in front of them.

The street had six houses and was narrow and unpaved. It was a dead-end street that accessed a walking trail leading to a stream. Most people driving on the main road wouldn't see the street unless they were looking for it. I unintentionally passed it myself on numerous occasions in the early years of living there.

From the house you could hear the animals in the Olympic Game Farm and see beautiful birds flying up close. I saw my first eagle in the wild. That was a sight to see. There were eagles, hawks, ravens, doves, and other birds. The four-legged animals were there too—coyotes, bobcats, and a few others. None of them were in captivity. There were also cows that belonged to the dairy that wasn't far away. All of the creatures were a blessing. The back of the house faced north, as did most of the rooms in the house, so we had a clear view of nature for miles—as far as the eye could see.

As it turned out, my living in Sequim was one of the biggest blessings of my life. I just didn't know it for a while. I had been put in a safe, beautiful environment with neighbors who were kind. And at 40, I was the youngest person in the neighborhood. The average age when I lived there had to have been at least 60. The retired people who lived there were more active than a lot of much-younger people. They hiked, ran, fished, swam, volunteered, golfed, traveled . . . any day of the week. Because of this new environment, I had the opportunity to do deep psychological work. I used my time there to heal.

In January 2002, right after the holidays were over, Bill said we should try in vitro again. I was fine with this, because I wasn't getting any younger. I would be 41 that summer and felt this would be my last opportunity to have a child. Even though I didn't want to raise a child on my own, at least he or she would have a name. So I went through the procedure again, this time in Seattle, and it was successful. It would be three months before we could be confident that it was viable, but the fertilization was a success. Bill was steadily declining in strength and was sleeping much of the time. I spent my time taking care of his needs and the house and reading spiritual books. It was a form of isolation that I had not felt before. I was all alone, with very little emotional support.

What little support I got came from my friends elsewhere. I'd occasionally get to talk with Gwen in Memphis or Wanda in Chicago. I wouldn't talk to them from the house, because Bill would be able to hear the conversations. So I'd sometimes call one of them on my visits to the grocery store. Back then cell phones weren't commonplace, so I'd use a phone booth. I couldn't see the big picture of the direction my life was taking, nor could I see what would happen next. I had to stay present in each moment.

Around the middle of May, Bill ended up in the hospital due to complications from the cancer. It was actually good that he was in the hospital, because I needed to go to Seattle for a doctor's appointment and wouldn't have felt comfortable leaving him at home alone. It was during his hospital stay that the doctor approached me about hospice. I had known about hospice but wasn't ready to talk with Bill about it, nor was I previously at the point where I felt the service was needed. So far, I had managed on my own to care for him. But, at that point, I had to admit I needed help. The bigger issue for me was "giving up." To put Bill in hospice meant I was giving up—that he was really going to die. I didn't want him to die. Yes, he acted like a complete ass, even with the cancer—but I also knew he was scared. He was vulnerable and had no control over his life at that point.

As Bill got sicker, his verbal attacks intensified. Once, he told me he wished he hadn't married me. I ignored the comment, just like I ignored most of his outbursts. The comment did hurt, though. It cut me to my core; but I wasn't going to let him see that. Sometimes we would sit and talk about death. He would ask me where I thought he would go. He said he knew there was something out there but that he didn't believe in God. I had started watching *Crossing Over with John Edward*. Bill would watch with me. I used the show as a conversation starter about the afterlife. It was never my intention to coach him on death. I had my beliefs about the subject because of my experiences with the other side, but I didn't want him to be afraid and I told him what I knew for sure.

Before the hospital visit in mid-May, we had visited a couple of the local cemeteries. This was something Bill wanted to do. He wanted to walk through them, reading headstones and I guess getting a feel for the place. I've never been fond of cemeteries and was glad to leave when he was ready. Going to the cemeteries helped him decide to be cremated. Actually, I think the real reason he wanted to be cremated was the cost. He never saw the need to spend thousands of dollars on funeral expenses. I agreed with him about this. He also didn't want any type of funeral. He wanted his ashes taken back home to Sage, Wyoming, and spread on the land.

Everything shifted when hospice got involved. A hospital bed was brought in and set up in the living room, nurses began visiting daily, and someone even came to bathe him. I would have done this, but he wouldn't allow it. Until hospice, he would take showers on his own. It would take him a long time, but he insisted on bathing himself. With hospice, I still was the primary caregiver, but I wasn't alone anymore. When I needed to go to the store, there was someone to sit with Bill until I returned. Bud was the hospice volunteer who would come sit with Bill. In hindsight I should have called hospice earlier, but I wasn't ready.

Bill's pain was being managed with morphine patches, and one of the side effects for him was hallucinations. Thank goodness he couldn't walk very far. The thought crossed my mind that if I left him alone for any reason, I might come home and find him walking in the street naked. He also wanted to kill himself. He told me that if he could get to his gun, he would blow his brains out. He hated the position he was in, and I didn't blame him. However, I was glad he couldn't get to his gun.

The hospital bed had been set up in the living room at both our request. Bill could look out the large window onto the landscape that he fell in love with. He could also see the ships going past on the strait, headed into or out of Seattle. He wouldn't be isolated in the bedroom. I started sleeping on the couch so that I could hear him if he needed anything during the night. I became a light sleeper.

One day, about two weeks after hospice was called in, Bill decided he wanted to go to the bathroom. I guess he was tired of staying in bed to use it. He wanted to walk there himself. He got himself to the bathroom but couldn't get back to the bed. All of his energy had been spent. I tried picking him up from the toilet, but he was dead weight. I had no choice but to call Alf, one of the neighbors. He and Virginia came over, and Alf got Bill back into bed. I put his oxygen back on. He was out of it, unconscious. He had been off the oxygen for a while. When he regained consciousness, he asked me, "What the fuck did you bring me back for?" I didn't know he had been gone or going. He also told me to inform his sister Iris that he didn't see any damn light. I chuckled at this. Not that I don't believe in the light, but I was amused that he didn't see it. "Maybe he wasn't going to the light," I thought.

Three days after this incident, I had a doctor's appointment in Seattle. I called Bud to come sit with Bill, plus Bill called his brother and asked him to come over from eastern Washington—which he did. After the bathroom episode, both of us knew it wouldn't be long, and Bill wanted to see his brother. He also wanted to see his son, who was on his way up from Salt Lake City. I had to leave early that morning, so Bud sat with Bill until his brother arrived. His son was due to arrive later that day. I went to the doctor and got a clean bill of health. The pregnancy was at three months and considered safe. There would be no need for me to go back to Seattle for checkups. I could transition to seeing a doctor in Sequim or Port Angeles. I was thrilled about this. At least I would have something I wanted.

When I got home, Bill's brother had come and gone. I never got to see him. He left when Bill's son arrived. He was at the store, and Bill was alone watching something on TV. I told him what the doctor said, and he was pleased about this. At about this time his son came back from the store. This was a little after 3:00 p.m. The three of us didn't really talk much. There wasn't much to say. We just watched TV. One of my favorite shows came on at 4:00 p.m.: *Hart to Hart.* I loved the lighthearted crime-fighting husband-and-wife team. As the show was ending, I noticed the rate of Bill's breath change. I told his son that I thought this was it—that he was going. Both of us went to his bed and watched him take his last breath. He was gone.

I called hospice, and they sent one of the male nurses over to take care of his body. Because I used hospice there was no need for me to do anything else. They called the funeral home to come pick him up and had the death certificate signed by the doctor. I was so grateful to have the hospice team helping me. It made things much easier for me.

I remember watching the nurse bathe Bill's body, and in particular the fact that there was no life force. I had never seen a dead person being bathed. I was fascinated that just an hour earlier he could move his own arms and legs—and now it was a shell. It had no use.

After the funeral home took him away, I called Mary to let her know, and she contacted everyone else. Bill's son called his mother, Bill's ex-wife. She wanted to talk with me, and at first I didn't know why. We had never spoken. She was very kind and offered her condolence. She made a comment that endeared me to her. She said she understood what I had gone through over the years living with him, because she had lived with him for seven years. That was all she needed to say—she had validated my experience.

His son stayed with me for a couple of days then went back to Salt Lake City. He was a wreck, which was understandable. I was just numb. After he left, I was all alone. The house was so quiet. This was the first time in my life that I had lived alone, and I was extremely uncomfortable. I began to leave the lights on at night. My fear of seeing people who had crossed over was never that far away, and now it was in my face. Someone had now died in the house I was living in. My childhood memory of sleeping in Uncle Hayward's bed after his death came back.

I wasn't sleeping much, and during the day I began to lie in bed and watch reruns of *Law and Order*—all day. I stopped cooking and ate meals out. I'd get up in the morning, go to breakfast, come home, and go back to bed. Then in the evening I would go to a restaurant for dinner, come home, and watch TV in bed until I fell asleep. There was no one knocking at the door, and the phone didn't ring much. It was the most alone I've felt in my life. And I was pregnant. I cried a ton too, thankful no one could hear me. I cried so much one day that I had to change the sheets. I didn't know a body could create so many tears.

I did, however, do something constructive a few days after Bill died. I had clipped an ad out of the newspaper a few months earlier for a feng shui practitioner and put it in the drawer of my bedside table. I knew that I wanted to rearrange the house after Bill died, and I thought someone with expertise in furniture placement would help. So I called the number and spoke to Jan, the owner. We talked for a while and decided on the best time for her to come over. I had just talked to someone who would become one of my dearest friends.

Jan and her husband, Red, came over to feng shui the house. I had no idea what was involved. I thought it was just about furniture placement, but I was totally wrong. It involved checking ley lines for energy patterns, blessing the house, clearing old energy out, and resetting the energy pattern to me. All of this was done before Jan started talking with me about colors and the meaning of each part of the house based on the Chinese bagua. I walked with her through the house with pen and pad, taking notes on what I needed to do for each area. My plan was to have the interior house painted and everything together before the birth of my son. Yes, I was having a boy, and I had picked his name. It would be William Austin. I had always loved the name Austin and gave him his father's first name—William. Bill didn't like the name I chose but didn't interfere.

I was still depressed, but I had stayed in bed long enough; it was time to get something done. I went to one of the local furniture stores and began my search for the items Jan said I needed. There was an interior designer available at the store, and she agreed to help me. I wanted a new bedroom set. One of the things I learned from Jan was that if you have slept in a bed with someone and you break up or they die, you should change the mattress. This is because their energy is in the mattress. Well, I was going further with this: I wanted a bed that was mine, not ours. The designer was wonderful. She had a great eye for color and a style I liked. She also had the contacts I needed for furniture movers, a painter, and other services. I had planned on turning the office, which was next to the bedroom, into a nursery and would need help moving the office furniture, too. I ordered a new bedroom set and hired the painter. He would paint the upstairs while I was in Utah and Wyoming for Bill's services.

I flew to Salt Lake City and drove to Sage to meet Bill's family at the homestead. His youngest brother had called me a few days earlier to say it would be hot and asked if I minded him going ahead with spreading the ashes before I got there. Bill wanted the ashes spread on top of a hill that had to be climbed. I gave my consent. In hindsight, this was a mistake on my part. I should have told him to wait until I got there. It turned out Bill's son wasn't there either. So his brother went up the hill alone and spread the ashes. None of the other family members went up either.

It was the quickest service I had ever participated in. I think Mary said a few words about her brother; a prayer was said; and that was it. We piled into our cars and went to Kemmerer for lunch. It was over. I went back to Salt Lake City and stayed for a few days, seeing friends and having a session with Gillian, my healer, before flying back to Washington.

Something interesting occurred during this session. While I was with Gillian, lying on the table, through my mind's eye I saw Bill being brought into the session by a Guide. He had been curious about what I was up to, and the Guide thought it was a good idea for him to witness the session. They didn't stay long.

I called Bill's brother a couple of times, and he never answered the phone nor called me back. I guess he didn't want anything to do with me after his brother died. I stayed in touch with Mary, Iris, and Bill's son. He and I are still friends and talk periodically. Iris called me to get information about Austin. She was the genealogist in the family.

During the last couple of years of Bill's life, I got to know Iris better. And I liked her. She was firm in her Mormon beliefs and compassionate. She didn't dislike me; she just didn't approve of Bill and me living together without being married. Bill had been extremely cruel to her over the years, which meant she didn't come around much, which in turn meant I only had his opinion of her to go on. She died a few years after Bill.

Mary stopped calling after Iris died. I sent flowers to the funeral home for Iris, and that must have upset her. I don't think anyone outside of the family knew that I was an O'Neill. This is only speculation on my part though. I have no idea what the real reason for not talking to me was, and I didn't reach out to her to find out. Except for Bill's son, my relationship with Bill's family was over.

26

Feeling Extreme Emotional Pain

After Bill's service and my visit with friends, I flew back to Washington and continued to decorate the house. My intention was to stay there for a year. I was a city girl and didn't think a town with just over 5,000 people would work for me. However, I knew enough about grief to not make any big decisions for at least a year. Plus, there was the birth of Austin to look forward to.

At that point, I hadn't concentrated on being pregnant. It was just a fact—meaning I hadn't bonded with the child. I hadn't had time. What I needed was a vacation. So I called my best friend, Gwen in Memphis. I told her that I wanted to go someplace; I didn't care where. I just needed to get away. We decided to go to the Bahamas. The trip was set for July. Then the unthinkable happened—her mother died. I had already planned to be in Memphis, since Gwen, Omari, and I were flying to the Bahamas from there. I was glad to be able to pay my last respects to her mother. She had been very kind to me over the years, making my dress for the pageant, letting me stay at her home when I came to town, and offering advice when I needed it.

A week after the funeral, Gwen, Omari, and I boarded a plane for the Bahamas. We spent a week there. We didn't do much, but it was fine just to be away. Once the trip was over, we went back to Memphis. I hung out for another week, helping Gwen go through her mother's things, and then I flew back to Seattle and took the shuttle to Sequim.

When I got back to Sequim, Bud's partner, Jane, asked me if I would go to Arizona with her. Bud had called me right after he heard about Bill's death and invited me to lunch at his home. He was retired, and Jane owned a bed-and-breakfast but was trying to sell it. Jane was gracious and mentioned that she liked to travel but didn't get to go many places because she didn't like traveling alone. She had another friend who would go with her but was sometimes unavailable, and Bud wasn't a big traveler. She asked me if I liked to travel and I said, "Yes, I love exploring new places." So when Jane called to ask me to accompany her to Arizona in August, I said yes. Of course, I had been to Arizona many times with Bill, but I thought it would be nice to go back with someone new.

People often say, "You never know someone until you live with them." Well, there's another saying that I think deserves more use: "You never know someone until you travel with them." I assumed Jane was well traveled and therefore comfortable with putting the logistics of the trip together. This turned out not to be the case. The trip, as it turned out, was a huge lesson for me. Jane was easy to get along with; she just wasn't organized and didn't want to drive the rental car, so I drove. We flew into Las Vegas, picked up the car, and headed to Sedona.

I had been to Sedona a few times and was familiar with the town. It was nice to get back to the red rocks. I loved hiking in the hills and visiting the various vortexes. It was around the 8th or 9th of August, and we planned to fly back on the 13th.

The first place I wanted to visit was The Church of the Red Rocks. I wasn't religious, but at the same time each visit to the church touched my soul in a palpable way. I loved the feeling of walking through the doors and seeing the huge windows at the front of the church with the red-rock vista beyond. On the day of our visit, the song playing as I walked through the door was "Ave Maria." It couldn't get any better than that.

Jane and I went in and walked around before finding a seat. We didn't sit together because each of us—or maybe it was just me—wanted privacy to pray and meditate. This was where I bonded with Austin. I could finally feel his Being. At the church I relaxed and began to feel again. It was a beautiful experience.

Jane and I visited other vortexes during the trip, ate good food, and walked around the town. We didn't venture into Phoenix or Scottsdale as Bill and I had on trips to the area.

After a few days, Jane and I headed back to Vegas to catch our flight the next morning. We had booked a room at an airport hotel. When we arrived at the hotel that evening, we got a bite to eat, repacked our luggage, and went to bed.

During the night, I woke up feeling wet, so I went to the bathroom. There was blood—I knew I needed to get to a hospital. I've never been a person to panic in crisis, and I didn't panic then. I woke Jane up and told her what was happening and that I was going to the hospital. She asked me if I wanted her to go with me. I said no. In my opinion—and this is only my opinion—when you tell someone that you are going to drive yourself to the hospital because you are pregnant and bleeding and they ask, "Do you want me to go with you?"—they don't really want to help.

I got dressed and drove myself. I left the hotel without knowing where the hospital was. I didn't think to ask the desk clerk at the hotel, so I stopped at a convenience store. I got directions and made my way to the nearest hospital. The hospital had a neonatal unit. I would later learn that not all hospitals are equipped to handle emergencies such as mine. I knew I was in trouble.

I was rushed into a room and put on a table. One of Austin's feet was slipping through my cervix. I was placed on an incline with the hope of reversing the situation. Jane came to the hospital that morning to see me. She didn't know the full extent of my situation until the nurse informed her. I could see that she was nervous and didn't know what to do. She told me she needed to get back to Sequim for a sailing trip she and Bud had planned. I also knew that if she stayed, I wouldn't be able to count on her. So I told her to go and that I would be okay. I gave her the keys to the rental car and explained to her how to return it at the airport. She went back to the hotel, took my luggage to the front desk to be held until I could collect it, and left for the flight back to Seattle.

I lay there on an incline in a kind of dazed existence. I never asked how this could be happening. It just was. Eventually, I was moved into a private room. Two female doctors who specialized in premature births came in to talk with me. They said there was no chance for Austin to survive. I was only five and a half months along, which wasn't enough for any hope of survival. I thought they were cold and unfeeling. This probably wasn't the case—however, in my state of mind and situation, I didn't feel any compassion from either of them. They sat in chairs away from the bed with their legs crossed, giving me the facts.

I heard the doctors but dismissed everything they said. I didn't want to give up. I am not a quitter. I called Gwen in Memphis to let her know the situation. She couldn't talk because she was headed someplace. I remember calling someone else, but I don't remember who that person was nor what was said. I spent that night on an incline, in bed—going over and over the situation and asking for guidance on what to do. I hoped that by the morning there would be a change for the better. There wasn't.

The next morning another doctor came to visit me. I have no idea what happened to the two other women. This doctor was one of the kindest men I have ever encountered. His approached my situation with compassion, which helped me relax. We talked, and I made the decision to release Austin. For me, that is what I was doing. The physical process was clinical, but the emotional process was quite another thing. I didn't cry or feel sorry for myself. I just surrendered.

When it was over, the nurse took Austin away, cleaned him up, and brought him back to me so that I could say goodbye. He was a cute little boy all dressed in blue. I held him for a while. The doctor came in and sat with me while I held Austin. We chatted a bit, and he stayed for a while.

The nurse came in and took Austin, the doctor left, and I was faced with making plans to get home. The hospital wanted to release me, but there was no one to release me to. So I had to stay for another night. I needed to be able to care for myself. The extra day gave me a chance to begin healing physically. I spent the afternoon changing my flight and making shuttle reservations to get back to Sequim from Sea-Tac. This was August 14th. The next morning, I was well enough to be released on my own. I took a taxi to the hotel, picked up my luggage, and headed to the airport for my flight. At the airport, I called Bill's son to let him know what had happened and then flew home.

I have never felt so empty and alone as I did going through the door of that house. I had been through tremendous pain before, but this was different. It was akin to being out in a desert naked, without water or directions to find your way back to civilization. I didn't know how I would survive this loss. I knew how to keep putting one foot in front of the other—to keep going. I had learned to do this as a kid, and that was all I could do. I was at my rock bottom.

Jane called a couple of times to see how I was doing. I just said I was fine and not much else. I didn't ask what she thought about my situation. I just knew that she had left me alone to go sailing, and that wasn't how a true friend behaved. True, I was not giving her the benefit of the doubt, but I felt I had a right to judge her. I wouldn't leave a stranger in the situation she left me in. It took me years to forgive her for this.

I saw Jane a couple of times over the years when I was out in the community. I was always cordial to her but kept my distance. (Back then, I was afraid of confronting others. That fear is gone today, but it posed a huge problem for me in the past.) Eventually, I came to terms with her actions and realized she wasn't capable of being there for me if I was in trouble. For me, this meant we could never be friends. In my opinion, friends aren't there just to have fun with—

they are also there to support you through hard times. Anyone who doesn't do this for me isn't a friend—they are an acquaintance. I had to learn this the hard way, but I learned it well.

Before I had gone to Sedona, Jan (the feng shui practitioner) had given me the name of her astrologer and said I should get a reading. I had no idea what an astrologer was or did. I only knew what I had read in the paper concerning my Sun Sign. For some reason it never dawned on me that people went any further by getting a full reading. I had nothing to lose, nor did I have any expectations, so I thought, "Why not?"

I called and made an appointment to get my first astrology reading. David and his wife, Laura, lived in Port Angeles, which is the next town west of Sequim. Laura was so nice and had a big smile when I arrived, which put me at ease. I was also happy that she was there. After all, I was going to a male stranger's home. Having another woman there made me feel more comfortable. Laura didn't sit in on the reading, but she was in the house.

David came out and greeted me. He had piercing eyes that were also kind. We chatted for a few minutes to get acquainted, and then he took me to his office for the reading. To say that I was blown away by the reading doesn't do it justice. The man described my life experiences in a way that was shockingly accurate. I couldn't understand how he could know so much about me from looking at a piece of paper with funny-looking glyphs. I also knew that there was no way he could have gotten the information from someone else, because no one knew my life story—not even Jan. Nothing was written about me on the web because I had no profile. I barely had an email address. In any event, David knew more about me than he should have, which caused me to trust what he was saying to me. He even explained what was going on with me at the time. It had to do with a planet that I hadn't heard of, Pluto, opposing my Sun. He explained how this might manifest in my life and what its purpose was. At the end of the reading he gave me one of his books on the various forms of divination and loaned me a set of cassette recordings for *The Tibetan Book of Living and Dying*. I hadn't asked for either; however, I accepted both with gratitude. I needed all the help I could garner.

I was so impressed with David's reading that I decided to start reading astrology books to learn more. I wanted to know how he knew what he knew. I also wanted to learn other tools that might be able to help me heal. David and Laura became my friends, and for several years I went to astrology workshops that they hosted. One was in Greece and another in Italy. Both trips were fantastic.

During that first summer in Sequim, I also took a trip to San Francisco to attend a Journey workshop. This was a workshop based on a book written by Brandon Bay called *The Journey*. A friend and ex-coworker in Salt Lake City had recommended the book for Bill. She thought it might help him with his cancer. I bought the book and offered it to him, and as would be expected, he refused to read it. So I read it instead. I was fascinated by the story and the healing technique listed in the back of the book and wanted to try it out. The workshop was good, and I learned how to do the process. The only problem was that at home there wasn't anyone to work with. I ended up listening to Brandon's cassette recording, which walked me through the process. That worked a bit—but my mind is fast, and I moved through the layers much quicker than the recording.

The other thing that happened that first summer was being introduced to a medicine woman. Jan's teacher, Pat, was coming for a visit, and Jan wanted me to meet her. My meeting her was fortuitous. After losing Austin in August, I had decided to take a trip to Taos. It was one place that had come to mind in 2000 as a possible town to live in. When Bill said he wanted to move, I had asked God to show me where we were supposed to go. The name Taos kept appearing in signs on billboards, TV, and other places. Bill refused to consider the town or the state. So I decided to have a holiday there to check it out for myself. If God said I needed to be there, then that was where I would move.

One of the things I would learn over the years is that there is a window of opportunity for everything. And once that window closes, the person has to wait for the next window—or should I say, door—to open. Anyway, the night before I was to leave on my trip, I met Pat. She was going to do a smoke at Jan's house. (A smoke is a Native American practice for sending prayers and receiving messages and blessings from The Great Spirit.)

I went to Jan's house not knowing what to expect. After all, I hadn't had any contact with Native Americans other than the one I met on the film set in Utah, nor did I have any experience with Native ways. Pat was really nice, and I felt that I had known her before—I mean in another life. I learned that she had planned on leading a water journey that summer, but something happened and it didn't take place, so she decided to visit Jan instead. (A water journey was a pilgrimage Native Americans used to visit various hot springs and water sources for healing practices and rituals. I would participate in the water journeys over the years, but I didn't know this at our first meeting.) We went into Jan's garage, sat on the floor, and began the ritual smoke. A few days earlier I had begun to bleed again from the miscarriage and was concerned about boarding the plane the next day because the flow was getting heavier. I hadn't mentioned this to Jan or Pat. After the smoke we sat and talked for a while and I went home. The next morning the bleeding was almost nonexistent. I was amazed. I knew it was due to the smoke, but I wondered how a smoke could do this. I called Jan and told her about the bleeding and how it was almost gone. She wasn't surprised. She just said, "Smokes are very healing."

I went to Taos that day without worry of bleeding all over myself. I didn't do a lot in Taos. Mostly I walked around the town, visited the Pueblo, and went to a powwow. It was the beginning of September, and the weather was gorgeous. It was nice to be on my own doing what I wanted to do. I stayed at the Taos Inn, which is in the center of town. It was a nice week and my first real taste of being free—not emotionally, but physically. Emotional freedom would take years to achieve.

Blossom

The flower bud is the protective casing for each petal that is developing within and has a rougher, thicker coating for protection. Facets/petals inside the flower bud are like the developing facets within people. A person who is accomplishing the great work of "knowing thyself" becomes the bloom and no longer the bud. Each petal opening represents one facet of our past being purified. The encapsulated flower looks like two hands praying. The harshness of life can disrupt the flower from fully blossoming, and this is the same for us. The harshness of our lives can prevent us from reaching our full potential.

27

Learning How to Heal

When I got back from Taos, I called Gwen in Memphis. I wanted to tell her about the trip and catch up. What I didn't know was that I had lost a friend—someone who had been in my life since junior high. We had rarely gone more than a couple of weeks without talking, and I had no indication that our friendship would end. It never crossed my mind. When she didn't answer my initial phone messages, I began to wonder if something had happened to her or Omari. I didn't have the phone numbers for any of her brothers, and her mother had died. The only thing I could do was to keep calling her number. On the fifth call, Omari answered the phone. I asked how he was doing, and he told me that he was fine. He then went to tell Gwen that Aunt Marie was on the phone. I heard her in the background tell him to tell me that she would call me back, which he did. I never heard from her again. That was years ago. My phone number and address stayed the same for years afterward. If she wanted to reach me, she could have. The only explanation I could come up with was that she didn't want to be my friend anymore. I have no idea why, but I will say this about myself: I will never beg a person to remain friends with me. If the other person wants to end the friendship, I accept it and move on. That doesn't mean the loss doesn't hurt—because it surely does. What I came to understand years later was that mine and Gwen's Karma was over and it was time to move on. I have a hard time releasing people from my life. So I guess her contract with me was for her to do the honors. That said, there were better ways she could have ended our friendship. In my opinion, she took a coward's way out.

As far as longtime friends were concerned, I only had Wanda left. At that time, we had been friends for 20 years, and we rang in New Year's of that year together. That holiday season was my first one since Bill's death, and I didn't want to be alone. It would turn out that I would be surrounded by people but still feel alone.

My neighbors and I had begun to get acquainted, and one of them invited me to their home for a holiday party. I went and had a nice time. All of the neighbors were nice to me, and we would become friends over the years.

After the holiday party, I went to Bogalusa for Christmas for the first time in years. That was nice, too. I spent a few days with family and then flew back to Washington State to leave again for Vegas. I had talked Wanda into meeting me there for New Year's. She loved Vegas, and I just wanted to get away—to be anywhere but home. It didn't take much convincing to get Wanda to agree.

On New Year's Eve near midnight, I went outside to watch the fireworks ring in the New Year. Wanda wanted to keep gambling, and that was fine—she was happy, and I was happy for her. I watched the fireworks with throngs of people and felt completely and utterly alone—more alone than I had felt in my life. I was running from that feeling but couldn't hide. It enveloped me right there—while watching others celebrating. I had no one who cared about me to say "Happy New Year" to. I felt like being in the fetal position in a corner of a room someplace. Instead, I watched the festivities for a while and then went back into the casino to find Wanda still at the same machine. She was in heaven. I told her that I was going to bed, which is what I did.

That year, 2003, was a year of beginning the process of finding my footing. I was still suffering and finding myself in tears sometimes, but not every day. David, my new astrologer, had asked me during the reading if I could wait a few years before going to work. He said that I was in a huge transition period and needed time for some impending changes to occur. I was being sent in a new direction, and neither of us knew specifically what that was. He advised taking no action concerning work or any other aspect of my life until Pluto had cleared my Sun by several degrees. He suggested that I just work on me. This was a profound suggestion—and looking back on that period of time, it was accurate. If I had jumped into working or another relationship or moved someplace else, I would have been making grave errors. Who I am today is not who I was back then. Every aspect of me has shifted. I told David that I had about five years' worth of funds to live on and could wait a year or two to find the "right work."

After the miscarriage, I was adamant about doing in vitro again. I still had frozen eggs and sperm stored and had planned on going through in vitro in 2003. I felt I didn't have much time because of my age, and I really wanted a child. However, as time passed, I began to realize I was holding onto a dream that I needed to let go of. It wasn't that I didn't want kids anymore—I just knew that this wasn't one of the blessings I would be given. I had to surrender the dream. I didn't come to this decision right away—it took months, maybe even a year. But I eventually let go of the frozen eggs and sperm being stored.

I had begun the long process of healing a few years earlier with Gillian and reading books. Now it was time for more action. It was time for me to act on the practices I had learned through reading. One of the first things I did was decide at the last minute to travel to Australia for a weeklong healing intensive put on by The Journey. I had to delve deeper after the previous workshop I had attended.

I talked an ex-coworker from Salt Lake City, Michele, into meeting me after the retreat. Since I would be in Australia anyway, I wanted to see as much of the area as possible. This is how I would travel for many years—combining classes and retreats with vacation. I thoroughly enjoyed the retreat and began to discover deep-seated issues that needed clearing. No one told me these issues were there; I either saw them through my mind's eye or felt them myself. I'm not one to believe what is being told to me by another person. I have to experience things myself.

Because the weeklong intensive was rewarding, I decided to become a Journey Practitioner. Though David had said not to do anything for a few years, I thought I could do this anyway. My intent was to help others do what I was doing. It turned out I needed to know the process for myself, not for others.

The summer of 2003 I went back to Australia and stayed seven weeks to finish the certification program. In hindsight, I had what I needed already, but this was the certification requirement. As I said earlier, the only issue I had with the process was not having anyone to work with at home. The process is usually done with two people. I learned to go through the process alone while listening to it on a recording. At some point I became very good at taking myself through a process without the CD.

The other big thing I did that summer was go on my first water journey with Pat. This was an amazing experience. We started in northern New Mexico, going to various hot springs to do ceremonies and Native American healing practices. This was my first introduction to The Great Mother—the mother of us all. Being raised Christian, I had only known about God, Jesus, and Mary. I didn't know that there was a female aspect of God.

That first water journey helped to change my life, and I am forever grateful to Pat for her teachings. She took me on as a student and taught me how to read and interpret Sign and Symbol, The Directions, The Medicine Wheel, and other Native ways. All of the teachings have become an integral part of me. I pay attention when I see an animal behaving oddly or look at the formation of clouds. I learned so much that helps me see and hear the messages coming from The Divine.

One of the ways The Divine talks to us is through nature. It's not the only way, but it is a primary mode of communication. I learned to ask a question and listen for the answer. This might seem odd—it did to me at first. Pat said trees could be asked questions. I didn't believe her. How could a tree talk? I was proven wrong. She taught me a method for releasing emotional baggage, which I use to this day for myself. Jeez—it seems I had a bottomless pit of emotional baggage stored in the astral plane.

I studied with Pat for four years. I wouldn't have been able to clear out so much emotional trauma without the practices she taught me. I combined one of her practices with what I learned through The Journey to release issues. I begin with one practice, and after it is completed, I begin the second practice and complete it. I found putting them together helped me to move through issues quicker. Now when I have an issue staring me in the face, I know what to do to heal it at its core and release it.

As an example, one day I was sitting on the upper back deck at the house, not thinking about much. I was just looking at the vista. My view was to the north—the place of the ancestors. All of the sudden there were seven hawks flying from the north to the south, right at me. When they got to a certain point, they banked right and went to the west. This was an odd behavior, which meant I needed to figure out the message—so I did. The ancestors were telling me that a healing opportunity was coming soon. I was being given a heads-up, so to speak. It was nice to get this message because it was now in my conscious mind that something big was about to happen. I still didn't know what, but the hawks were saying, "Pay attention and look closely." If I didn't pay attention, I could miss the opportunity.

About a week to a week and a half later, Jan was meeting me in town for some reason. She had been working for this couple in their booth at local fairs and shows. Her boss saw her and came over to say hello. She introduced him to me, and we shook hands. I took an instant dislike to the man. Of course, being polite, I shook his hand and said hello. I didn't say anything to Jan. At the time, I wasn't thinking about the message I had been given by the ancestors. It never crossed my mind that this man could be a part of my message and ultimately a key factor in my healing.

Jan was planning to work one of the local shows and needed to work closely with him and his wife during this time. As luck would have it, I saw him a second time a few days later when Jan and I were again out together. I had never met this man before, and after this part of my healing concluded I never saw him again, even though we lived in the same town. The second time I met this man, my dislike for him had grown exponentially. I can't say I hated him, but I sure didn't want to be around him. Still, I shook his hand and was polite. But this time, my curiosity was piqued. What was this about? I still didn't catch on to the message. I went about my business and didn't think to dwell on my feelings about him.

On the day of the dog show, Jan was working and I went to see if she needed anything. She was working alone; maybe she needed to go to the bathroom and I could stand at the booth until she got back, or maybe I could go get her something to eat. While I was there, Jan's boss came by and stuck out his hand to shake mine. I couldn't take his hand. I was having a visceral response. I had an aversion to him that I hadn't felt in my entire life. It was palpable. I told Jan I had to go and rushed off, leaving both of them baffled, I'm sure.

I had to get to the bottom of this. This man had never done anything to me. What was going on? I knew that I needed to get to the root of it and clear whatever it was. I went through the process and figured it out: he represented every man who had ever violated me in any way. This was *big*! I had to *forgive*!

One thing I have learned is that when issues are ready to be released, you don't have to go looking for them. They come to the surface, saying, "Hello, I'm ready to go. I no longer serve who you are. Release me." The problem is that the issue surfaces and triggers the trauma. I spent seven days releasing this issue. I'll never forget on the eighth day I did a burn ceremony to release the source of the issue and asked for a sign that it was complete. I received the sign that the issue was complete through nature, which made me tremendously joyous. I couldn't wait to tell Jan. She had filled me in on her boss and confirmed what I was picking up from him—not that he literally raped people that I am aware of. What he did was rape people through the way he treated them.

I told her that the issue was done; that part of me was healed. She said, "I don't know. You won't know that it is cleared until you see him again." I said that I didn't know how that would happen, since we didn't travel in the same circles. For me, it was done. However, the ancestors had one last meeting up their sleeves. The next evening, I went to a theater event, and who was sitting at one of the tables? Jan's boss and his wife. I got up from my table, walked over to them, and held out my hand to shake his, which he accepted. I felt nothing—no aversion, no attraction. It was done. I was over the moon and couldn't wait to share the news with Jan.

This is the way it went for years—an issue would surface and I would clear it. It got to the point where I asked The Great Spirit, "Please give me a few weeks without an issue coming up." There was just so much to work on and release. From time to time, I still have issues that arise from my subconscious needing purification—just not as frequently.

One of the many gifts Sequim gave me was the theater. It was the theater that helped me adjust to living there. The town was and still is filled with all kinds of creative outlets. The symphony in Port Angeles wasn't far, and there were several theaters there, too. Sequim had one theater that put on shows about four or five times a year. This gave me a creative outlet, plus I gained friends to do things with. I'm still friends with people I met in that theater.

It was over a year after Bill's death before I found out about Olympic Theater Arts, as it was called back then. Up until that time I had spent my time redecorating the house, learning The Journey, traveling, and getting to know the neighbors. But I still hadn't settled into living in Sequim. I hadn't found where I fit in the town.

Sequim has never had much of a minority population. In fact, when I lived there, I would joke with people who came up to me saying they saw me someplace or heard me sing in church, when it wasn't actually me they saw. I would say, "No—that wasn't me. That was the other one." But it was a testament to the woman named

Marianne who was putting on a show that I was cast in. She decided to direct a play that had two Black people in the cast: a male and a female. She just knew it could be done. Marianne was a feisty woman in her late 70s or early 80s at the time. I didn't know this when we met. She was a lioness in a petite, very slender body.

I found out about the play through a friend of Jan's who I had gotten to know—Lori. Lori was a retired massage therapist who had this uncanny ability to see right to the core of who people were. She was another lioness—also petite and fierce. Lori called me one day and told me about an audition being held at the theater and that they were looking for an African American female to portray Addie. The play was *The Little Foxes*. Lori didn't ask me to consider auditioning; she told me to audition and then promptly hung up the phone before I could reply. Without realizing it, I was beginning to gather strong, opinionated, obstinate, loving female elders around me.

I had the time, so I went to the audition. It had been years since I was on the stage, and I thought it might be nice to get back into theater. Auditions were being held in the old Howard Wood building downtown. The theater would move a few doors down the street to the old Boys and Girls Club building after *The Little Foxes* was over, but I didn't know that at the time.

When I entered the building for the first time, I wasn't sure what to expect. What I found was a cadre of people who were serious about putting on a show that could rival a New York production— with Marianne at the helm. I saw her sitting in one of the theater seats giving directions to an actor who was auditioning for one of the parts. I sat and watched until she was done. She then looked around and saw me. I'll never forget the huge smile she had on her face. She told me that I was her Addie. I thought, "I haven't auditioned yet; how does she know I'll be the right fit for the part?" I didn't realize at the time what the minority population was in Sequim. As it turned out, I *was* the perfect fit for the part. If I must say so myself, I nailed the role. I had found my place in Sequim—where I belonged. Being in plays also gave me a high profile in town. Most people knew who

I was even if I didn't know them. It was nice. Most of the friends I developed over the years came from the theater, too.

Marianne began to invite me to the monthly lunch she and several other theater people had. I had already met two of them: Charlotte and Carol. Charlotte handled anything that had to do with sound on a show. She was also an excellent actor. Charlotte and I met at the auditions for *The Little Foxes*. When she saw me for the first time, she looked me straight in the eye and said, "We are going to become very good friends." And we did—we still are. Charlotte was a retired school principal from California and had a no-nonsense attitude laced with compassion. She never suffered fools lightly, as the saying goes.

Carol was Marianne's stage manager for every show. She was the churchgoer of the group. I love Carol—she was and is so nice. She reminds me of a beloved aunt who could give practical advice over a cup of tea. That said, if she gets mad, she will say it to a person's face. She also has a wonderful sense of humor. I remember playing a joke on her during one of the plays I was cast in, *Proposals*. It was Carol's job to make sure the actors were ready to go on stage on cue. It was about 60 seconds before my cue line would be said. Carol was standing next to me, behind the curtain waiting, when I leaned over and told her I had to go to the bathroom. She glared up at me and said, "You had better hold it," to which my reply was a giggle. I loved the look on her face. I could act like a kid sometimes.

A couple of other women were initially a part of the lunch group, but it soon became Marianne, Charlotte, Carol, and me. We cherished these lunches and had them every month until I moved away. Even when one of us couldn't make it, the others would still have lunch together. These women were my elders; yet we not only enjoyed each other's company, but we also respected and trusted each other. We also supported each other through difficulties. We had deep philosophical conversations for hours during lunch. Carol and Marianne knew nothing about metaphysics or astrology but were fascinated with what I was learning. Charlotte had studied metaphysics, and this made it easier for her to grasp the language. Each of us gave our viewpoints about most aspects of life.

In addition to the monthly lunches, when we were rehearsing a show, we would meet after rehearsal at Oasis—one of the bars and grills in town—to unwind before going home. When Applebee's opened, we quickly relocated there because they were open much later. Most theater people are night owls. Shows were over at 9:00 and nobody wanted to go home, so we went to the only place open late. Over the years, I have eaten more hamburger sliders at 10:00 p.m. than I care to mention.

Interestingly, every show that I was in served as an opportunity for me to clear an issue from my past. My style of acting isn't to "act"—it is to "become." When I am cast in a show, I have no idea who the character is that I will portray. I have to get to know her. It's called character development. It's not quite an organic process, because I work at it and she begins to show herself to me. I then have to allow her to inhabit me. I'm not talking about a split personality; I'm talking about me being the observer on stage and allowing this character to speak through me, using my body, gestures, voice, and expressions. I am fully aware of everything but have surrendered to the character. This can only happen if I don't block the character. For the character to be authentic, I must let her flow, unobstructed.

After I did *The Little Foxes*, Marianne was so thrilled to have a Black female actor in town that she decided to do another show that required a Black actor: *Proposals*. Marianne had wanted to do these shows for years but didn't have the cast required.

The character in *Proposals* that I would portray was Hattie. She was the lead. The show was set in the '50s. Hattie was the maid for a single father and his daughter. Because it was the '50s, I decided to use Granny as my muse for the character. She was about the same age as Hattie during the '50s, and I knew who she was—or so I thought—so I assumed it would be easy to have her portray the character. The process proved to be a challenge. I was having difficulty getting over the fact that Hattie was a maid. Granny had been a maid in real life, and I had witnessed an incident as a kid that confused me, to say the least. What I didn't know was that I had stored up resentment in the cells of my body, and this acted as a block for the character portrayal.

As a kid I was taught to say, "Yes, ma'am" and "No, ma'am" to my elders—which I did. After all, I was raised in the South; this was—and I think still is—proper etiquette. One day I saw and heard Granny saying "Yes, ma'am" to a Caucasian woman who was clearly not an elder. Granny was the elder. I didn't understand. The young woman should have been saying "Yes, ma'am" to Granny, not the other way around. I asked Granny why she had said this to the lady and all I got was "You will understand later." Although many thoughts and questions came to mind, I knew not to question her further. But my respect for her was tainted. I was angry at Granny for doing such a thing, and I internalized that anger. I recall saying to myself at the time that I would never, ever say "Yes, ma'am" or "No, ma'am" to someone younger than me.

Fast-forward to *Proposals*. The resentment and anger with Granny were blocking me from portraying Hattie in an authentic way. Most shows took six weeks to put together before opening night. I discovered the block during that six-week period. I had to face Granny, and my anger with her, head on. This involved being able to forgive myself, too. I was able to finally see the situation from her point of view and realize the inner strength she had to be able to survive as a Black woman during the times she lived in. Once I was able to let go of my anger, Hattie came through flawlessly for me. Every night during the run of the show, I received a standing ovation.

As I said before, every show I performed in Sequim presented me with an opportunity to heal an aspect of my past. This hadn't happened before, and I am immensely grateful for having been cast in those shows.

28

Astrology and Buddhism

After a couple of years in Sequim, it became clear to me why I was there. Bill had his motives for moving me there, and those motives played into the hands of my Higher Self's intent. Bill's motive was to isolate me from my friends and the life I was beginning to build with acting. He also wanted to make sure I would not get into another relationship—or at least reduce the possibility—thus the attempt to give me a child to take care of. He knew me well enough to know that caring for a child would take precedence over any other relationship. My focus would be on raising the child.

My Higher Self's intent, however, was to give me every opportunity to heal from the trauma of my life—and there was a lot of it. My Higher Self also knew that I needed a bit of isolation to be able to get the work done. If I had stayed in Salt Lake City, I probably would have just gone back to work, continued to act in shows, and hung out with my friends. That would have been fine, except that I wouldn't have focused on healing my past. In addition, being that it was my Higher Self, it also knew what level of physical comfort I needed. So I was put in a beautiful, peaceful neighborhood with neighbors who acted as a surrogate family. They didn't interfere in my life, but I did interact with them frequently, celebrating birthdays, checking in on them, sharing dinners and parties, and basically being helpful to one another. And even though I never felt the house I lived in was completely me, it was beautiful and served as my personal retreat.

I still don't know how everything works as far as the Other Side is concerned. I only know what I am shown, which I don't think is very much. It's always on a need-to-know basis. As an example, it was a few years after I moved to Sequim before my Guides felt I needed to know Bill's intention for moving me there. I don't know why they waited to tell me—maybe they thought I would move away before my time there was done. I do know that when I learned of his intention, I was furious with myself for not seeing it before.

One of the ways I get information is through dreams. Some things are better discovered this way—such as the fact that Bill also intended to kill me. It made sense when I took a look at his actions during the move to Sequim and compared them to the dream. As mentioned earlier, he wouldn't let me help him with the drive from Salt Lake City to Sequim. Well, in my dream I saw Bill driving in his SUV. I was in the passenger seat. He began to speed, and I told him to slow down—that he was going too fast. He then sped up more. In front of us was my car, which was parked. Bill gunned the engine and headed straight for the driver's side of my car. His intent was to kill us both. When I realized his intention, I turned in the seat, into a fetal position, and called out to God to save me.

After that dream, I verified with my Guides that Bill's intention was, in fact, to kill me. His thinking was that if he was going to die, he was taking me with him. I don't know why he didn't follow through with his plans, but I'm certainly happy he didn't. He was a sick man—in many ways. I had to forgive him for this and see who he was, which was not easy. Both of us needed to be free of each other, and this would take years after his death for me to accomplish.

As I was saying, I'm not sure how everything works on the Other Side, but I do know Angels, Guides, and other beings are working hard on our behalf and that maneuvering to relocate me to Sequim had to be a piece of genius on their part. I didn't want to be there, and I also think they had to plant the seed in Bill's mind to move away from Salt Lake City. It just seems odd that a dying man would have wanted to move to an isolated place away from his family. Plus, I do think they intervened to keep Bill from offing me en route to Sequim. But all of us have free will, so I'm not exactly sure how much help they provided with this.

Although David was my first astrologer, my first real astrology teacher was Don. Don and I met at one of the local grocery stores, Sunny Farms. Don and I were standing at the butcher's waiting on our orders to be filled and began to chat. I would learn that he was an astrologer and had been one for many years. He invited me to his house to talk astrology, and this is how he became my first teacher. He had not taught astrology before, but since he had been practicing for years, he thought it might be nice to teach. Another woman had been after him for a while to teach her, so he decided to teach both of us together. I asked him if we could also include my friend Jan, and he said yes.

Once a week the three of us would sit at his dining room table and talk astrology. (Jan ended up having to stop due to family issues, but the other woman and I stayed with it.) Don was old school, which meant no computer programs. We learned to create charts by hand. In hindsight, it's amazing how quickly astrological concepts and meanings were integrated by not using computer programs. I'm glad I began learning astrology the old-fashioned way. It took a lot longer to create a chart by hand, but by the time I was done, I had a good sense of who the person was.

Years later, when Don was moving to Oregon, he gifted me a few of his old books—which I still have—and told me that I would become an astrologer. I didn't believe him. I just wanted to learn astrology to help myself. But he was right—I did become an astrologer. It took years for me to own it and integrate this fact. But when I did, I felt more at peace with myself. I'm sure Don would be proud of me.

In 2004, I felt the need to go back to work. It had been three years since my move to Sequim, and I felt ready to get back into being productive. That year I asked my astrologer David what he thought about this idea. He suggested I wait one more year, so I did. I was still dealing with an intense configuration in my astrology chart, which would begin to ease up in 2005.

In this astrology session with David, we talked about careers that I would thrive in, and both of us settled on life coaching as a good road to follow. For years my friends had been coming to me for advice about various aspects of their lives. I would help as much as I could. It usually entailed a lot of listening and asking questions to help get to the root of the issue and formulate a plan to resolve the problem. This is also what a Life Coach does.

I searched the Web and found an online school with a program I liked. Classes began at the start of 2005, and it would take about a year to become certified, which suited my needs nicely. When 2006 arrived, I had my certification as a Life Coach and had decided to specialize in life renewal coaching for widows and divorcees. I chose these niches for two reasons: first, I was a widow and felt being divorced was also a death; second, I lived in Sequim, which had a sizable population of widows as well as some divorcees. So in the fall of 2006, I opened my business as a Life Coach.

Of course, I could have easily gone and worked for someone else, but I didn't want to work for anyone else. One of the traits I realized about myself was that I needed to be in control of my destiny, and the best way for me to do this was to work for myself. I had never run a company but felt I had the skills to do so. I had the MBA, plus I had watched Bill run his company for years. I was up for the challenge.

If I had known then what I know now, I never would have done it. Hindsight is everything. There were a couple of fatal flaws in my plan.

Flaw #1   I learned that having a quality product that people need isn't good enough—they have to not only want it but also want to pay for it. I marketed my services to all the groups in several towns and received wonderful feedback about how I would benefit widows and divorcees in the community. Some people did come to me for coaching; however, never were throngs of folks asking for help. It was a couple of years before I figured out what was wrong. The issue was the age group. These people were mostly retired. Some were of the WWII generation, and others had been kids during the war. That particular generation tends not to talk about their problems to outsiders much, if at all. Most of the time they have a "suck it up and take it" attitude. I admire that generation; they have done a tremendous service for the world. But when I started my business, I missed the fact that they don't seek help for emotional issues as readily as the younger generations.

Flaw #2   I'm stubborn and at the time was slow to change or tweak my course. I knew in my heart that I was a Life Coach—the problem was the niche I chose. As I said, I learned this in hindsight, but I stuck to my guns for far too long.

Flaw #3   I refused to put myself out there as an astrologer to expand my niche. Astrologers are actually Life Coaches, too. My problem was that, at the time, I didn't think I knew enough to be a professional astrologer. Although I felt this way, it was also an excuse to cover the fear of rejection I thought I would face from the community. Plus, my original intention was to use astrology only for myself.

I didn't admit to this problem until another professional astrologer with more than 40 years' experience called me out for not having astrology listed on my website. Her name was Jan—the same as my friend. I'll call her Jan #2. Jan #2 was perusing my website one day and lamented on the fact that I only had life coaching listed as my profession. She knew that I was also an astrologer and felt I was selling myself short by not having it listed. I told her my concern, to which she replied, "Rubbish! You are an astrologer, and the Universe is going to keep holding you back until you own this fact. This is a part of your destiny." I contemplated her words and knew she was correct.

Because of Jan #2's words, I finally came out as an astrologer. Doing so did alienate me with some of the people in the community, but not everyone. The Universe also presented me with another astrology mentor, Steven Forrest. I took a giant leap of faith and was rewarded for it. Steven's style of teaching fit wonderfully with the way I learn. He is a terrific teacher of evolutionary astrology, and I am blessed to have had him cross my path.

Buddhism was another piece of the puzzle that helped shape who I am today. At the time, I had no intention of ever being involved with any religion in any form. I guess The Divine had other ideas on the subject.

Before we go any further, I need to explain something. We set up possible experiences we want to have before we incarnate. These experiences are best described as "possible," because we have free will and can reject the opportunity for an experience. I must have wanted the experience of Buddhism. I used to say I was coyoted, or tricked, into it. (Coyote is the trickster animal in the Native American tradition.)

There is a mountain range in Sequim called the Olympic Mountains. If you are headed anywhere in town, they are visible. Sometime during the fall of 2006, while driving and looking at the mountain range, they began to look like the Himalayan Mountains. I had only seen the Himalayas in photographs, but there they were. Every time I looked at the Olympic Mountains, they felt and looked like the Himalayas. I found this odd but didn't contemplate it too much.

One night—it had to have been January or February of 2007—I had a dream. In the dream, David, my astrologer, was climbing up a ladder at the front of my house. His purpose was to take a green bottle cap off the roof. He showed me the bottle cap and I woke up. I wondered what the heck that was about.

I called Jan and told her about the dream. We both figured out its meaning but had no idea how it would manifest. In dreams, houses represent the Mansion of the Soul, which is the person. The roof is the head. So in my dream, my mind was being opened to something new—maybe a new way of thinking. I was going to have the opportunity to transform my mind in some way. It didn't take long for the opportunity to materialize.

I had subscribed to the *Shambhala Sun* magazine a month or so earlier but hadn't had a chance to read it. At the time, I wasn't sure why I had ordered it—but I had, and I didn't want to waste my money. So when the second issue arrived, rather than put it on the coffee table without reading it—as I had done with the first issue—I decided to read its content.

I'll always remember what happened next, because it was like the bottle cap coming off my head. I poured myself a cup of coffee and sat down at the kitchen table with the magazine. When I opened it, I turned a few pages and began to stare at an ad. The ad was for a trip to Bhutan. Something inside of me short-circuited. I slammed the magazine shut on the table, looked up angrily to the heavens while pointing my finger up at The Divine, shook my head, and said loudly, "I'm not going and you can't make me go!" I'm sure the Angels are still laughing about that outburst. But at the time, it wasn't funny. I was bound and determined not to go. I had just opened the life coaching business the previous fall, and I didn't even know where Bhutan was located—had never heard of the place. Plus, it was a Buddhist trip. I knew nothing about Buddhism, nor did I have any intention of learning anything about the religion. I actually said to myself, "I'm not about to shave my head, put on one of those funny-looking robes, give all my money away, and live in poverty. No way!" Little did I know, that's not what was being asked of me.

As the day progressed, I could feel the pressure of my Inner Self intently. It wouldn't let up. It was similar to a loud noise that wouldn't stop. Because of the pressure, I decided to call the tour company to get information. I thought this would stop the internal pressure.

I called and spoke to the owner, Tina. She was so nice. Before I knew it, I was giving her my credit card number for the deposit. Six weeks later, I was on a plane to Thailand. This was where the group met for the final journey to Bhutan aboard Druk Air. There were six of us on the tour, including our guide, Nick. It was one of the best trips I have ever had, and every one of my fellow travelers and I are still friends. That trip changed my life. The people of Bhutan are marvelous. They don't have much in the way of money or possessions, but they are happier than any other group of people I have ever encountered.

On the plane ride to Bhutan, Nick sat next to me and asked me why I was on the trip. It was that moment when I realized why I was being sent there. I told him that I had left a piece of me there and was going back to get it. I was amazed at what I said and had no idea where it came from, but it was a truth—I could feel it. Nick said he would do what he could to help me with this. I thought that was nice of him to say, but at the same time I felt just being there meant I would get the lost piece back.

Nick ended up giving a gift that I am grateful for. At the end of the trip, he had arranged for all of us to go through a soul retrieval. I was in shock when he informed us of this. It wasn't a part of the tour. One of the high-level Lamas would perform the ritual with his monks in residence. There were nine of us going through the ceremony: the six of us on the tour, plus the driver and the two Bhutanese guides. The number nine represents completion.

Everyone who went through the ceremony said they felt the energy and felt the shift within themselves. I didn't feel anything— at first. It was peaceful for sure, but I still felt the same afterward. About a year later, I realized something had changed within me. I was different. I felt that all my pieces were back where they belonged. The ceremony had actually worked.

One of the things I learned back then was that each time we suffer a trauma on any level, we leave a piece of us in the location where the trauma occurred in the form of an energy pattern. This is why, in my opinion, people who are sensitive to energy can go to a particular location and sense what happened there—because the energy left behind by trauma is strong. And for the person to be whole again, they must retrieve that part of themselves. There are various ways to do this, but it can be done.

Within a week of returning home from Bhutan, I had a dream in which I visited a Lama who lived in a cave. I found myself sitting on the dirt floor of the cave in front of him, next to a caldron. He was ancient but didn't physically look ancient. The cave was not large and not small. However, there was an opening to my left that seemed to be endless. I didn't walk over there to take a look—it was something I felt. The Lama picked up a ladle, dipping it into the liquid inside the caldron. He then filled the ladle with liquid and handed it to me, telling me to drink. I drank the liquid and handed him the ladle. He then said I wasn't quite ready. Instead of asking him, "Ready for what?" I asked him what was in the liquid. He listed off the herbs, and I woke up. As soon as I woke up, I regretted not asking him the proper question: "I'm not quite ready for what?" Then again, in hindsight, maybe I wasn't supposed to ask the question that was burning in my mind.

I immediately called Nick to relay the content of the dream and ask what he thought. We both agreed that the Lama in the dream had to be my root teacher. And my not being ready for something—whatever it was—was a truth. All I could do was to keep working on myself to hopefully become ready.

I would learn years later through my studies in esoteric astrology that there is a hierarchy, and the Lama is most probably a part of this group of teachers. It was a while before I would see him again, however. I knew he existed and was watching over my development. Right after the dream, I thought I could find him in human form. I knew he was my root teacher, and I would search for him. That wasn't quite a good idea, but it wasn't a bad idea either. Some people do search and find their root teachers after having visions or dreams of them. I'm just not one of those people.

Because of my experience in Bhutan and this dream about my Lama, I thought it would be a good idea to start learning more about Buddhism. In my library of books, I had a copy of *The Tibetan Book of Living and Dying*, which I had read a couple of years earlier. David had made me aware of it during my first astrology reading. I pulled the book off the shelf and looked in the back to see if there was a website, and there was. I saw on the site that online classes were available, so I signed up. The name of the organization was Rigpa, and it was run by Sogyal Rinpoche, the author of the book. *Rinpoche* means "teacher." I took online classes through the organization for years, learning the fundamentals of Buddhism.

A couple of years after the Bhutan trip, all but one of my friends from that trip went on a sojourn to Nepal and Tibet. It was also a magical trip, though I learned that very high altitudes don't work for me. I must have burned off some serious Karma in Tibet. I had no choice but to move slowly. It was as though oxygen wasn't reaching my extremities. Still, I went on the hikes I could do and visited the temples and the Potala Palace, which is 12,000 feet above sea level. We flew to Nepal after visiting Tibet, and I bounded off the plane. I could move easily again at a mere 7,000 feet above sea level.

In 2011 Nick suggested that we attend the Kalachakra Initiation with His Holiness the Dalai Lama in Washington, D.C. He couldn't go, but four of us did. We rented a house in D.C. for the 10-day event. It was the first time I had been to an event like this. There were thousands of us at the indoor venue, yet most of the time the only sounds being made were from the monks and His Holiness performing ceremonies. Because the event was being held during the Dalai Lama's birthday, there was a live feed from his best friend, Desmond Tutu, offering a birthday wish and teasing him. It was an amazing event. I believe that anyone who gets a chance to attend an event with the Dalai Lama will be blessed by being in his presence.

A couple of things happened to me during the Initiation. Most mornings, my friends and I would eat before leaving the house. However, one morning I was running late and didn't eat. When we got to our seats, the Dalai Lama and his monks were already there performing rituals. (I was told that he got to the center hours before the rest of us to begin the day's rituals.) I was hungry and told my friend Christy that I was going next door to one of the restaurants for breakfast and would be back. There were fast-food places at the event center, but I'm not much of a fast-food person. As I was approaching the exit for the building, I felt an energy field. It was a protective field, and I knew I wasn't supposed to pass beyond that field. Whatever rituals were being done must have included protection, because I felt it. The hall was virtually empty, so I wonder if I would have felt it if the hall had been filled with people. Well, that morning I ate fast food for breakfast and was grateful.

The second thing that happened wasn't apparent until I returned home. When two people are in a relationship, an energetic cord attaches them to each other. This cord isn't necessarily severed when the relationship ends. My Native American teacher, Pat, used to say that if you have sex with someone, it takes a year for the cord between the two of you to be severed naturally. And it might not happen even after a year—it all depends on our thought process. Therefore, she advised to be very careful whom you sleep with and to wait a full year after a relationship ends before sleeping with another person. Otherwise, you are bringing your previous partner into the bedroom with you and your new mate. I've found her words to be true.

Shortly after I got home, I found out that the energetic cord connecting Bill and me had been severed. Before this revelation, I hadn't realized the cord was still attached. Bill had died in 2002, and this was 2011—nine years later. Eventually, I figured out why it took so long to be severed. After Bill died, I could feel him in the house still. He would frequently come and go. I would also wake up sometimes and find him lying next to me. I would consistently tell him to leave—that he was dead and shouldn't be there. Sometimes I would get angry and yell at him, especially when I saw him looking at the checkbook to see what I was spending. He never paid any attention to what I was saying when he was alive, and this carried over after his death.

Jan asked me if I wanted to seal him out of the house. There is a ritual for doing this. I had seen her perform this ritual—it really works. I said no. This was still his house, and I didn't want to shut him out. After all, he had paid for it. I didn't want to be cruel; I just wanted him to behave.

A couple of days after D.C., as I was standing on the back deck, in my mind's eye I could see him trying to attach a cord to me. He was throwing it like a whip at me. It wasn't attaching, and he was not happy. In that moment I knew what had happened and how it had occurred. I knew I had felt lighter after arriving home—and now I knew where some of that lightness came from. I hadn't realized the cord attaching us had not been severed years earlier, and the Initiation in Washington caused it to be severed.

I didn't want that cord reattached to me. I was done with him, and I was tired of being kind. I called Jan and asked her to help me seal the doors to keep him out. Intention is everything with rituals, and my intentions were off-the-chart strong. Bill knew what I was planning and tried to get me not to do it. As I have said before, everyone has free will—and my free will said he was getting the hell out of my life. We sealed the doors, so he couldn't enter the house anymore. There are rules that have to be followed, even on the Other Side. The use of my free will and intention were sacrosanct—he couldn't override them.

What Bill did next was ludicrous. I only learned about it through a dream. A couple of weeks after the sealing ritual, I had a dream in which one of my Spirit Guides appeared. She told me that Bill was being "contained" for his own good. I had never heard of such a thing. How could someone with no body be contained? She said that he blamed them—my Spirit Guides—for my locking him out of my life. Of course, he would—I would have been too stupid to think of such a thing on my own, in his opinion. He felt this whole "spirituality thing" I was on was their doing, and the solution to the issue was to do them harm. How can anyone harm a Spirit Guide? Well, they can't—but Bill was trying anyway. So he had to be contained. I was told that he would remain in this state until I crossed to the Other Side. He wouldn't be able to reach me in any way, not even through his thoughts.

This was an amazing revelation and told me so much more about Bill's tenacity and delusion. I haven't felt, heard, or seen him since then. It's all quiet where he is concerned. There is so much we don't know about what happens on the Other Side of the veil—or should I say, so much that *I* don't know. I had no expectation when I went to the Initiation with His Holiness, and what I received I couldn't have thought up, even if I had tried.

29

Being Prepared for a New Life

When I moved to Sequim, I knew it wouldn't be my permanent home. What I didn't know was how long my stay would last. One of the issues I have had over the years is not knowing when to let places, people, and things go. I have gotten attached and held on—to my detriment. This should be quite evident by now.

I knew several years in advance that my stay in Sequim was coming to a close. And yet I wanted to hold on to the town and neighborhood. It had been my refuge, my safe haven. I had done a lot of healing there and felt comfortable. My neighbors, for the most part, were supportive. There was so much ease in living there that I didn't want it to end. But everything ends at some point.

When I think back on when the "beginning of the end" started, my mind goes to when I painted the house in 2008. I had never liked the color of the exterior but didn't want to paint it until it needed a new paint job. I'm all about home maintenance, so I tackled one big project a year to keep the house looking good and running smoothly. One of the neighbors once asked if I kept my yard so neat because

I was Black and maybe felt the need to go above and beyond to be accepted. I told him no. My desire to keep things looking pristine doesn't have anything to do with being Black—it is just how I am.

The house was built in 1998, and I've always felt a house needs a paint touch-up every 10 years. Thus I decided to give the house a fresh coat of paint in 2008. The paint still looked good, but it was time. And I wanted to change the color anyway. I called the interior designer who had helped me pick the interior colors to assist with choosing the outside color. She chose was a warm, vibrant green. I loved it. The front door would be changed from teal to red with a black trim. The house was stunning when it was completed.

One day after the house was painted, Jan came by for something. She told me that when she drove up the street and saw my house, she had to stop and stare. The energy of the house had changed, and she knew in that instant that I would need to move. She said that I didn't fit anymore. A house reflects the people living in it, and by that time I had done a lot of work on myself, releasing the parts of me that didn't serve my highest and best good. My painting the exterior of the house reflected the internal shift that had occurred.

I pondered what Jan said about me needing to move and knew that when The Divine was ready for me to leave, the door and the way would present themselves. What I didn't realize was that doors would begin closing in Sequim to help prepare me to move when the time was right. I have to say, the next period was painful. The more attached I was to something, the greater the pain was in letting it go.

One of the things that happened to help loosen my grip on Sequim was the loss of the theater. It had been a vital part of my life in Sequim. For several years the building the theater was housed in was going through a remodel, so shows had to be held elsewhere in the community. A big gala event was planned for the reopening. The center of the event would be a musical—*Cabaret.*

Initially, I wasn't going to be in the show because I felt I couldn't sing. I had taken singing lessons for four years with a retired opera singer who lived in Port Angeles to get over my debilitating fear of singing. As the gods would have it, shortly after I stopped taking singing lessons, Marianne approached me to be in *Cabaret*. I said no. I informed Marianne that a show I was cast in with the local reader's theater would prevent me from making rehearsals for *Cabaret*. Marianne, being who she was, persisted. She said I would only need to sing one song and it would be sung by everyone on stage. I wouldn't have to do it solo. To further appease me, she told me I could begin rehearsals after the reader's theater show closed. I had no more excuses—she had won.

The show was a huge success. And because of this, the theater decided to add a musical to its yearly lineup of shows: *Nunsense* would be the next musical production. *Nunsense* was a show about nuns, and the director asked me to play one of the nuns. I was shaking in my underwear, but I said yes. I wondered how in the hell I would pull it off. There was a vocal solo, and the whole cast had to tap dance. The tap dancing was the easy part.

There wasn't much I could do to prepare for singing rehearsals, because the music wouldn't be given to me until September. I talked to Marianne, who had been in a previous production of the show. She said that she "couldn't sing a lick" and had memorized all the songs from a recording. She was confident that I could do the same. All I needed to do was approach the music director and ask him to record the songs so that I could play them over and over again. I went to the music director and told him about my problem: I couldn't read music very well and needed to have the songs on a recording that I could memorize. He was happy to help and felt that I would be fine.

On the first night of rehearsal, the music director began working with us on the songs. I was the only one who couldn't read music. Plus, my eyesight was deteriorating. This meant that not only could I not read the music, but I was also struggling to read the lyrics on the page. I didn't say anything about this to anyone in the show. It was my problem, and I would deal with it.

I had insecurities oozing through my pores during the first rehearsal. I couldn't stay on pitch, read the music, or see the lyrics clearly; I was intimidated by the singing skills of my fellow actors; and I still feared singing solo and looking like an idiot in front of people. That first night was awful for me, but I didn't give up. I felt if I could learn the songs by listening to a recording of them, I would be fine.

There was another, bigger issue that was laid at my feet that I felt was unfair, and I wasn't sure I could pull it off: the music director's expectation of how I was to sing. I didn't learn of this until a few rehearsals had passed. He wanted me to sing the solo like a Black woman in church would sing it. That wasn't fair, and it was a hell of an assumption on his part to think that I could do this. First, not all Black people can sing, and second, not all Black people grew up singing in church. I sang in a choir as a kid for all of a minute and had never sung a solo in my life. Not to mention, I am reserved in most things I do. And finally, for most of my adult life I had lived in a white culture, which had affected how I moved through life. I will say this: the music director wasn't racist—he simply had a perception that was flawed. All the same, I was hurt by his expectation. And all I could offer was to do my best to portray the character he envisioned. I had no idea where to find her.

One day, I was sitting at a table by the window in my favorite coffee shop, when who should walk through the door but my double in Sequim. She came over and sat down. I talked to her about the part I was playing in the show and asked her for advice. She gave me a pep talk and said she knew I could pull it off. That conversation helped me quite a bit. She gave me the courage to not only *believe* I could do it, but to *know* that I could—plus she agreed to work with me on the delivery. I felt much better and tackled the script and music with much more vigor. The music director and I had also begun to meet for private rehearsals weekly, which was a big help.

What happened next threw me for a loop. I went to the music director's house on the night of our usual lesson. His wife answered the door as she normally did and ushered me in. Her husband asked me to sit down rather than go to the piano to begin working. I knew something was wrong, but I didn't know what it was. He told me that he had to fire me from the show. I was in shock. I couldn't believe what I was hearing. I had never, ever been fired from any show. Not only that, but I was working hard to get up to speed. Didn't he believe I could do the part? Obviously not.

I listened intently to what he was saying and knew it wasn't his doing. Someone else had pushed him into firing me. I sat there quietly while he talked and took what he was telling me graciously—at least outwardly. He told me that I was being too kind to him, letting him off the hook, but it's never been my style to throw tantrums. I think he was as hurt as I was—that's what I saw in his face and felt coming from him. I'll never know who was behind my being fired, and it doesn't matter. What I do know is that I was crushed by it, internally. And I vowed never to do another show for that theater. The theater had been my anchor, and it was gone, just like that. A big door in Sequim had closed.

After being fired from the show, I decided to join the Christmas Choral Group. I was bound and determined to rid myself of the singing fear. On the first night of rehearsal, the choir director mentioned that there would be auditions for soloists. So seizing the opportunity, I went home, memorized a song, and auditioned to be a soloist. I would be damned if I was going to let that fear lick me.

I was given a spot as a soloist, and every night I worked that song. The Christmas Choral Group event was the kickoff to the Christmas season in Sequim, and the church where it was held was packed for every performance. When it was time for me to walk to the front of the choir and sing, I was nervous and I was ready. I just let go, and the song came through me. I was able to be vulnerable. It was magical for me up there. The music director from the theater was in the audience during one of the performances. I got to see the shock on his face when he saw me sing—that was an unintended checkmate. I went on to sing with the group for two more years and enjoyed every minute of it.

After the solo, my fear of singing was almost gone. I would later realize that my singing fear was a symptom of a bigger issue: fear of speaking my mind without fear of rejection. I had healed maybe

85 percent of the way in this area. The rest of the healing occurred by singing in another show and singing in front of my astrology tribe at Steven's Apprenticeship School. After one of the events at the astrology retreat, I realized my fear was completely gone. I was free. This meant it no longer mattered what my singing voice sounded like—I wasn't and am not afraid to raise my voice in song to others in public. The side effect of this was that I also found my true voice again—it had been dormant all my life—which in turn helped me get over the fear of being rejected. There was more work I needed to do on this fear; however, finding my voice was a key component.

The other thing that helped to loosen my grip on Sequim had to do with my neighbors. They had become a part of my family, and one by one they began to die or move away.

Dick died a few years after I moved to the neighborhood. Even though I was affected by his death, I wasn't devastated.

The next person to go was Ted, and then Alf. Alf died a year or so before I moved, and it was tragic. He and Virginia had planned to put their house on the market so that they could move back to the city to be near the kids. They loved Sequim, but Virginia had some form of dementia, and it was getting worse. Alf was in the process of readying the house. One day he decided to change the smoke detector battery at his house. The smoke detector was located over the stairs. I had been out someplace and came around the corner, headed home, when I saw the paramedics and an ambulance outside of their home. I stopped the car and went inside to see what was happening. Virginia was standing at the top of the stairs in a daze, and as I looked down, I saw Alf lying at the foot of the stairs being worked on. He had fallen off the ladder. I took Virginia to the hospital, and by the time we arrived, Alf was gone. Within a month, Virginia's kids had moved her into an assisted-living facility near them.

The final person to die before I moved was Wayne. His death was hard to take because he was like a second father. I loved him, and everything changed for me after his death. My bond to the neighborhood was almost gone. There was an energy shift.

There had also been two vacant lots on the street for years, and both of them had been sold and houses built. There was a house next door to me now, and the ladies who lived there were nice. I liked them. But the writing was on the wall for me. It was nearing the time for me to leave.

I even mentioned this to Steve when I saw him for my biannual reading in 2013. He told me that I stole his thunder. He said the window for me to move was open, and it was time to move forward. I told him that I thought I would move in 2015. Steve said that the window would still be open then, but he felt the move would happen earlier. He also warned me about what would happen if I didn't move before the window of opportunity closed. It was pretty clear in my chart that I would have problems if I stayed.

I had no idea where I would move to. I didn't want to move back to any of the places I had lived. My initial thought was California, but I didn't think that I could afford to live there. My bank account was dangerously low on funds, and even selling the house wouldn't give me enough money to buy another one in California. So I set my sights on Bellingham, Washington, as I had before. It wasn't far from Seattle, and I now had ties to the astrological community there. In addition, I wouldn't be too far away from Sequim and could always visit. My logic was sound, but it wasn't where The Divine wanted me to land.

I put the house on the market in September of 2013. Because I used astrology to pick the listing date, I was sure it would sell fast. I had enlisted the help of Jan #2 to help me pick the date. The house just sat there—no lookers. I was perplexed as to why it hadn't sold.

By March of 2014, I was at an all-time emotional low. I wondered what I was doing wrong. My friend Jan asked me one question that changed everything: "Are you sure you are supposed to move to Bellingham?" I had picked it out of logic, not love. I really wanted to be in California but had put it out of my mind due to cost. I thought I would go to Bellingham and earn enough money to move to California at a later time. By the time Jan asked me the question, I was very low on money and was using all the spiritual tools I had learned over the years to keep myself in balance emotionally. There were times when all I could do was take things a minute at a time.

Because of Jan's question, I told The Divine, "Okay—you know what is in my bank account. If you want me to move to California, you are going to have to get me there." I surrendered where I would go to The Divine.

I decided to send a Facebook post out to all my friends. I told them that I was selling the house, putting everything in storage, and moving to California. I requested that if anyone knew of someone who would rent me a room or mother-in-law apartment to please let me know. I was shocked to get an answer from one of my friends in California who knew someone who rented rooms out in his house. This was April. I contacted her friend, who lived in Santa Rosa, spoke to his wife, Alicia, and the rest is history. I had a place to stay. All I had to do was sell the house.

Shortly after this, people started looking at my house, and I had an acceptable offer over the Fourth of July holiday. The house sold, and I loaded up the truck and moved to Bev-er-lee. Okay—that's a joke—I moved to Santa Rosa.

Perfume

When the flower has bloomed, it gives off a fragrance
that is carried on the wind and can be smelled by
anyone nearby. This is the same for the human
Soul. Once it is in full bloom, it can now be
a teacher for others. The human Soul does
this by radiating its true self out into
the world, which inspires others to
achieve their Soul agenda.

30

Experiencing a New Sense of Self

By the time I moved away from Sequim, I had recovered my personal power—my sense of self. The only part of me that resembled who I was before moving there was my physical features, but even they had shifted. I had spent years releasing past pains. I still didn't know the ultimate plan for my life, but I knew the plan would present itself when I was ready. Being ready meant healing the trauma. I still had a little more work to do, but most of it was behind me.

When I consciously began to do my spiritual work, my dreams became more intense and vivid. The issue with dreams is that it can be difficult to interpret them correctly. This is because each culture and person has their own meaning for items. For example, the color white in the West means purity, while in the East it means death. This difference has to be taken into consideration when interpreting a dream with this color as a focal point.

Dreams were a major part of my healing process. In one dream, which occurred while I was in Australia going through the certification program to become a Journey Practitioner, I saw a black snake. This snake was long, sleek, fast, and smart. In the dream I was doing all that I could to outrun it. Every place I'd run, there it was—just looking at me. Once while running, I thought I had gotten away, only to find it in front of me, standing with half its body off the ground, looking at me at eye level. I woke up terrified.

At that time, I wasn't well versed in dream interpretation, so I called Pat to ask for help. When I relayed the dream to her, she roared with laughter. "What's so funny?" I wondered. She said, "You are running from your personal power. Everyone has a snake in their root chakra, and this is yours. You are afraid. Why are you afraid of who you are?" I had to ponder the answer. And it took years for me to own my personal power, partly because I still feared rejection. I also brought a bigger part of the fear into this incarnation from various lifetimes. The dream gave me direction concerning what I needed to work on, and I did work hard over the years. Every trauma worked on brought me closer to owning all of who I am.

Another dream, which was reoccurring, was also related to personal power—and it terrified me, too. One thing is for sure: Spirit Guides and your Higher Mind are tenacious when you step onto the Path. They will use any and every means necessary to help you progress. In my case, it's not that I didn't want to do the work; sometimes I just didn't get the message clearly. Plus, at times there was an element of procrastination involved. I've learned over the years not to procrastinate when it comes to figuring out a message and taking the action suggested.

Over the course of a year or so, I had been periodically waking up to find myself in various parts of the house. I had been running from something in my sleep, and it must have been terrifying for me to get out of bed while still asleep. One time I woke up while standing up in bed with my hands on the ceiling. Waking up in various places began to concern me. I worried that I would go outside or do something that would cause me harm, and I wondered if I would have these occurrences when traveling.

It never dawned on me to ask my Guides for help getting to the root of the problem. And I guess they were growing tired of my inaction. Whatever it was that I saw in my sleep, I didn't remember when I woke up. This soon changed. One particular night I saw it and remembered what it was—and I was more than terrified. Standing next to my bed was a skinless torso—no head, no arms, no lower extremities. I could clearly see all of the inner-working parts of the torso. This time my escape route was via the foot of the bed. My feet got tangled in the duvet and I went flying, waking up in midair just as the back of my head hit the wooden footboard.

I landed softly on top of the duvet, on the floor, arms stretched out to the side, eyes open, staring up at the ceiling. I lay there for a few minutes quietly integrating what had just happened. After doing a mental check of my body to see if I was hurt, I promised my Guides that I would get to the bottom of the dream, and I did. It had to do with me running from an aspect of my core self. It was still about me owning my personal power. And this didn't involve my head—thus a torso without the head—I had to work on my heart. Not having any skin signified a great deal of vulnerability. I must have gotten the interpretation right, because after I figured it out, that dreamed stopped. Not only did I get to the bottom of the dream, but I took active steps to work on the issue, which involved setting the intention to heal that part of me. It was not easy work, but over time I achieved the goal of owning my personal power.

The ultimate goal of this journey was and still is to allow the Soul to lead rather than the personality—aka the ego. This was, in fact, what I meant subconsciously in the comment I made to Bill all those years ago regarding what I was looking for in the books I was reading. I was looking for me. I was looking for the authentic me—which is the Soul. I have come a long way on this journey.

Each of us is given tests on the Path to discovering our authentic selves. They are designed to not only show us where we are in our development, but also to tell us what still needs to be worked on. There is no passing or failing grade. If we don't do well on the test, it is just given again at a later time, after we have had more life experience.

Case in point: after consciously working on myself for years and developing self-esteem, personal power, trust in The Divine, etc., it was time for a midterm test. (I say "midterm" because I know there are more on the horizon.) As a Taurus moon, I don't do well when funds are low. I know most people don't, but we Tauruses *really* don't. I designed my test perfectly. (That's right—each of us designs our own tests, with the help of those who will act as our Guides, long before we incarnate.) The point of the test was to see how much trust I had developed with The Great Mother. You can use God, or Divine, in her place. Whatever works for you is fine.

In the beginning of my conscious journey to get to know and trust her, I took baby steps. It's not easy to trust someone, at least not for me. I had been hurt many times by people I trusted—especially by the people responsible for my upbringing. I was like a wounded animal who limped into The Great Mother's campsite—hungry for the sustenance of love and acceptance and fearing being brutalized. Thus the challenge of her being able to feed me. The Mother feeds us through our heart, and the amount of food we receive is determined by how open our heart is. At first, my heart was closed shut, and as it opened, I was able to take in more love. An aspect of this love is trust. I had to trust that she would feed me—that I didn't have to do anything to receive her love and the many blessings she had for me.

To begin building this trust, I asked her for something small and insignificant. This way, if I didn't receive what I was asking for, I wouldn't get hurt. What I found was that most requests were granted. It didn't matter if I felt worthy of the request, either. All I had to do was ask. The only thing that I added to my request was the statement "if this is in my highest and best good." Some things clearly wouldn't be in my highest and best good, and I might not know what these were.

Over time, I began to trust her more and more. Not 100 percent, but more than at the beginning of our relationship. And now it was time for me to be tested on just how much I trusted her.

The test came in the form of a desire at the beginning of 2014. The house had been on the market since September of the last year, with no lookers, and I was under tremendous emotional stress. I had stretched my money as far as it could go, and the bank account was virtually empty. I had done well over the years managing the finances, especially since my original calculation was that the funds would last five years after Bill's death, and here I was, 12 years later.

One of the astrologers I knew, Alan, was having his 70th birthday. He had planned a party plus two one-week classes to be held in Santa Fe, New Mexico. Alan and I had met in 2003 at one of the annual astrology conferences held in Seattle. He was an esoteric astrologer. When I first laid eyes on him, he looked familiar. I had known him before—in another life. I had the thought to study with him, but for some reason the opportunity didn't arise.

Fast-forward 10 years later—2013. Alan was teaching a class in Seattle at the local astrology club. I attended the class and became reacquainted with him. When I learned of his birthday celebration the next year, I knew instantly that I was supposed to be there. It was the same feeling I had with the Bhutan trip. This time, however, I wasn't flesh with cash. How would I pull this trip off?

My first step was to ask The Great Mother to provide the means for me to go. I didn't specifically ask for money, because I had learned not to dictate how she accomplished the goal. I had also learned that I only needed to ask once. There was no need to beg or plead.

The second step was to wait until she provided the opportunity for me to take action. The tricky part was the waiting. One of the components of trust is knowing something will occur and therefore not worrying—waiting patiently, with emotions balanced and calm. Thus my emotional strength was also being tested. My nature is to take action when I see a problem and a possible solution. But this time I had to wait patiently for The Great Mother—which I did.

The first order of business was paying for the class and the banquet. The funds for this came in the form of new astrology clients. I hadn't had new clients in a while, and suddenly there they were. I think it was only about a week after I had asked The Mother for help.

The next thing to be paid for was the airline ticket. So what did The Mother do? A few weeks after I paid for the conference, I received a call from a friend who had moved away from Sequim a few years earlier. She needed a place to stay for an event she was planning to attend. I, of course, said yes. When she arrived, she asked me to give her a reading and also said a friend of hers needed help with a life issue. She gifted her friend a reading with me. I now had the funds for the airline ticket.

Now I needed to pay for the hotel and transportation and have money for food. I wanted to stay at the hotel where the event was being held but knew that I would need a roommate to be able to pull this off. I also knew that I prefer being on my own, without roommates. I had heard about Airbnb but didn't know how it worked. So I did a bit of research, surfing the Web and looking for places in Santa Fe. I found one that was about two miles from the hotel. Now all I had to do was wait until the money came to pay for it.

Out of the blue an astrology friend, Glenna, gave me a call. She simply said, "I got this feeling that you are supposed to be at Alan's party," to which I replied, "Yes, you are right, and I am in the process of pulling things together to get there." She then said, "So what do you need? I'll loan you the money; you can pay me back whenever." I was in shock. I had never had anyone voluntarily offer to loan me anything. Usually, it was the other way around. I was so truly grateful. She loaned me enough to pay for lodging. Now that was taken care of.

The only things left to pay for were food and transportation. I was flying into Albuquerque, and another friend would pick me up and take me to her place for a day to visit. Afterwards, she would drive me to Santa Fe. I'd take the train back from Santa Fe, and she'd pick me up from the station. We'd hang out that evening, and she'd take me to the airport for my flight home the next morning. On the Sequim side of the trip, I planned to leave my car at the casino on Banbridge Island. They had an airport shuttle and free parking. Transportation handled.

I had a few weeks left before the trip, and the only thing I needed was spending money for food. I had calculated how much I needed per day. My total estimate was $300. So far, The Mother had come through, and I had no reason to believe she wouldn't continue providing for me. Still, there was doubt.

One of my coffee-shop friends, Maureen, was privy to the saga. I needed someone to talk to—someone who wouldn't worry about me but would just be supportive. Maureen and I talked daily about what had occurred. It was like a real-life soap opera, except without the commercial breaks and music. I told her why this situation was happening and what the goal was. Over the years, Maureen and I had had many conversations about spirituality and beliefs. I knew she was nervous concerning whether or not I could pull the trip off. Every time I made progress, she was awestruck by the occurrence— as was I.

I don't remember now how the money for food materialized, but it did. I was all set. It had been stressful, to say the least, but my trust in The Great Mother had grown. So far, this had been the biggest test in my life concerning trust and emotions. I was trusting something that couldn't be seen; she could only be felt. I had passed the test—or had I?

Four days before I was due to leave for Albuquerque, I learned that I had made a timing error. I needed to be at the party a day earlier. Somehow, I had read the date of Alan's party incorrectly. I had scheduled my flight for the right day but the wrong time. I needed an earlier flight. This was a huge problem, because airlines charge to change flights and I didn't have the extra money. Plus, I was booked into the Airbnb a day later, and it would cost to add another day. Talk about turning the pressure up—it was all I could do to stay calm. Staying calm and not panicking were key in this situation. I wouldn't be able to hear The Mother if I was panicking.

I called the airlines and told them what had happened. The change fee plus the difference in the cost of the ticket was a little over $200. I agreed to the amount, but because I had bought the ticket through a third party, I would need to go through this third party to make the changes. The third party would have to contact the airlines. Jeez—it got complicated.

I was on hold for more than an hour with the third-party travel company. I called the airline back, and they tried getting through on the phone for me—with no success. After being on hold for at least a half hour, the customer-service person said, "Okay—this is ridiculous. Here is a suggestion. Go to the airport at the time of the flight you would like to board. If seats are available, you can pay $50 and get on the flight." I had no idea this was an option. Why hadn't she told me this before? She confirmed that there were still seats available; I just had to pray that they would still be available when I arrived at the airport. I had to keep trusting.

The flight I needed to take departed Sea-Tac in the morning. This meant that I had to catch an early shuttle ride at the casino. I left the house around 4:00 a.m. The casino was more than an hour away. When I arrived, I learned the shuttle didn't run that early. This mistake on my part cost me a taxi ride to the ferry. Taxis aren't cheap—even short rides. There went $20.

I arrived at the airport early and asked about the flight I needed to be on. It was overbooked due to spring break. Now what would I do? I stayed steadfast and strong. I wouldn't give up.

Because I had a boarding pass for the later flight, which left a few hours later, I was allowed to go through security and went to the gate to wait for the customer-service desk to open. When it did, I informed them of my dilemma and was put on standby. I was told that the flight was overbooked and that I probably wouldn't get on. I sat down to wait and just said, "If I am supposed to be at Alan's party, you—The Mother—will take care of getting me on the flight. If I am not supposed to be there, then so be it."

The stress was gone. I let go of expectation and just waited. One of the customer-service people came over to me after the flight had been filled and told me that I couldn't get on the flight. I thanked her and continued to sit. After about 10 minutes there was an announcement over the intercom. They were calling for a person who was supposed to be on the flight but hadn't gotten to the gate. There were three people on standby, including me. Only one seat.

After calling for the person a third time with no response, the customer-service person came over to me and gave me that person's seat. I had made it on the flight. And, in the nick of time, the doors to the plane had to be opened for me to board. I was shaking when I sat down from the adrenaline that rushed through me. My trust in The Great Mother increased. She had come through—again.

My friend picked me up at the Albuquerque airport and straight away took me to Santa Fe for Alan's birthday banquet. The party was terrific, and it was nice to connect with old friends and meet new ones. Two things happened that night. First, I had forgotten to pay for something. I don't remember what it was, but I had to pay an extra $50 that wasn't planned. Second, I didn't have a place to stay for the night. I couldn't check in to the Airbnb until the next day. I considered sitting up in the lobby of the hotel but thought better of that idea. I would just have to leave it to The Mother to take care of.

As The Mother would have it, I sat next to an astrologer that I knew from Steven's Apprenticeship program—Lisa. She was on her own. As we caught up on what was happening in each of our worlds, she offered to have me stay with her that evening. Problem solved. I was more than grateful for her kindness. We had a slumber party, talking most of the night. The next morning we went to breakfast, walked around the town, and at the appointed time I checked in to my abode for the week.

In the mornings I would leisurely walk to the hotel for class, stopping at the local store for a breakfast burrito and coffee. It was tasty, I saved money, and I got daily exercise. I was happy. That said, I was concerned as to how I would stretch the money further so that it would last until I got home. My original calculations went out the window due to the extra expenses. I asked The Mother for the extra money needed. I wouldn't have needed to ask if I had trusted she was on the job and handling the situation. But, as I said, my trust factor in her wasn't 100 percent.

Because it was dark when we finished each evening, one of the ladies in the group offered to take me back to my place every night. I didn't mind walking back, but it was dark; if I didn't have to walk alone at night, why would I?

One night, a few of us decided to go swimming in the hotel pool. When we got there, there were a few other people in the pool. All of us started talking and having a good time. One of the ladies asked me what I did for a living. I told her that I was an astrologer and tarot reader. She had been wanting a reading for a while and was thrilled to know I did tarot readings. She asked how much I charged. I replied, and she hired me on the spot. We met the next morning before my class. She was so happy with the reading that she told a friend, and that friend met me the next morning for a reading. Money problem solved. The Great Mother had come to my rescue. The rest of the trip was wonderful, even more so because I wasn't worried about money.

By the time I arrived back in Sequim, my trust that I was taken care of by The Divine was much stronger, and I had kept my emotions mostly balanced. There were a few tense moments, but overall, I had done well. I couldn't wait to tell Maureen about the trip. When I saw her at the coffee shop, she said she had thought of me every day and was wondering how things went. I told her what happened, and both of us were amazed by how the trip went.

For me, the journey to trusting The Divine had to be carried out in the way that it was. I had to take one step in faith and trust, and then another, and another. This is the way I built that muscle, and this is why now, for the most part, I don't *believe* I am taken care of—I *know* I am taken care of. As I said earlier, I'm a tough cookie in the trust department—so I would say my *knowing* is at 97 percent.

So there you have it. My life has taken so many twists and turns, and I've never known what was waiting for me around any corner; I just had to take a leap of faith and keep going—trying to follow my own compass. There have been failures, successes, and some not-so-sures. This is how a Black girl born into poverty and raised in the South away from family became who she is today. I've learned so much over the years about myself and about people. I've grown in ways that I never expected, and the growth continues.

Any questions? You must be hungry after all this; I sure am. Let's go eat.

Afterword

As I reflect on my life, I am struck by the myriad of experiences and what I have learned about myself and others from them. I've also finally found where I belong. I found Home. Yes, I am in California and love being here. California fits my temperament, and that is important. However, that's not what I'm referring too. Places we live are not really Home; they are temporary dwellings. Home for me has been with me all along—I just didn't know it. It's within. I discovered who I am at my core. And nothing or no one can take that away. I am secure no matter what happens externally concerning my circumstances in the world. That is real security. It has nothing to do with the house I live in, how much money I have, who I love, or what I look like.

My true foundation is more solid than the strongest mineral. Life brings us many experiences, some wonderful and some we'd rather not have. And, if we know who we truly are, we move from one experience to the next with grace; as I have so often read in the Buddhist text and been told, this is non-attachment. That doesn't mean we don't feel love or have compassion for ourselves and others. It means we see the big picture and the purpose of it all, which is to "know thyself." We see the interconnectedness of everything and our place in it.

One of the advantages of living from a knowing of who I am at my core is that my mission, or what you might refer to as "right work" in the world, has been revealed. We don't have to go looking for our right work in the world. It is revealed to us when we are prepared for it. My mission is to help others discover their true selves, where Home is for them. The journey each of us takes to discover Home is unique to the individual, but each of us is, in the end, seeking the same goal. I chose the lotus plant to reflect my journey through life. You also have a plant in nature that best reflects your journey. You might even know what it is. If you don't, wouldn't it be rewarding to learn what it is? It's your plant teacher, and knowing what it is will help you learn more about yourself.

My journey continues. I will keep learning and developing for as long as I breathe and beyond. Not long ago, in two separate meditations, I had two visions. In one, I was visited by the Buddhist Lama I saw in the cave many years ago. He simply popped in and said, "You are ready—to FLY." In the other meditation, I was shown an open door. There was a being standing there watching me. I could simultaneously see from the side view many more doors, which were closed. I knew instantly that a door had opened for me and that once I had gathered the experiences it offered, another door would open. The journey never ends.

Acknowledgments

The saying that no man is an island is true. No one does anything on their own even when it looks that way. This is the Universal Law of Interconnectedness. There have been many people who have supported my quest to write and publish this book. My intention is to acknowledge a few of them here. I say "a few" because to mention all of them would take a chapter, at least.

First, to my editor Andi Reese Brady of Personal History Productions LLC. She has been a brilliant, efficient, capable, and compassionate shepherd, guiding every aspect of the production. Having her as an editor immensely reduced my stress level.

To all my friends who have supported me from the beginning of this writing journey—offering encouraging words and sometimes direction—I offer a huge amount of gratitude. Daneris Moran, Wade Hyde, Deborah Forrest, Leslie Neal, Tony Navarra, Alicia Wray, Gordon Marlette, Barbara Martin, Marilyn Babcock, Karen Bergin, and Moll Fothringham were all cheerleaders for this book. They listened, gave hugs, insight, pushed and sometimes pulled me forward with their words.

Special thanks to my comrade and friend Jan Butler, who knows most of the stories of my life and who gave me the idea for the title and cover. It just popped in her mind while we were talking one day, and it felt goosebump right. And to my astrologer, mentor, friend, and dharma-brother Steven Forrest, who encouraged me to write my story. He also helped lift me up with his heartfelt advice when I felt discouraged.

About the Author

M arie O'Neill, MBA, is the founder of Padma Life Coaching, located in Santa Rosa, California. Marie has many years of experience as a Life Coach, astrologer, speaker coach, healing retreat facilitator, and past life regression facilitator. She also lectures on astrology and is known for her motivational speeches. She is a Distinguished Toastmaster through Toastmasters International, on the board of directors with TEDx Sonoma County, and an astrology mentor with Forrest Center for Evolutionary Astrology (FCEA). In addition, Marie lectures at numerous astrology conferences and has now added published author to her list of achievements. Marie's passion is helping others achieve their dreams, reach their goals, and learn to shine brightly in the world.

To book Marie for a consultation, session, speech, or workshop, please contact her at (800) 337-7682 or padmalifecoaching.com.